*International African Library 9*
General editors: J. D. Y. Peel and David Parkin

# TEARS OF THE DEAD

For the memory of my mother

# International African Library

### General Editors

### J. D. Y. Peel *and* David Parkin

The *International African Library* is a major monograph series from the International African Institute and complements its quarterly periodical *Africa*, the premier journal in the field of African studies. Theoretically informed ethnographies, studies of social relations 'on the ground' which are sensitive to local cultural forms, have long been central to the Institute's publications programme. The *IAL* maintains this strength but extends it into new areas of contemporary concern, both practical and intellectual. It includes works focused on problems of development, especially on the linkages between the local and national levels of society; studies along the interface between the social and environmental sciences; and historical studies, especially those of a social, cultural or interdisciplinary character.

Titles in the series:

1 Sandra T. Barnes *Patrons and power: creating a political community in metropolitan Lagos*†
2 Jane I. Guyer (ed.) *Feeding African cities: essays in social history*†
3 Paul Spencer *The Maasai of Matapato: a study of rituals of rebellion*†
4 Johan Pottier *Migrants no more: settlement and survival in Mambwe villages, Zambia*†
5 Günther Schlee *Identities on the move: clanship and pastoralism in northern Kenya*
6 Suzette Heald *Controlling anger: the sociology of Gisu violence*
7 Karin Barber *I could speak until tomorrow: oriki, women and the past in a Yoruba town*★
8 Richard Fardon *Between God, the dead and the wild: Chamba interpretations of religion and ritual*★
9 Richard Werbner *Tears of the dead: the social biography of an African family*★

★ *Published in the USA by the Smithsonian Institution Press*
† *Published in the USA by Indiana University Press*

### Editorial Consultants

Kofi Agawu
Pierre Bonte
John Comaroff
Johannes Fabian
Paulin Hountondji
Ivan Karp
Sally Falk Moore

# TEARS OF
# THE DEAD

The Social Biography of
an African Family

RICHARD WERBNER

EDINBURGH UNIVERSITY PRESS
for the International African Institute, London

© Richard Werbner, 1991

Edinburgh University Press
22 George Square, Edinburgh

Photoset and printed in Great Britain by
Redwood Press, Melksham, Wiltshire

British Library Cataloguing in Publication Data
Werbner, Richard P.
  Tears of the dead: The social biography of an
  African family.—(International African library
  I. Title   II. Series
  305.896

ISBN 0 7486 0304 2 (cased)

# Contents

# Preface

In writing this social biography about a Kalanga family, the family of Lupondo, I have tried to keep their lives in the foreground. The family is a large one: Lupondo's own living offspring and their spouses numbered, in 1989, more than 350 adults and children and those of his brothers at least another 150 souls. Their history from the beginning of colonial Southern Rhodesia to the present in post-independence Zimbabwe has been my main concern. Yet my own history is very much a part of the account. When I first came to know Lupondo's family, over a period of fifteen months in 1960–1, I was a young student. I was fresh from a year of studying social anthropology in England at the University of Manchester, after having graduated from Brandeis University in America.

Like most students, I had in mind a long-term project that was influenced by the work of my teachers. At Brandeis University, as a student of Paul Radin's, I had read and reread *Crashing Thunder, The Autobiography of an American Indian* (1926). Paul Radin taught me the importance of recording life histories and personal narratives. Under his direction, I attempted a summer's fieldwork among Winnebago Indians, in 1958, primarily for the purpose of recording life histories. Max Gluckman and Victor Turner, my teachers at Manchester, taught me the virtues of the extended case method and the rich interest in studying observed events as sequences in historical processes (on these contributions of the Manchester School, see Werbner 1990). Clyde Mitchell, my fieldwork supervisor at the University College of Rhodesia and Nyasaland, did his best to get me to appreciate the impact of state intervention on the people's lives—he urged me to study current social problems, most importantly the attack on African agriculture and the social consequences of measures under the Land Husbandry Act.

There was, to my knowledge, no book which gave a rounded portrait of several generations of an African extended family, largely in their own words. African grandparents, children and grandchildren of the same family had yet to give their own accounts in our literature. I hoped that my research would document the insiders' views and that it would illuminate the historically different courses of their lives from generation to generation.

Aiming to bring together the study of personal narratives and the extended case method, both of which required close rapport with a fairly limited number of people, I made my home in Lupondo's hamlet in the Chiefdom of Bango for most of my first visit among Eastern Kalanga. Buka, Lupondo's eldest son, gave me the use of two of his huts, freely and generously, without rent, one for my assistant and the other for me. On my return visit in 1989, Buka's surviving full brother, Gwati, was equally generous in providing me with a hut. I remain greatly indebted to Buka, to his brother Gwati, and to the rest of Lupondo's family for their kindness to me, despite what were all too often, I now realise, my failures to be truly *nnu we kanyi kwedu*, 'a person of our home'.

It was only after I left Bango, and had time to reflect upon the personal narratives and life histories, that I recognised many of their limitations. I had only begun to elicit the basis for understanding how family members rework the past in the light of the present. To pursue that, I planned to resume my conversations with the same members of Lupondo's family in the hope that they would recall their memories of times we had known together and the intervening years since 1960–1.

Alas, my plan was not to be realised.

I did try to return in 1964, unsuccessfully. It was not long before the Rhodesian regime made its unilateral declaration of independence, and I became a prohibited immigrant. That prohibition was lifted, of course, soon after the independence of Zimbabwe. This allowed me to give a lecture at the University of Zimbabwe on a very brief visit in August 1980.

From 1964 onwards, I made repeated visits to Botswana for research, first among Western Kalanga in the borderlands to the west and north of Bango, and later among Tswapong, to the south-west. News of Lupondo's family and my other friends at Bango continued to reach me. But I still could not return to Bango, as I had hoped.

The violence continued, even after the guerrilla war was won, and independence declared. Peace remained sadly beyond the reach of the people of western Zimbabwe. At last, peace did come to that troubled part of the country, when an amnesty was declared in May 1988. Soon after that the government of Zimbabwe gave me permission to take up my research at Bango once again. I am particularly grateful to Mr A. C. Mpamhanga, then Under-secretary of the Ministry of Local Government, Rural and Urban Development, for arranging my affiliation to his ministry. Chief Charles Bango found the time to accompany me from Bulawayo back to Bango; like his late father, Chief Jeremiah Ngugama Bango, before him, he opened the way for my research by his thoughtful assistance. I am indebted also to Michael Bourdillon and Angela Cheater for their helpful suggestions and hospitality while I was preparing for my research.

Nearly thirty years had gone by since my first visit, when I returned to Bango in June 1989, for a period of six weeks. Few of the first and second generations of Lupondo's family had survived. Some had died of old age and disease, among them Lupondo himself and his eldest son Buka. Lupondo's senior son Dzilo had been killed by guerrillas during the war, after they had accused him of being a sorcerer. I mourn his death along with those of my other friends at Bango, and prominently among them I mourn the late Chief Jeremiah Ngugama Bango. The death of Chief Jeremiah Ngugama Bango, after independence, was an atrocity officially attributed to 'murder by dissidents', although the people themselves blamed the Fifth Brigade of Zimbabwe's National Army.

In writing this book I have been very much aware of the undertaking I gave family members and other friends at Bango to tell the world the truth about the ordeals they endured. I thank them for their trust, and I hope they will recognise that I mean *Tears of the Dead*, as Kalanga do, to convey the respect of the living in remembering the past.

My acknowledgement of help must be greatest to two friends, Saul Gwakuba Ndlovu and Timon Mongwa who, in turn, were my assistants in my first fieldwork. Saul and Timon, who are both roughly my own age, were former schoolteachers then in their early twenties. Their conversational and personal skills counted heavily for our establishing rapport with members of Lupondo's family. My own inexperience and, at times, raw insensitivity led me to make very great demands on their time, their good humour and their personal strength. Both of them had their homes in the London Missionary Society's trust, Dombu Dema, to the north and very distant from Bango. They were themselves virtually strangers to the people of Bango, although their notable fathers—one a highly skilled carpenter, the other a celebrated preacher, and both among the earliest of literate Kalanga—were well known in the Chiefdom. Timon's father, Reverend Mongwa Tjuma, had been one of the first evangelists for the London Missionary Society; along with Saul's father, Gwakuba Ndlovu, he helped translate some of the gospels into Kalanga. My research benefited greatly from the love of learning, the cultural sensitivity and the feeling for nuanced translation which their fathers' example inspired in them. On reflection about our co-operation, I must admit something else, although I find it embarrassing. I suspect that from their own and their fathers' experiences with European missionaries they learned the art of managing other awkward, curious and obstinately intrusive strangers, such as I was in my early fieldwork.

Over the years since we worked together as young men, Saul Gwakuba Ndlovu and Timon Mongwa have continued to encourage me with their friendship, their intellectual interest and in various ways their practical help. Each in maturity has made a major contribution to public life. Saul, currently an editorial consultant for the multinational company Lonrho, has been a crusading journalist, editor and emissary for the Zimbabwe African People's Union (ZAPU). Timon, formerly Mayor of Francistown in Botswana, is a prosperous, large-scale entrepreneur. I wish to thank them, above all others, and I hope that they will consider that this book, which is largely a product of our early research together, is a worthy record of Kalanga lives.

The texts of the life histories from my first visit are edited versions of the translations which I made with the help of one of my assistants from tape recordings, while we were living in Lupondo's hamlet. Saul Gwakuba Ndlovu helped me record and translate Buka's life history and parts of Tobela's, and Timon Mongwa, each of the others in Chapters 2, 3 and 4. I alone am responsible for the translations from my later visit. To protect the family's privacy, I have changed their names and concealed certain details of their identities. For married women, I use the convention of respectful address, Baka, 'mother of' (a first born). At the end of the book to help readers keep in mind who the main individuals are, there is a list, giving a brief profile for each. The officials discussed, such as the Chief, the Native Commissioner, the Land Development Officer, were public figures, and in accord with that I have kept their own names.

I gratefully acknowledge the scholarships and grants which made my study possible: a Brandeis National Scholarship, a Fulbright scholarship for my year at Manchester and for one year of my first research among Eastern Kalanga, and awards from the University of Manchester, first a postgraduate grant for three months in 1961, and second a Staff Travel Grant for my return research in 1989.

I wrote the final manuscript during a sabbatical from the University of Manchester, while I was a Senior Fellow at the Smithsonian Institution in Washington. William Merrill, my host at the Smithsonian, never tired in his support for my project, despite the pressing demands I made on his time. He encouraged me greatly by giving fine, critical comments on each chapter; he arranged a very helpful seminar to which I presented some of the chapters in early drafts. I thank him and the other seminar members: Michael Fischer, Jack Goody, Ivan Karp, Robert Leopold and Tony Shelton. With much personal kindness and professional efficiency, the Anthropology Department librarians at the Smithsonian, Mary Kay Davies and Mayda Riopedre, made it a pleasure to use the Smithsonian libraries and the Library of Congress. Linda Werbner brought her editorial skills to bear for a close and helpful reading of several chapters. I also wish to thank Elizabeth Colson, Kingsley Garbett, Isaac Schapera and Marilyn Strathern for their constructive responses to early drafts.

To Terence Ranger I owe not only a great deal of intellectual stimulation in argument over many years but also the heartening encouragement which he gave us all by going ahead with his own research in Matabeleland so soon after the amnesty.

My wife Pnina has been my closest reader. She took part in my fieldwork among Western Kalanga in Botswana, although not among Eastern Kalanga in Zimbabwe, and her contributions, enabling me to reach greater insight and clarity, resonate throughout the best of this book.

Mabuyani.

Richard Werbner
Washington, D.C.
June, 1990

# List of illustrations, maps and genealogies

# Introduction

This book about Lupondo's family from the Chiefdom of Bango recovers memories. They are my own, and they are the memories of the several generations of Eastern Kalanga who told me their life stories. *Kanyi kewdu*, 'our home' was a remembered reality. It was not a world of experience that Lupondo's family and their neighbours among Eastern Kalanga could always take for granted, for they had needed to recreate it around themselves, repeatedly. They did so under pressure. White settlers had driven them out of their original homes and lands within the central highlands of western Zimbabwe. Colonial officials had subjected them to imposed resettlement. Invading armies, guerrillas and regular soldiers forced them to suffer until terror and violence in war and in the aftermath of war remained stamped upon their memories. To survive in their Chiefdom of Bango, when it was a part first of colonial Southern Rhodesia and later of post-colonial Zimbabwe, was to endure dislocation, often arbitrary and never easy to forget or forgive.

Yet in their own stories, as they originally chose to tell them to me, before the recent guerrilla war, they left many of those unsettling experiences in the background. What they did tell me, however, regains more of its implicit and understood resonance, the more a wider history, which is the social and cultural struggle over their land, becomes known. This history helps us to make better sense, also, of their outrage against personal violation, their painful disillusionment, and the bitter reproaches they later voiced against their own government, nearly a decade after independence.

The first part of this book gives my account of the making of Bango Chiefdom in the face of large-scale eviction, displacement from home, imposed resettlement, guerrilla war and its violent aftermath. To understand the strategic action by the people of Bango themselves, from negotiation and passive resistance to civil disobedience and war against the state, I consider the force of their own concept of public authority. By quoting extensively from memos, correspondence and reports, I intend to make accessible an official world which the people of Bango were not intended to see clearly. That world was

based upon the closed premise that government on the inner circle by bureau-
crats and technocrats was best. Despite their awareness of being at times
'hopelessly in error', such officials convinced themselves they knew what was
in the people's interest better than the people themselves. For the sake of a
rounded view of the impact of the state on Bango Chiefdom, I present portraits
of officials, including the Native Commissioner, the Land Development Officer, and Chief, who in their different ways sought to redirect the dislocation.

Lest the significance of the Chief, in life and in death, be mistaken, I show
how he managed the contradiction between his private and public stances, how
he came to support acts of civil disobedience, and how he has been remembered after his murder. That leads me to consider the installation of his son
Charles after independence, towards the end of the civil violence which
involved 'dissidents' and the Fifth Brigade of Zimbabwe's National Army, and
which threatened to tear Zimbabwe apart. To conclude this part of the book, I
reflect upon the said and the unsaid in the official rhetoric at this post-
independence installation of the young Chief, a renowned freedom fighter yet,
in the rhetoric of the day, merely 'a keen farmer in deeds not words'.

Upon the basis of that political and social history of Bango Chiefdom, I turn
in the second part of the book to the personal narratives I was told during my
first visit to the Chiefdom. I begin with accounts from the oldest generation;
first the reminiscences of Lupondo's cousin Tobela, who gave the richest
commentary upon the early struggles over the land. Tobela looked back over
his roughly seventy years, from the European conquest and the end of Ndebele
rule over Kalanga to the following decades of colonial domination. After
having been a pioneer as a migrant worker, a kitchen boy then a cook, in
Bulawayo and later Johannesburg, Tobela had served the colonial administration as a clerk in charge of the dipping of cattle; he had observed whites
closely. By nature given to being outspoken, he voiced strongly the people's
grievances about land and alien domination.

The life histories that follow in Chapter 3 from Lupondo's own generation,
and in Chapter 4 from his sons' generation, are more about personal loyalties,
the loves and hates of relatives, than about the struggle over the land. At one
extreme, a brother's wife, Baka Chedza, testified to the unremitting and
ongoing struggles within the family, struggles her memories traced back to old
faults and debts, to quarrels over bits of property, and to crises at birth and
death. Out of the quarrels of mothers as co-wives came the rivalry of their
leading sons. Her realistic stories about the past were full of moments about
which one had to be cautioned as a family member. At another extreme, a son's
wife, Baka Sala, virtually disregarded any major conflicts; she told her life
history as a romance leading up to marriage with the man she loved. Lupondo
himself presented a nostalgic recollection of the good old days, culminating in a
time when his wives were obedient and considerate, followed by times when
some of them were the opposite and most, including his brother's widows,

were virtually at each other's throats, or at his. Each of the leading sons, the rivals Buka and Dzilo, recalled his experiences as a labour migrant and told of his attitude towards town, but these sons, too, were most interested in looking back upon family events in their lives at home. They represented themselves as the heroes who achieved a characteristic of manhood, *masimba*, 'force, power authority', despite the undermining efforts of family rivals and other antagonists. Here my own discussion moves from my earlier concern with the struggle over public authority to the struggle over authority within the family.

This inward-looking concern of both generations reflects the fact that Lupondo's family had reached a crisis of maturity. How the family would split was uncertain. To decide that, family members pored over past rights and wrongs, repeatedly resorting to divination to reinterpret their afflictions; they constructed truths of character, truths of self-justification; they argued about a whole series of family quarrels. They carried on a fine, highly personal discourse among themselves, drawing upon the debris of family history. The life histories were both effect and cause: they grew out of such a personal discourse, and they also carried it forward. Only through knowledge of the sensitive, sometimes petty, personal discourse among family members can we understand the moral argument resonating in each life history and between all the life histories. That is why I devote so much of my own discussion in these chapters to other expressions of the family's personal discourse, particularly the pointed expressions in frank or biting gossip and the coded memorials in familiar names and nicknames. 'The names speak', as I was told: forming a whole series in Lupondo's family, the names of children evoke memories of mothers' histories, their quarrels and their grievances at the time of childbirth. Located in this context of personal discourse, my appreciation of the styles of the life histories explains the kinds of personal narrative that different family members use according to their personal image or sense of self, their place in the family, and their rapport with me.

My approach appreciates the life histories in a context of history, no less than in a context of artful, even stylised discourse. Besides taking account of the dislocation and reconstruction of their Chiefdom, I analyse the importance of changes in property relations, in the value and organisation of family labour, and in the circulation of workers between town and country. Elsewhere I have discussed other trends of development, widespread among Kalanga, by which groups of kin split or come together, wax and wane within localities; and I do not repeat the discussion here (see Werbner, 1964, 1975, 1982). Instead, my historical analysis prepares the way for the third part of this book, on the most recent changes. There I show how the second and third generation recreated the family, and particularly the bonds between brothers and sisters, across town and country. Having abandoned polygeny in favour of monogamy, they organised security circles of a new kind around some of Lupondo's granddaughters, the first women of the family to be permanently based in town.

Much of the third part of the book, arising from my return visit in 1989, reflects upon wartime terror as a remembered experience. It testifies to the grief in bereavement, the anger, and the degradation that family members felt. They had survived a vicious war for the liberation of their country only to be terrorised even more brutally by the Fifth Brigade of their own state in its post-independence campaign against 'dissidents'. I try to make some limited sense of that terrible campaign by a brief historical account of the rise of quasi-nationalism as a violent movement produced in the formation of the nation-state in the twentieth century. In the light of their powerful concern with remembering the past, I ask how and why family members took part in a certain kind of religious revival: on the one hand, focused on aggression and the violation of the person and on the other, centred upon *sangoma* mediums as healers speaking in Sindebele with the voices of the dead. Here, and indeed throughout much of this book, I seek to understand the force memories have in sentiment and passion, their force in the creation of family knowledge, and thus their force in the actual making of the family itself.

The literature on family life in Africa suffers from a great poverty of social biography. The need is not merely to make the voices of the people heard. Even more, it is to make them heard, and understood, as voices which talk with, against, and about each other. After all, as the voices of family members, they are the voices of people who come to know themselves, in highly charged and significant ways, by knowing each other. Yet despite a growing interest in African life histories and personal narratives, the subjects of even the most illuminating biographies have mainly been single individuals such as *Nisa a !Kung woman* (Shostak, 1981), political figures such as King Sobhuza of Swaziland (Kuper, 1978), the Dinka Paramount Chief Majak Deng (Deng, 1986), and the Berber judge Hajj Abd ar-Rahman Mansuri (Eickelman, 1985), or social categories such as *Three Swahili Women* (Mirza and Strobel, 1989).

To meet that challenge of personal discourse within families, a different kind of biography is needed. In my view, it is a biography which is social not simply because it documents social contexts and social processes (for a contrasting view see Eickelman, 1985, pp. 15–16) but, above all, because it places at the very centre of the description, interpretation and analysis the personal narratives of the people whose lives are actually interdependent and mutually significant. My own approach to social biography owes much to the extended case method developed by anthropologists of the Manchester School (for my account of that see Werbner, 1990). However, that method has rightly been criticised for stopping short: it developed the use of case histories without either a full record of the people's own stories or an explicit analysis of their narrative forms (Rosaldo, 1989, pp. 140–2).

My approach relies upon close attention not only to the said but also to the suppressed and the implicit, the taken for granted yet unsaid. This enables me to recognise how, from generation to generation and from one period to the next, family members changed the ways they told about their lives, giving fresh significance to the remembered past. My interpretation of their discourse discloses significant changes in their consciousness of themselves and the world around them. My analysis explores what are the links between the specifics of family history and wider social movements in order to show how one generation has actually come to replace another.

The collection of family members' accounts is of course no more than a first step towards an appreciation of the same events and people, from very different points of view (for a limited attempt at such a presentation, although recorded virtually without the biographer's account or interpretation of the family relationships, see Munson, 1984). By going further, I intend this social biography to be a narrative of narratives. It means that the book has to move between different kinds of narrative: one that documents moral sentiment and passion; another that examines or analyses such documentation; still another that argues, explains or criticises as it unfolds the context of other narratives. My list is not exhaustive; different readers will find their own variations.

I am aware that such multiple engagement, moving through different narratives, poses a problem for the overall coherence of this, and perhaps any other, social biography (for a perceptive review of *Nisa* as a 'braided narrative' of multiple stories, see Clifford, 1986, pp. 103–9). There is a tension between the unfolding of each life history and the development of my own account. There is also a tension between the different subjective perspectives, including my own, and a perspective that attempts to encompass them, in an overview. But problematic as all that is, it nevertheless opens to a greater depth, rather than foreclosing, the argument about the significance of change in the lives of members of an African family.

I am aware of a further problem of my own responsibility: who am I to criticise? The moral problem is sharp for any outsider, once the subject of much personal kindness, who as a social biographer must write not only about a painful family crisis in the colonial past, now distanced from us all, but also about a catastrophe still grievous in the post-colonial present. Even more, the post-colonial state, like the colonial state before it, gave me permission and facilitated my research (my affiliation to the Ministry of Local Government, Rural and Urban Development was nominal). Yet I am obliged to testify to what, in his novel of the liberation war and its aftermath, the Zimbabwean novelist Shimmer Chinodya calls the 'Harvest of Thorns' (1989). Vicious as the liberation war was in itself, its aftermath has brought fresh social wounds, festering and still unhealed, if ever they can be. Of the truth of that, members of Lupondo's family and other close friends have made me painfully conscious; and that is why, within the limits of such consciousness, I write critically about the impact of the post-colonial state upon Matabeleland. *Tears of the Dead* are tears of Lupondo's family, of the people of Bango, and they are also mine.

*Map 1*   Bango Chiefdom, 1989

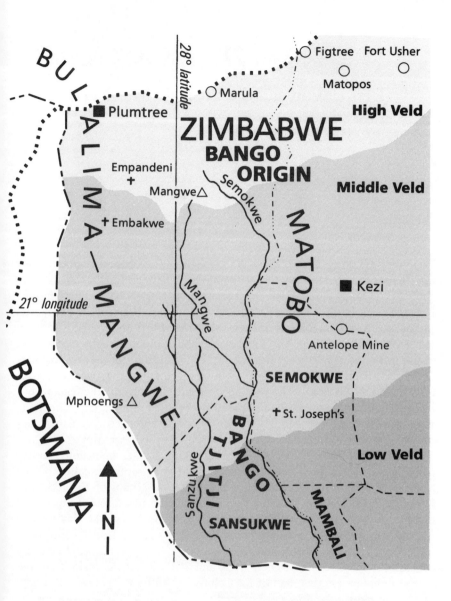

Map 2 Southwestern Zimbabwe

# 1

## Dislocation and the Struggle over Land

From the beginning of the colonial era to the present, a changing struggle over their land shaped the ways that generations of African families made their homes in western Zimbabwe. For members of Lupondo's family, Eastern Kalanga living in the Chiefdom of Bango, this struggle began when Europeans encroached on the highlands or high veld to establish ranches and farms in Matabeleland. It reached one crisis, at the time of my first visit in 1960–1, in open confrontation over measures planned by technocrats for the sake, primarily, of conservation. In the people's own view, however, they were measures for 'carving up the land'. The popular resistance was against the fencing and the resettlement that was to be imposed under alien domination. The liberation war of the 1960s and 1970s carried forward that struggle: to regain control of lost lands was a main reason for going to war (see Moyo, 1986).

Bango Chiefdom, like a large number of others, lost its nineteenth century home in the central high veld of Matabeleland to European ranches (on the history of other such chiefdoms, also peopled by Nyubi of the hills, see Ranger, 1989a, and forthcoming). This dislocation down to the peripheral hinterland, to the more marginal, less fertile lowlands or low veld, was part of a vast displacement: the countrywide appropriation of the land by European settlers (see Garbett, 1963; Ranger, 1970, 1985, 1989a). Legally sanctioned by the Land Apportionment Acts of 1930 and 1941, it left the majority of the people rights in less than half of the Colony of Southern Rhodesia. Roughly 51 900 000 acres, including most of the best land, was legally set aside for the European minority, leaving 41 000 000 acres for the African majority in reserves, in special native areas (areas like the reserves in modes of tenure, but not places originally designated for Africans under the Colony's constitution) and in African purchase areas.

Eastern Kalanga recognised, and rightly feared, the danger of dispossession by European ranches from the very start of the colonial period, towards the end of the nineteenth century. It took some decades for them to feel the full force of dislocation, however. 'Squatters' was the label landlords and colonial officials came to use for many of the Kalanga in Bango and nearby chiefdoms. Even after independence, the label for unwelcomed residents stuck, or was once again made to stick, in the usage of post-colonial state officials and landlords.

Eastern Kalanga themselves witnessed, and readily told me about, a change in farm exploitation. It marked some of the early settlers apart from their successors. Some of the early settlers were content to receive labour, rent and tax in return for allowing the people to remain living at their homes. Later landlords wanted the land free of the people and rid of the pressure from their herds (on the landlords' squeeze by raising rents, see also Ranger, 1970, pp. 37–8). Lupondo's cousin Tobela recalled:

> When we were still living there at the mountains, we saw a European coming one day to tell us, 'This is my farm. I have been told to look after this farm where you are settled.' We said, 'That is alright but where shall we settle?' He said, 'Just settle here. But what you'll have to do is give me money.' That was Kesbaum Teit. We paid tax to Teit, we really paid tax to him . . . he took all the country from our place at Bango up to Malaba, there at Mbakwe near Mpandeni Mission . . . that was our good European . . . we lived there; and then we found the farm had been cut and an Afrikaaner had come in . . . He came when we were at Nswebetani and said, 'There have never been two chiefs. Get up and go. Your cattle are too many; your goats are too many; they are living in this country. This is my country. I have bought it. It is now mine.' It was then they chased us away. We removed and came this side of Ndadza. While we were behind Ndadza, we lived there for a time before one named Kala came, 'Hau! This farm is now mine. Remove from here. I don't want you anymore.' Ah, we were tired of carrying burdens.

Following the initial period of settlement, European settlers began to develop their ranches in ways they considered to be more rational. One result was that they reduced their need for farm labour. Another was that Europeans competed even more fiercely with Africans for land in the high veld, especially grazing land. The colonial policy was, dominantly, to protect European agriculture against competition from African agriculture. In accordance with that policy, landlords, bothered by 'squatters' and unwelcome tenants, were given greater powers of eviction. The colonial authorities enforced the landlords' powers, despite appeals against them, and the people of Bango, along with others, were harried from place to place.

Eventually, in the 1930s, the colonial authorities demanded that the people of Bango resettle at Lupane in the far north. They would have had to return from the south and go past their original homes to remote land in an even more arid and agriculturally risky zone. The burden of this further move was more than the people were ready to bear. They had already been pushed from the high veld to the low veld and the marginal borderlands, along the Shashi River, where it runs as the international boundary with Botswana.

The resistance the people of Bango put forward was based upon their reading of legitimate authority. The order to remove to Lupane, given by the Native Commissioner of their district, had to be a matter for appeal to his *wola*, his senior. On that basis, a delegation, headed by Chief Luposva Bango and including Lupondo's cousin Tobela along with two other prominent, literate, 'smart' and 'modern'-looking men, got the Native Commissioner's permission for an appeal to the Provincial Native Commissioner. The appeal was successful.

Bango Chiefdom was allowed to relocate in the nearby Sansukwe Special Native Area 'C'. There, historically in certain seasons, some Eastern Kalanga had hunted game, or even grazed their herds. There the water was more scarce, but the grazing better (at least at the beginning of their relocation in 1939) than at their original home in the high veld.

### RECONSTRUCTION IN THE LOW VELD

A period of reconstruction followed, for most of the next two decades. For purposes of resettlement, the ruling policy in this part of the low veld remained largely *laissez-faire*. Technocrat planning was yet to come to Sansukwe Special Native Area 'C'. It was also a period, therefore, when the people of Bango were able to negotiate among themselves how and where they were to live. All of this was underwritten by the colonial authorities' promise of permanence on the land.

The idea of public authority over land and people was expressed by *buxe*. Chiefship is one translation; sovereignty, rule, dominion are others. There is a sense, among other things, of rightful, and thus qualified, command. It is accepted authority, to which is owed obedience. It implies a hierarchy, within which the everyday exercise of command is qualified by the reality of effective appeal from inferior to superior. It implies also, that decisions taken in public, or at least presented to the people in public, are not to be reversed in private, as if they were at the discretion of an individual.

*Buxe* was conferred by the people: no man could take it for himself. Nor did it belong to one man by himself, although it was a man's to deploy by virtue of his office. Other people, such as his potential successors, in the case of a chief, his close patrikin, are the 'true owners of chiefship', *beni be buxe*. The expectation was that the chief would take their opinions into account; that some of them would be his advisers, and in an inner council which he would consult about important issues and upon which he would rely for mobilising wider consent among his people.

The idea of *buxe* as such was constitutional orthodoxy, somewhat apart from political practice. But it was the constitutional orthodoxy that still prevailed during my first visit, though in the face of increasing challenge.

Typical of this constitutionalism and its orthodox premises is the homily

given to me by a prominent patrikinsman or 'uncle' of the Chief, when I asked
him to reflect upon his own life:

It is good to live with a person who will obey. If you are not obedient you
will not remain well with people. You will always be a person wandering
about in the country, saying the people hate you, when actually you are
the one who makes them hate you. That is how I live in my hamlet. And as
I am living in this way, I think there is no-one here who can argue with me.
If he argues with me, I send him to court; I have that right. We were given
the powers to be the 'eyes of the chief' [that is, as headman]. If there is
anything that has gone wrong in the hamlet, even if it is at night, I stand
up, and put on my shoes, and go to the Chief. I knock at his door, and I tell
him. He also gets up, and puts on his shoes. He comes, and sees what the
wrong is. If he wishes, he may then take it to those at the head. That is
what I say, we live so. If I am in a hamlet and see a thing and hide it from
him, then I ought to have a case at court. I will be arrested. 'Having seen
such a thing, you did not come to report. What is wrong with you?' Even
forward to Europeans, I would not have a way out. How can I have a way
out? I know I am wrong. It is good that I go and report when I have seen a
thing. I mean, as we live here at Bango.

In arranging themselves in their newly re-established chiefdom within
Sansukwe Special Native Area 'C', the people brought to bear certain organis-
ational skills. They had developed these in local nobility within and between
chiefdoms, and during successive evictions. They made use of personal links to
create chains of immigrants. Each immigrant in turn brought in others to join a
headman established in the relocated chiefdom. In addition, they brought
certain proven cultural resources to bear, proven in defining trust, loyalty,
authority and interdependence between kin and neighbours in the face of
much wider social mobility, including the increasing circulation of migrant
workers between town and country.

The result was that the reconstructed chiefdom came, in a limited number of
ways, to resemble certain chiefdoms in Botswana which escaped displacement
from the high veld. I make this observation on the basis of my study of the
Western Kalanga in the high veld of Botswana in the early 1960s (see Werbner,
19175, 1982, 1989). In Bango Chiefdom, as in the high veld chiefdoms of
Western Kalanga, the densest settlement of hamlets, people and herds formed
around the Chief at the centre. If not a clearly nucleated village, it was a
popular area for many to live in, because it was near the meeting place of the
Chief's court, the largest primary school (originally under the care of the
London Missionary Society), and a substantial store which was part of a chain
owned by Asians. At this core, outnumbering others, were the relatively close
patrikin of the Chief along with some of his maternal kin and affines. Each
major locality or neighbourhood had a focal group of kin; they provided the
central links in the chain to which other immigrants attached themselves. In

addition, in conformity with colonial regulations, clusters of hamlets consti-
tuted 'administrative villages', registered under tax headmen or *sebuku* ('men
of the book', the book being the tax register).

A major limitation in this low veld area was the lack of many small rivers and
valleys. The contrast was to the high veld containing a watershed and dissected
by numerous streams or sand rivers. Given the more limited access to water in
the low veld, the people of Bango confined their settlement to a narrow belt of a
mile and a half to roughly two miles along their main river, the Semokwe, to
the east.

At first, their settlement was more divided than it had become in the high
veld. Rather than being finely mixed together, main areas of residence, pasture
and arable land became roughly separate, though not totally so. The hamlets
tended to be in the middle; they were strung out between the arable lands to the
west and to the east, the main year-round pastures extending to the river. To
the west, the interior of the river valley remained somewhat inaccessible and
largely virgin land, until it came to a belt of settlement, again about two miles
from another river. Here along the Sansukwe River lived the people of the next
chiefdom, Tjitji, some of whom arrived first, in 1936, shortly before the people
of Bango.

During this period, under the policy of relatively minimal intervention by
the colonial officials, some of the people, including Chief Luposva Bango,
prospered. They had been prominent among Kalanga in making a long-term
shift from an emphasis on keeping goats in the high veld to a greater emphasis
on keeping cattle in the low veld. It was a change that was said to have been
influenced by Ndebele and to have begun in the keeping of cattle for the
Ndebele king during the pre-colonial period. These owners of the increasingly
large herds of cattle at Bango found fresh areas of grazing in the Sansukwe
Special Native Area. But there were some people, even among the cattle rich,
who yearned at times for the high veld.

> 'Our old home was better,' a rich patrikinsmen of the Chief said, 'in
> drought years, it was better for maize, and we had the swampy pans [vleis]
> where maize thrived [on the Nyubi use of vleis, see Ranger, 1989]. There
> bullrush millet used to keep for very long, as much as twenty five years.
> There the weevils kept to the top layers in the granary, and left the rest
> untouched,' he paused, and then added, 'but sorghum keeps better here,
> and here it is much better for cattle.'

Waves of evictions from ranches and Crown lands in the high veld and its
environs continued throughout the decades of reconstruction. The mounting
influx of people and their herds, along with the natural increase of the existing
population, brought increasingly severe pressure on the accessible belts of land
in the valley between the Sansukwe River to the west and the Semokwe River
to the east. Increasingly, the interior became a prize competed for by people of
Bango coming from the east and their neighbours, advancing from their side of

the valley in the Chiefdom of Tjitji to the west. Such competition, once established, was to continue even in the post-colonial period. The competition intensified all the more, during the colonial period, when a new pipeline, providing water primarily for cattle, enhanced the value and potential use of the interior at the frontiers between the chiefdoms. This pipeline was on a ridge at their frontiers.

In public meetings, many people of Bango spoke angrily against encroachment from Tjitji Chiefdom. They put their own claim in moral and legal terms, blaming their neighbours. It was a claim which the colonial administration had refused to recognise despite repeated efforts by Chief Jeremiah Ngugama Bango, the successor to the chief at the time of relocation. According to the Native Commissioner writing to the Provincial Native Commissioner, Chief Bango had insisted 'that all Sansukwe Special Native Area east of the Sansukwe was "promised" to his tribe' (4 April 1961). Who got there first mattered most to the Native Commissioner and according to him, people of Tjitji, 'were on both sides of the Sansukwe (in 1936) before the "Bankos" were moved in from the farms (in 1939–40)' (4 April 1961).

PLANNING, MUDDLING THROUGH, AND POLITICAL OPPOSITION

But how many people and animals could or should this area hold was a central question that had to be answered when the Bulalima-Mangwe district policy shifted towards greater control and intervention by colonial officials. The Native Commissioner at Plumtree, the district headquarters, gave his superior an opinion about the carrying capacity of the Sansukwe Special Native Area in August 1957. He thought it adequate to receive a large number of Africans about to be evicted from nearby Crown lands which were to be turned into ranches. A year later, he admitted to his superior that this opinion was 'hopelessly out':

Up till the end of 1956 very little was known about the potential of the Sansukwe Special Native Area . . . when it was gradually opened up there were (in the interior of the major river valley) many square miles of almost virgin country ungrazed because of lack of water. All the kraals were along the Semokwe and Sansukwe rivers [the opposite sides of the major river valley]. Using [the colonial administration notice on regulations for destocking of livestock] as a basis for a similar and adjacent area, I was sure I could take the people from the Crown lands. Since Assessment Committee have sat and the area has been properly examined, it is clear that the destocking regulations on which I base my opinion are hopelessly out. This is my explanation. I would also say that without any reference to this office a Land Inspector turned up and proceeded to cut up the Crown land into ranches (29 August 1958).

Such official confusion came to be a characteristic feature of this second period. It was, from the colonial authorities' point of view, a period of active planning, more rational and more technically informed; and yet in good measure because of that very technical rationality, the district officials were constantly having to make *ad hoc* arrangements. Their 'muddling through' and their being at times 'hopelessly' in error, was what the officials admitted and excused among themselves, often in correspondence or in private, rarely if ever in public, or in the presence of the people they administered. The Matopos Government Experimental Station provided these officials with an apparently scientific rationale for land use planning based on a trusted formula for the precise calculation of the carrying capacity of grazing areas. As Ranger points out.

> [The] experiments [of the station's leading scientist] lent a largely spurious exactness to those calculations of excess human and cattle populations which gave ideological justification to the mass evictions of Africans from central Matabeleland after 1945. (1989a, p. 225)

The people of Bango, and their Chief, in defending themselves against 'the man on the spot', such as the Native Commissioner, deliberately made use of hierarchy, of the placement of each official within the grades of the colonial administration. They appreciated that in certain issues the Native Commissioner was not the official of last resort. His permission had to be gained, they believed, for a lawful appeal beyond him, but the possibility of appeal was held to be vital. The people of Bango attempted that repeatedly, when it came to communal grievances over land.

Chief Bango made such an appeal, unsuccessfully, in May 1960. The plans for resettlement demanded a drastic reduction in herd numbers. It was to be harsh, too severe a destocking, Chief Bango objected. His objection was based upon standards fixed for his chiefdom by the Assessment Committee of 1958. The committee's members included, along with Chief Bango himself, the Provincial Native Commissioner, the Native Commissioner (the predecessor of Dawson, the official in 1960–1), the Land Development Officer, another agricultural officer, and a representative of the Native Reserve Board. Given that prior agreement, Chief Bango was unwilling to accept the harsher policy of the current Native Commissioner, and appealed against it, with the Native Commissioner's permission. The Native Commissioner wrote to his superior:

12 May, 1960

To Provincial Native Commissioner
S.S.N.A. (Sansokwe Special Native Area)
Application of Land Husbandry Act: Grazing Permits
We have got to the stage of having the grazing permits written out ready for the final Land Husbandry Assessment. Chief Banko has been with us at our camp and seen that drastic reduction of present stockholdings will be necessary. The Marketing Officer wishes to have all the excess taken out this year, and to do this a six-month period for sale is all that can be permitted although final decision as to time allowed must be his. Now

Chief Banko has intimated a wish to approach you on the subject of what he thinks a harsh reduction of stock programme. I have tried to explain the details to him but he keeps mentioning the standard number of 15 set by the Assessment Committee. He is of the opinion that every man should have at least 15 animal units as being in accordance with Assessment Committee Policy.

I welcome Banko's wish to discuss the matter with you, and if possible, during his visit to Bulawayo, I would like him to go and discuss Land Husbandry Planning with the Provincial Agriculturalist and Mr. Jordan to see that only a limited number of animal units can be permitted in Sansukwe, i.e. 6,500.

Note the error on pg. 2 of the Assessment Committee Report—10,186 is wrong. It included stock owners on European Crown Land.

|  | 1956 | SSNA<br>End of March 1960 |
|---|---|---|
| Owners | 540 | 609 |
| Animal Units | — | 12,006 |

On the 1956 declaration, there were 2,155 excess stock. Today there are 5,500 in excess and the herds are growing all the time.

To get rid of the excess this year the sales must run at an average of 700–800 whereas the numbers offered have only been on an average of 350 to 375.

The matter of the standard number is puzzling Banko, and I find it very difficult to explain that it is impossible for everyone to have at least 15 head. To allow everyone to have 15 head, then only 400 owners can be allowed in S.N.A. 200 owners must give up stock altogether or find a new home.

I gave certain owners at Banko tank, on Banko's assurance that they would sell certain of their excess stock, permission to go and Lagisa [make a cattle post] in the European Crown Land. They did not sell what I asked them to do, and I have given five their grazing permits and de-stocking orders to dispose of certain excess stock by 3 June after the next sale. If they do not comply with this order, I propose to prosecute.

The Provincial Native Commissioner replied on 17 May 1960, after he met Chief Bango:

His main worry seemed to be that people had to reduce to their permitted holding in one year and as some were very large owners and would have to dispose of a considerable number this would cause hardship. . . . if you think it would do any good I am prepared to come down to discuss the matter with Banko and two or three people but I will not have any mass meeting and in fact would prefer to meet them at Plumtree and not in the Reserve where it would be difficult to keep people away.

The outcome of this negotiation was a delay, mitigating the severity of the destocking but not eliminating it from the plans.

'The Government is always asking us to "cooper" [cooperate],' Chief Bango complained to me, 'but ahh, this British rule! It is not good when one man can change the things that many people talked over and decided [Chief Bango referred to the changes in destocking, in the allowed animal units, and in the location of settlement] and that same man Greeff [the Land Development Officer] is always coming with his quarrelsome attitude and saying, "Bango is not sticking to things."'

The encroachment politics of land eventually reached a watershed. The intensified competition was the culmination of the first period in the Special Native Area, the period of *laissez-faire* reconstruction.. It was at once, also, a force advancing the next period when there was, above all, the threat of technocrat planning for imposed resettlement.

For the Chief, the situation of the interior as a prize yet ambiguous frontier was highly problematic. If the Chief exercised tight control over movement, settlement or the allocation of land—and he was under considerable pressure to do that by the Land Development Officer and his Agricultural Demonstrator—he risked losing ground. The initiative would be gained by the competing chiefdom. On the other hand, to be seen to authorise removal to the frontier would be dangerous insubordination. It would jeopardise the Chief's standing in the district. An open, damaging confrontation with the District's colonial officials would be the result. Yet doing nothing, actually coming to a standstill, was also unacceptable. The people of the Chiefdom themselves reached a moment when they were unwilling to wait any longer for permission or for an authorised allocation of land. The Chief had to have a pre-emptive strategy.

Chief Bango's choice was to do one thing in public, and another in private. In public, he affirmed the Land Development Officer's instructions and his warnings against unauthorised removal. At the same time, the Chief turned a blind eye to new settlement at the frontier. The more people from the competing chiefdom advanced forward, the more he covertly encouraged counter-movement from his side. He managed to let his collusion be understood, at least by some, and yet not publicly known or acknowledged by all; he always conveyed his encouragement carefully in private and freely denied it in public.

All of this situation had important implications for planning as a political exercise in this second period. It was not merely a matter of disagreement over the content of the plans. Even more fundamentally, there was a conflict over the very nature of planning, over the intent, the premises, and the actual participation in planning. Of course, misunderstandings arose, sometimes because of ignorance, sometimes because of deliberate attempts to deceive by concealing motives and actions. Nevertheless, the conflict over planning was carried forward somewhat reflectively by the different sides in that each had some consciousness of the underlying disagreement about the nature of planning. One side, the politically weaker, grounded planning in political strategy. The other and dominant side made planning out to be detached from power, and grounded, as it were, in technocrat rationality. But both sides took into account the other's grounds and perspective.

Seen from the side of the Chief, planning had to be strategic, given the intensified competition. Chief Bango tried to get the Native Commissioner to accept a plan that would allow the people of his chiefdom to move inland. He told me that he wanted a protective 'pad' [paddock] of land around them on both sides, so that European or other groups would not be able to encroach. His premise was political; that a tactical campaign had to be waged and it had to be won to secure the permanence of his chiefdom against threats coming to the land from outside. His intent was to get his people to be placed to the best advantage in the struggle over the land. The analogy he drew, in explaining this to me, was a comparison to a battle. 'In a battle you go to the place of fewest soldiers', he said. In addition, to cope with the perspectives of the district officials, such as the Native Commissioner and Land Development Officer he had argued with them that on the high ridge in the interior the soils were best for an arable block around homesteads. Having that location would give the further benefit of a domestic water supply, if taps were added to the pipeline.

On their side, the European district officials recognised the fundamentally political nature of Chief Bango's perspective. For that very reason, however, knowing his perspective to be strategic and political, they vilified him.

'He's a little Hitler' the Native Commissioner said, describing Chief Bango.

'What!' I exclaimed in considerable astonishment.

'Yes, he is trying to grab bits here and there like Hitler did Sudetenland.'

'Why?' I asked.

'For status and money, he gets more salary the more followers he has.'

From their own perspective, such district officials were above the rivalry between African chiefs. It was as if they had convinced themselves that they alone were not in any battle; that being disinterested, they were the true judges of what was in the best interests of all the Africans in the different chiefdoms. Such conviction legitimising a lack of accountability was, of course, a great advantage in the assertion of authority by alien officials. Not surprisingly, there were differences among the district officials themselves about specific measures, such as the extent of necessary destocking, but their views met in being, above all, conservationist.

Dawson, the Native Commissioner at the time of my first fieldwork, was an old hand, distinguished by long service among Shona in other parts of the country. A paternalist, an autocrat, and in his own eyes, at least, a model senior civil servant, he carried himself in the manner of a man used to being obeyed. Yet he prided himself on his ability to know Africans and their opinions; he made it his business, in the manner of an abrupt, no-nonsense Southern

*1* Women smearing the compartments of a granary

Rhodesian, to ask them what they thought and did. Even after a long and tiring drive across country, some 140 kilometres from district headquarters, Dawson created an impression of considerable force of personality and restless energy.

Dawson was firmly convinced that government on the inner circle, internal planning and internal decision-making by the administration, was best for Africans. That is why, he warned me, I must not interfere in district administration or offer plans to 'the local Africans'. Any criticisms I would write in my papers would be welcome, but I must write them, not spread them to 'the local Africans'. Allowing that there might be differences about the best policy to be pursued, he told me, 'the facts will show that we have little to be ashamed of in the administration of the country'.

After our first meeting, Dawson came to Lupondo's hamlet on a surprise visit, unannounced and unrecognised at first. It was the day after a health inspector had inoculated children against diphtheria. The message I received was that another 'man of injections' had come to meet me. Our greetings and introductions, when I found the Native Commissioner waiting by the fore-court of Lupondo's hamlet, were brief. There abruptly vanished before the Native Commissioner's quick stride all the politeness of entry, the great divide between the public space of the front and the private space of the back and the granaries. His haste dispelled an unquestioned reality of public and personal

2 Unthatched granaries showing open compartments

space which I had come to share with Kalanga. He rushed to the granaries at the back of the hamlet, as members of the family gathered, hearing that their visitor was the Native Commissioner. Even his sergeant major, who accompanied him, was taken aback, and muttered that a person should not just run ahead to the granaries, but should wait to be led along there.

'How much will this granary hold?' The answers Dawson got to his question were clearly as unacceptable as the question itself. Exasperated by the answer of Lupondo's son Buka, 'It will barely suffice a year', the Native Commissioner turned to me, exclaiming in an audible aside, 'Typical Kalanga response! They are suspicious. You only want to help them, and they don't trust you.' He snapped an irritable complaint when he noticed one granary in disrepair, but seemed to accept that it was because, as he was told, the owner was away.

Then, he went on to admonish the people not to sell their grain now. They must keep it for a poor year, he insisted. Otherwise, they would lose by having to buy the same grain at nearly double the price later. They must sell cattle, not grain. They must build up their granaries. He lectured them as if he believed that they would be improvident, and allow crops to waste, unharvested, in the fields, because their granaries were too small.

When I asked him about this later, he admitted that he had never heard of people actually doing that. But he did believe that they might delay in reaping, and would not thresh so rapidly or so well, if they found their granaries to be already full. He accepted also that in a year of foot-and-mouth disease, while cattle sales were stopped, people in need of ready cash had to sell some of their crops. But dismissing all that, he seemed most interested in finding out whether a ritual had to be performed for a new granary. I pleaded ignorance, and he went on to ask, 'Are these people spirit-ridden?' That was so in Mashonaland, where he was really from, he believed.

Kalanga had explained to me their own conservation and storage methods. They divided their granaries into different compartments, so that they could draw on the reserves of previous years in different ways according to how good or bad the present year was. Much careful planning went into the arrangement of a granary. The ideal was to prepare for the future, to save, to be provident. It might be, some guessed, that the present granaries would not suffice, if all the standing grain could be harvested. But actually much would be lost to birds. And if there were need for more granaries they could easily be built, even if there was no grass available at present, for there would be little or no rain to threaten crops in an uncovered granary, for some months. In a good year, people expected to build temporary granaries, for storage by the threshing ground. If some granaries had fallen into disuse, this was after the past run of hard years. No one I spoke to could see people playing about with grain after several years of hardship.

The Native Commissioner announced, after his inspection of the granaries, that he wanted to go to see some of the arable lands. At that moment Lupondo's son Mfila was closest, by his own granary; he scurried to get out of the way and avoid being chosen. (For his and others' brief biographies, see the list of profiles at the end of the book.) Another son, Buka, pushed himself forward, and offered to show the way to his fields. We went together in the Native Commissioner's Land Rover, which he drove at some speed, and with the air of a sportsman enjoying his mastery of awkward, even dangerous, hurdles.

Buka's fields did not please the Native Commissioner. 'A sensible man wouldn't have these in his fields', he remarked, pulling up witchweed. It was, unhappily for Buka, the one patch that he had overlooked. In response, he muttered to himself, characteristically in a way that no one could quite hear, and in a way that the Native Commissioner chose not to hear at all. The last time I had come to his fields Buka himself had ripped out some of the witchweed, and complained what a menace it could be. The Native Commissioner turned to the agricultural demonstrator, himself a Kalanga, who accompanied us, and asked about the yield per unit of area. It was not as high as it should be. The plants should have been spaced further apart, to allow for the shading of one plant by another, the demonstrator explained. Some plants had also failed to yield, due to poor selection of seed. When I heard this, I recalled seeing Buka sitting so very patiently and carefully sorting out his own seed, and also preparing to use the hybrid seed that he had purchased.

The Native Commissioner was himself puzzled by part of what the agricultural demonstrator told him. While at Lupondo's hamlet, the demonstrator said, in answer to a question, that the soil would not take fertiliser, because it burns off in a few weeks, turning the plants yellow. At the fields, however, noting the heavily manured soil, he said that manure was good for this soil. The Native Commissioner wondered what the difference was between the soils at the lands and at the hamlet. Were they not the same type of granite soil? The puzzle remained unsolved. The Native Commissioner made other disparaging remarks, in Buka's presence, about the cultivation, 'The heads of the local variety of millet are large, yet they bear too little.' The need the Native Commissioner said he saw was to get the people to manage a shift from extensive to intensive cultivation.

I asked him who would have to bear the brunt of the shift. After all, even a model farmer like Buka required and exploited nearly *twice* the amount of acreage that he would be allowed in the future. 'He will have to bear it.' Conveying mixed emotions, the Native Commissioner seemed to sigh, as if he were someone whose pity exceeded his power.

Later, when we walked alone, the Native Commissioner tried to gauge my opinion of an alternative scheme that was being put forward for dry areas like this special native area. Under the proposed scheme, the administration was to allocate to a headman and his people a definite paddocked area. Further subdividing of the land would be an arrangement made by the people themselves, and not by the administration. The administration would first make contour ridges in the arable land. Anyone who damaged the ridges would be subject to a fine.

'They couldn't come complaining to me then for more land. They would have to go to the headman', the Native Commissioner said. When he asked my opinion about it, I replied evasively that I would have to consider it further.

The problem was, he said, that cattle experts regard this country as ideal for raising beef. A plough should never touch the soil here, they maintain. If there were only 25 acres per beast, the cattle would fatten up by themselves, grazing along without care. Dawson said:

> But using it as arable land, I can keep a family happy on 25 acres. To support that same family on cattle alone the herd has to be large enough to sell three or four a year, a herd of at least 15 to 20 head. Under the proposed scheme we would give them the land, then they would use it, whether it became overpopulated or not. But we would start by giving extra land over there.

Listening to the Native Commissioner, I began to realise that another emotion mixed in with his pity was the desire that the objects of his paternal care should stand up responsibly on their own. They should not keep expecting hand-outs. 'If you were in America,' he asked me as an American, 'could you demand free land as your right?'

Although he said there was still debate at the policy level, Dawson warned me repeatedly not to discuss these matters with 'the local Africans', as he termed them. He readily admitted that a preliminary scheme, which I had recently seen at the caravan of a Land Development Officer, had already been scrapped. But I should not create doubt, he cautioned me, about whether the present policy would be carried into effect. The technical work, he emphasised, was proceeding ahead.

Our parting words, shortly before he left to return to district headquarters, were about anthropology and anthropologists. Dawson was proud of having helped the anthropologist Clyde Mitchell, my fieldwork supervisor, to find the Njere tree, and he said that Mitchell would remember him. Asking me to speak of him to Professor Schapera, he recalled a 1936 seminar at Cape Town:

> We differed much but liked each other, though some of us from Rhodesia when we got back felt that anthropology was fine to play with after work but otherwise . . .

And here I am not certain whether he said it was gobbledegook, or hot air, or a waste of time, or what, but it was *not* flattering.

Dawson came to Lupondo's hamlet again roughly two months later. The initial plan for resettlement had now definitely been scrapped. The expectation, he explained, was that people would gradually move to the area of their lands, which would become an arable bloc. 'That is not where Bango and Co. think the soil is good. There is a shallow pan over there, as our tests have shown', Dawson said. Toward Tjitji's (Chieftain) on the west was to be a grazing area. Probably people would scatter along, some staying near the river water supply, others moving towards the lands. They would be allowed to take water from the watering place for cattle, but there would be no special pumpline for them—too expensive. One of the fences built in preparation for the earlier plan would have to come down.

'Don't tell the local Africans the news. They will think we do not know our own minds', Dawson said. Hearing his formula about 'the local Africans', I joked, 'they don't think, they know you don't know your minds.' And he laughed.

To get the rivalry between chiefs in a right perspective, he suggested that I visit the neighbouring chiefs, and not take Bango's view alone. He confided:

> On the other side, they call him a newcomer . . . I am telling you confidentially. You must not leak it out to the local Africans. But now Mapolisa [a headman in another chiefdom] is asking to come over here. I don't know what pressures are on him. I think he does not want to come alone, but wants to bring all his followers along. We have got to hear (Chief) Tjitji as well. He has been a good Chief, even though Bango thinks he is an old man behind the times.

Dawson added that between Bango and Tjitji there have been no definite boundaries, but Bango has now been given a map 'private to him', showing the area he will have. 'These people had settled on this river, and others on that one', Dawson said, 'when the Crown lands were given over as Special Native Area.'

From Lupondo's hamlet we went together to see the low-lying bridge. Then newly built across the river that is the district border, it was later named Posselt Bridge after one of the district's Native Commissioners, later a Chief Native Commissioner. Dawson said how eager he was to see it:

> There you see concrete results for the money, in land and animal hus-
> bandry all you see is resentment and no improvements. But we can't have
> a *laissez-faire* policy. We have got to go ahead with modern methods, or
> the country will be ruined.

At the bridge site, having treated me to tea, Dawson declined my lunch invitation, 'I never eat in the bush.'

Watching me closely, Dawson asked if there was any political activity in my area. My answer was that people were concerned about their lands and their cattle. He elaborated on the need for destocking and said, 'We can't make them understand animal units, that so many goats equal a head of cattle.' I had found that Kalanga had no difficulty in thinking of a ratio between goats and cattle. But their starting point was not a speculative estimate, such as the pressure of large as against small stock on grazing, but the actual economic value. 'Goats don't pay, a goat may be £1.10 shillings, a beast £15, so the number of goats for a beast should be much higher than now', Lupondo's son Buka told me.

The new conservationist measures within the district were part of country-wide schemes under the Native Land Husbandry Act of 1951. These were ostensibly intended, in the words of the Act, 'to provide individual security of tenure through the allocation of arable and grazing rights and the establish-ment of sound farming practice including adequate conservation of natural resources.' The minimum requirements of the existing human and animal population were supposed to be covered. In actuality, the conservation of natural resources was given priority by the officials implementing the act in the Bulalima-Mangwe district as a whole, and the Sansukwe Special Native Area 'C' was no exception to this higher conservationism.

Economic prosperity for many was out of the question, at least in the plans. This was because the resources of the special native area were known to be inadequate for maintaining a fraction of the population. If the officials talked about the need for the provision of more land, this was not actually to be granted. In 1961, the colonial administration estimated that roughly 7000 people lived in the 153 000 acres of the special native area. Bango Chiefdom had some 79 800 acres and somewhat more than half of the population, and Tjitji Chiefdom had roughly 73 200 acres, under half of the population. Only certain people were recognised to be registered owners of livestock in the area, a mere 648 residents. Yet, even these registered owners could not be allowed enough grazing for herds of an economic size.

In the initial stage of planning, when the Assessment Committee met in 1958, it was estimated that the area should sustain no more than 6500 animal units (cattle and their estimated equivalent in small stock). However, in 1961 the figure for the actual population exceeded this by at least a third. To cope with a situation that was worse than the planners' expectations, the Native Commissioner was advised to get the people to make a further reduction in the numbers of their stock.

Allowed holdings had to be cut. The reduction was supposed to be from an average of about seventeen animal units per registered owner to an average of less than nine animal units per owner. Yet, viable herds were larger than that, and the largest herds were the most profitable. The destocking demand simply made no economic sense for producers; it would have been devastating for the most viable and profitable herds.

Clear divisions of territory in the special native area were also called for in the plans. After decades of territorial ambiguity, it had become essential to have a public drawing of precise boundaries. The intent of having definite areas was to secure unambiguous accountability under chiefs, accountability in terms of regulations for conservation of the soil. Where each boundary was to be was considered primarily a matter of administrative or technical convenience. A road or preferably, given its greater permanence, the new pipeline would be best for marking the boundary. Any past agreement was virtually irrelevant. Administrative convenience did also include planning for some rough accommodation to immediate possession, which of course meant that taking possession was all the more vital for the future of a chiefdom.

The planned mode of new settlement was based upon the use of paddocks. There was to be a clear separation of pasture from areas of cultivation and places of residence, and these were to be in centralised or nucleated village sites. The Native Commissioner had in mind a radical departure from the people's own practice.

As the people recognised, and the Native Commissioner denied, it was actually a development towards a European settler model:

> . . . the development of the area [of the interior] as a large ranch in which there should be no villages or kraals . . . [otherwise] the damage done on the Semokwe and Sansukwe rivers would merely be shifted to the ridge where the pipeline exists (N. C. Plumtree, 20 May 1960 to Provincial Native Commissioner).

The official immediately responsible for implementing measures under the Land Husbandry Act was the Land Development Officer, at Bango an Afrikaaner named Greef and popularly known as Mavuka. Born and reared in Matabeleland, Greef was a huge, swollen-bellied, gross man, with an unenviable reputation among the people of Bango. One man told me:

> When we were boys, we hunted together, we played together, we talked with each other, freely. Now he tells me to call him Nkhosi (Lord, Chief,

in Sindebele). We must take off our hats before him. The people who disobey him he beats.

Many others complained that 'he has nothing to show us, he is troubling us with his fences.' Greef acted the demanding master as Land Development Officer, never the public servant. His part in the everyday implementation of the Land Husbandry Act at the local level gave him many occasions for bullying and petty tyranny.

On one such occasion, Greef found Lupondo's son Buka beginning to build a brick house at his new site by the pipline. It was a move that jumped the gun on the plans for the area, although by using the rationale that he needed to be near his work at a pump house, Buka had secured the Native Commissioner's permission. Greef shouted, 'Who gave you permission? How can you remove in my country without telling me?'

His arrogance was taken to be a deliberate insult to Chief Bango, who was present and kept silent. 'We try to teach him to be civilised', Chief Bango told me, 'He knows that we won't just agree, that we will talk up. Later when it is explained to him, he will know what happened.' In this instance, the Land Development Officer stopped the building of Buka's house for some time, despite Buka's efforts to explain about the Native Commissioner's permission.

Another occasion of the Land Development Officer's petty tyranny was the meeting to confirm the land registry listing all the rightful holders, who were to be entitled to fields under resettlement plans. The meeting was held near the tank for dipping cattle, on the morning when the veterinarian also came to inoculate the herds. Greef sat with his assistant. Chief Bango stood then sat on the margin, just outside the shelter, facing his headmen who were under a shade tree. The expectant hush of the headmen, among whom I sat, was overwhelming, and I found myself speaking only in the softest whispers.

'Bango,' ordered Greef, treating the Chief like an untrustworthy errandboy, 'make it clear that these books are from the old tax records.' Later, loudly enough for everyone to hear, he warned his assistant about a headman who had attempted to correct the list. 'Watch him, they'll always try and swing some fast one', he said. Some widows were missing from the list he read out for the Chief's own list, and the Chief immediately named them as missing. 'Bango, why weren't they registered in 1956? Why weren't they registered', he bellowed in fierce anger. Chief Bango insisted that they had been registered, and he did not know why now they were not.

Greef's assistant shuffled his papers at some length. Eventually, he found a list with the rest of the widows. But Greef himself wasted no time on an apology. Throughout the meeting he seized on any signs of what he could consider to be insubordination. If a headman stopped to consult with the men he represented, Greef would shout, 'Don't talk to him about it there. It is finished over here.'

In the eyes of the people of Bango, the Land Development Officer, more

than any other government official, represented both the threat against their
having their own land and the arbitrary use of power by the alien few against
them, the real owners of the land (on Kalanga ideas of land ownership see
Werbner, 1975, 1982). He embodied their dispossession, making them feel,
they said, that they were being hemmed in like donkeys in a pen. The fencing
and the cutting down of the land that kept their herds from moving to grass and
water was all his work. The Land Development Officer was the one they
blamed most for destocking, for the hardships they met when bringing their
animals to the veterinary tank for dipping.

One elder, who made these complaints about the Land Development Officer, also criticising the Chief for not doing something about it:

> How can the beasts go such distances and then have to wait there without
> anything to eat, from morning until afternoon, through the heat of the
> day? This thing of dipping is hard, hard. Spread out, the cattle can find
> grass, or something to nibble. Bunched together, there is nothing for
> them.

In the same vein a cousin of the Chief remarked:

> How can he come to destock our cattle, when whites have large farms they
> are not using? We are being crowded into a corner. They have the rule, a
> few men, and we have to obey.

Another close relative of the Chief's said, 'Before the good comes we must
suffer. It can't come like water to be swallowed without chewing.' He hoped
that the government would see the people's need for more land, and that it
would change its policy. He added:

> Many people might have built better houses, if they had known that this
> was to be their permanent home. Instead they had had to suffer removals,
> removals, removals. And was that finished?

Many of the people of Bango feared that they would suffer losses of land,
crops and cattle due to the measures under the Land Husbandry Act. These
measures required the amount of a man's land to be limited within units of a
standard area, 12 acres in the Sansukwe Special Native Area. For example, a
polygamist like Lupondo's cousin Tobela would be allowed one standard
area for himself and one wife, and a third of this for each of his other wives.
Tobela feared that because his large family worked a much larger than average
area, the new measures would force him to reduce the size of his fields,
beyond tolerance. Moreover, as Tobela explained it to me, a kinsman at home,
usually an elder such as Tobela himself, often had to take charge. He had to
provide or organise various services which were essential for keeping a wage
earner's fields cultivated during his absence at work in towns or elsewhere.
Yet, the land was to be reallocated by alien officials, such as the Land
Development Officer, who lacked very specific, local knowledge. Such reallo-
cation would be made in ignorance of the labour needs and the claims of owners
of nearby fields. The plans would disregard and, consequently, disrupt vital

arrangements between interdependent kin. No allowance was made for family arrangements to meet the diverse requirements of agriculture at home and migration to work elsewhere.

Severe and very sudden destocking was demanded by the plans, because enough land for the prosperity or even the minimal needs of the people was not to be provided. The threat of impoverishment was feared alike by owners of large herds as well as small ones. Some owners of large herds, including Tobela, spoke against the destocking policy because it meant ruin for them in particular along with great hardship for subsistence production. A similar conclusion was reached by the only economist in the colonial administration who had made an intensive study of prospects for the low veld under the Land Husbandry Act. This economist pointed out, in a report of June 1960 that 'in this respect [of destocking] application of the Land Husbandry Act is a retrograde step' (Hunt, 1960, p. 6). He argued:

> . . . proper use of the low veld areas is on the basis of a livestock economy, through the management of large herds over extensive areas of land. The Land Husbandry Act with its restrictions of herds to three times the standard holding perpetuates, on the basis of present standard numbers, relatively small herds. It completely eliminates the comparatively few herds large enough to provide a good income under efficient management (Hunt 1960, p. 6).

Years of preparation were needed. The plans required surveys and numerous meetings with the people of the chiefdoms. In the meantime, the people were ordered to stay put, or be tried and fined by the Native Commissioner or later a magistrate. Such threats were actually carried out, for political reasons, against an exemplary few among the many who did remove towards the interior. Later in this chapter I describe a direct confrontation between the technocrats and the 'fathers', the heads of families in Bango Chiefdom.

The implementation of the Land Husbandry Act had begun much earlier in the adjacent chiefdom of Bidi, across the River Semokwe and in the next district, Matobo (on the civil disobedience opposing the Act in this District, see Ranger, 1989a, pp. 244–5). The organiser of the National Democratic Party (NDP), the newly formed successor to the banned African Congress (ANC), came to Bango from Bidi on an organising campaign in late February 1961 (on party leadership, see Mlambo, 1972, pp. 136–64). I asked him why the African National Congress had not been so successful at Bango as it had been at Bidi. 'It was a matter of time', he replied, 'Congress had been organising there for a year before they came to Bango.' I was with a young cousin of Chief Bango, and the youth immediately insisted on his own answer, 'The Land Husbandry Act came in there long enough for people to have already felt it. Here the government has hardly begun to destock.'

When the party organiser tried to explain how and why it was that the NDP was fighting against many laws, the Chief's cousin voiced an opinion that I heard from many others at Bango, 'You are fighting just one law [the Native Land Husbandry Act].'

In a similar vein, another cousin of the Chief and a schoolteacher spoke out, when telling his neighbours, over a pot of beer, what he thought after hearing a speech by the nationalist leader Joshua Nkomo in Bulawayo. He reported Nkomo to have asked and then answered:

> What does Reserve mean? There are only urban and rural areas. Reserve! As if the land is someone else's, and a part has been reserved for us! How can the Government take away the rights of boys to land and throw them into towns where they cannot get jobs? And the chiefs, they must be warned, they must not be stooges.

The people of Bango became increasingly aware of the very severe impact that the measures under the Land Husbandry Act had elsewhere. Stories circulated about the damage done by the Land Development Officers to the north, especially in Nata. The stories also told about the riots and stone throwing the Land Development Officers provoked.

### CONFRONTATION: A TECHNOCRAT, THE CHIEF AND THE CHIEFDOM'S FATHERS

The sharpest expression of a growing political consciousness came in June 1961 at the confrontation between the heads of homesteads and hamlets, the 'fathers' of the chiefdom, and the technocrat planners. A planner, Wright, announced the specific proposals for the resettlement scheme without having fully briefed Chief Bango in advance. Nor did he give the people of Bango the opportunity to hear their Chief's understanding of the specific proposals and then discuss them among themselves. The Chief was informed merely of the general outlines. The simple fact that the proposals *were* radical, an attack on the mix of agriculture and pastoralism in favour of beef production for the market, was something the planner would not admit to the people themselves. After all, he was certain that he had the benefit of scientific experiments for looking after the land, technical knowledge of soil conservation, and a right understanding of the country. His certainty extended to the very definition of the country: it was 'cattle country'. He was quite sure that the local soil was not suitable for crop production, although neither he nor anyone else had made any study in depth of the productive economy the people had developed, under conditions of labour migration, through drought and depression or recession, in the face of the sharp risks and uncertainties of the local climate and the wider economy. In fact, his own certainty derived from agro-ecological categories, framed around commercial agriculture by larger-scale farmers, that dominated the official wisdom in the colonial period. The people had to fit in with that, mainly producing beef for the market: it was in their own best interests, for the sake of better yields from better farming methods, in brief for the sake of progress and development.

Although this technocrat presented himself as coming to consult the people, not to give orders, he was seen in a different light. The sense of the meeting was that he was approaching the people in a way that they could not be united among themselves. Their complaint was that had he really wanted what he claimed to want he would have let them sift through the proposals first. Some opposed him because they saw that his method of consultation, undermining the Chief and weakening his authority, also weakened them against the outside world. Others, less concerned about chiefly authority, could simply not contain their anger, being outraged by the proposals. It was striking that even the severest opponents took care to base their protest on an appeal to *buxe*, to chiefship and public authority, to premises of constitutional order which, they insisted, like the chiefship itself, were prior to European rule. They attacked the Chief, not the chiefship. They found fault with the Chief for having reached an earlier agreement, in 1958, on the official assessment of land use, without public discussion. While they upheld the ideals of the office of Chief, they rebuked the Chief personally for acting without the endorsement of the heads of homesteads duly gathered at the Chief's court for consultation. Their protest brought them into a direct, head-on clash with the Chief himself, whom they denigrated and whose exercise of authority they challenged in a way that he felt he could not tolerate on such a public occasion.

The following extracts from my transcript of the meeting document this protest and the unfolding of the confrontation. I give this documentation at some length, because there is a great need in our literature for substantial evidence to disclose the use of premises of constitutional order and chiefship by the people resisting dispossession as opponents of alien domination. Such documentation is all the more important in our present post-colonial period, when the discredited 'scientific wisdom' of colonial officials threatens to be revived, designed to be truths in an ideology of development, by the new technocrat officials as post-colonial successors of the old.

The planning officer was not happy about my own presence; he avoided my greeting, and made something of a demonstration of ignoring me. At the very end, he hurried off, as if not wanting to be seen in public discussion with me, and I had to find an occasion to come to his trailer to get a better sense of his own views.

Before the planning officer started, he asked the Chief:

You have no objection to this European [in an ironic tone] being in on this meeting?

The Chief replied without concern:

No, it's all right. He's just an anthropologist and we have nothing against him.

In his address to the people, the planning officer gave this introductory speech, appealing as if he had the best knowledge of the ecology and the technical grounds for efficient, proper land use:

I've already spoken to your Chief giving him general outlines of what we're going to do here. I presume he has passed on this information I gave him. I asked him to pass it on so we could come and discuss this ourselves. Many of you have seen us going about here asking questions, writing on maps and pictures. You have probably been wondering what we've been doing. All we've been doing is very simple, planning so you can use better farming methods. We've collected most of the information we want. Now we're down to the planning stage of laying out areas. That means telling how many people, how much arable, how much water.

Now what I asked you to discuss is the division of this area into units. Your Chief probably knows more about units than I do, for he's had units in an area across the way in his headman's [Headman Mgulatshane in the adjacent Matabo District].

One difference about these units is that they are large units, not small units. Large units have been developed because this is an area for stock and not for arable. According to climate and rainfall and soil, this area is not suitable for crop production. It should be for stock only. That's why we're laying out this plan on a large unit basis for the purpose of stock farming and beef production.

Now I don't know what you think of that. This area is laid out in three units, each to carry 1000 head of cattle. There is provision made for arable. The suggestion is made that each unit be divided into paddocks, two for grazing and one for living and arable. The most suitable way we see at the moment is to have the living and home paddock down this end near the river. The rest of the area right through to the pipeline is to be divided into two paddocks, one for the rainy season and one for the winter grazing.

The planning officer went on, making light of what in fact was radically wrong with the plan, because it failed to redress the shortage of land:

There's one slight difficulty. That is the amount of arable in what we call the home paddock. It doesn't have quite enough to give each man the assessed 12 acres. This would mean each farmer would have to accept reduced acreage for arable. I might inform you also that the area is very, very overstocked and according to all proper farming planning, it's over-populated, especially where Chief Bango lives. There it's the most heavily populated and overstocked unit. Other units further down are not so heavily stocked, for some reason. In fact, if we are to get a proper distribution, we'll have to get some people to move down there. I have to draw up a report on this very shortly and I should like to hear your views. I'd like anyone who wants to ask questions or discuss this to do so.

Chief Bango spoke very briefly:

They are chopping down land and fixing up fences. The area at Mak-wakwa [a section] is to be divided into three. They've already mentioned putting people by the river [in the opposite direction to the actual drift of the population inwards to the valley], and he says my people at Gwambi [the river near another section] are too many. He says some should be sent down there [further south]. What do you think? It is a proposal not a finished thing. This is the time to give your words.

The immediate response came from a young homestead head, rejecting fences and planning so plainly modelled after a European ranch, something alien from the planner's own home:

I personally do not like such a thing. We hear what the white chief [official] says. His words are heavy. If he now says we ourselves are to have fences like fenced cattle, and we're to have small farms, then he is making things in the way of his own home.

The planner replied, trying to minimise the fact that the plan aimed at increasing beef production at the great expense or neglect of arable agriculture:

This will make very little difference to your farming. It will improve it. You can rest a paddock and graze one and have more cattle for sale. It's the start of a programme to have better and fatter cattle for sale. It's not something to disturb you very much. It will help you for you can put cattle in paddocks and you won't have to herd them. You'll only have to bring them to the dip [tank], but instead of being locked up in the cattle pens they can graze for twenty four hours, and not for sixteen. The question is where do they want their arable, to move it or to leave it where it is now?

In immediate response came the one significant intervention by any one of Lupondo's sons. Lupondo's son Buka avoided any protest or criticism of the Chief but simply addressed the narrow issue of the location of the arable area; his concern was about the impact of the change on his own and his family's fields. I draw attention to this narrow concern because it fits the more inward-looking tendency of the family members' life histories which I discuss in Chapters 3 and 4. Buka remarked:

We hear of grazing for cattle. Up there it's better. Here [in the area where his own lands were], it'll be too near some people's lands.

In their further response, people of the chiefdom argued against the fences; they attacked the planner's claims to know about overgrazing and the grounds for destocking. The planner defended the fencing by saying:

It is not my wish, but a general practice of soil conservation and of looking after the land.

The Chief tried to direct the discussion to his own objections to part of the plan:

The talk is first that you are to be settled by the river. I want to tell you what you are to talk about. They say you are grazing along with Wobodo [in competition with people under a headman of the next chiefdom]. I don't want [arable] lands along the river. [People of] Makwakwa [another section] can plough near home. At the Makwakwa assessment committee [in 1958, see above] we decided that people should have twelve or more acres [contrary to the planners' current proposal]. I refused to let them send us near the mountains. If you talk like fools, where will we graze?

Another homestead head resumed the argument against fences and raised an underlying concern about the threat of further dispossession by European farmers, for whom the fences would represent an attractive development:

About making paddocks, we left the farms behind us near the Railroad. Are Europeans going to come here and again buy?

The planner answered:

No, I'm pretty sure that will never happen.

The homestead head continued, emphasising that herding had its own mode of efficient practice:

We are not satisfied. We do not want that way of building paddocks. Who will agree to mix up his cattle with those of others? They must be separate when they graze and when they water.

Others put further objections, questioning the motives of the planner:

Is he doing it for those who like the soil or for us?

The planner insisted:

This type of planning is not only here but it is everywhere in the world. I don't want them to think it is done only for them. It is done everywhere. We are passing on the information of experiments to show us how to do these things correctly. We are trying to pass this on to them so that they can build up this country and the land as well.

A prominent leader of the protest, who had recently returned from working in South Africa, argued:

Where is it that this has worked well? One thing I know is that there they agreed and were not forced. We refuse and we do not want wires. We told you, but you had already put up the fence. You did it without consulting us. We don't want it. In talking to Europeans about fences we are wasting our time. We grew up having cattle and we know about them; we don't want any European cutting down the land or moving us about. As for what was said by the Chief asking if we want to go over there, that is what we want to be asked by *him*. Then the answer will be from us and not from the European.

Other heads of homesteads took up his points, comparing the fences to rocks on the people's heads, a trick for the sake of more control and more destocking. The planner was criticised by a locally important activist of the nationalist party (NDP), himself a known friend of the Chief, for not writing down their words:

He's not writing to carry our words to the other officials. This means that the thing is already finished. It's like a bag that is already stitched up . . .

The Europeans are troubling us. Today we see them coming to cut this land. How are we going to live in this country of *God*?

The planner's interpreter missed the point, and many shouted at once, 'This country of God', emphasising that the country belonged to God, not to the Europeans. The speaker continued:

Where will we live, for we are always being pursued. We ask you to free us [from that] because we pay tax and we do what you ask of us. We don't want our lands cut down, and we don't want to have our fields interfered with. If my cattle get thin, I'll sell them and get £5, that's all.

After a barrage of similar objections from the people, the planning officer turned to the Chief:

Chief, I seem to hear that these people and those under them feel against my development taking place in this area with regard to improved farming methods and they are against paddocks. So if there's anything else you want to say?

Put on the spot, the Chief answered:

I want to tell you this. I personally won't run away from the way the plan is to work. The plans we are talking about have already been applied elsewhere. In other small places there is no wire [fencing]. On Monday, they were doing that [implementing such a plan] at Mbembeswani [beyond the Chiefdom]. I asked you [the people] to talk about how we are to be settled. If you say you do not want it, then you'll not be co-operating with the government.

One of his most prominent critics, a remote patrikinsman and 'uncle' of his (although roughly his age), rebuked him:

We are disappointed when the Old Man [the Chief] goes over what we have talked about. You were put in the chair by these people and not by the Europeans.

The Chief began to reply about the specific issues he considered could be and needed to be considered within the framework of the government's policy, 'He [the planner] asked if you want to have homesteads by the river and to have less than twelve acres', but he was drowned out by an uproar of voices:

We object and we refuse. The farms will soon be here, and the Europeans will say go. We thought our Chief was supporting us, but now he is killing us.

The Chief defended himself, saying:

I felt that we should go along according to the proposals. But if they come and drive us away, what shall we do?

The party activist and known friend of the Chief's spoke again:

Let them come and drive us off. Others will come here, and we'll get good land.

The Chief tried to continue his defence:

I wanted you to reach a good understanding.

But one of his prominent critics went further:

Our Chief is the one who should go to them and say our people refuse [to accept it]. Here we find fault with our Chief.

The Chief persisted:

I told them, as I told you, that we are ploughing on rocky places [unsuitable areas], and we want to move. I told the LDO [Land Development Officer] in 1958. When we had the assessment committee, we agreed that each family should be given not less than twelve acres. As a result of today, I see the twelve acres are to be reduced. To that I do not agree. I want the same acreage agreed on by the 1958 assessment committee. Also, it was recommended by the 1958 assessment committee that people should be settled along the pipeline at the ridge. There were to be two lines of settlement. There were to be paddocks, as he says. But today there is much change from the agreed suggestions. I had favoured the recommendations of the 1958 committee. I 'co-oper' [in English, co-operate] with the government. I stop there.

The planner himself turned to attack the Chief by flatly contradicting the Chief's account of the recommendations of the assessment committee:

I've got the assessment report right here. And the recommendation by the committee is this, paddocking on a pipe scheme for rotation of grazing. There's nothing said about land on the pipe scheme or people moving to the pipe scheme. [He turned in irritation to the Chief, and went on with heavy irony.] But your Chief has given me his view. He says it appears things, acreage and allocations, have changed. Let me assure you nothing has changed. There has been no mention of change. The discussion has been about planning. And we have been talking about a reduction only if they are satisfied. If they are not satisfied, then I recommend no change. That is why I asked the people to come, so I could see whether they liked it, or didn't like it. It appears I've now got their feeling, which is that they don't want any reduction in the assessment committee recommendations. They're not keen on a large paddock grazing system. They would rather carry on ploughing wherever they like by moving away from the broken down lands they're now using by the river. Is there anything I've left out?

I might also mention that I talked about paddocks and units in paddocks, but I never mentioned fencing. They are the people who mentioned fencing. No one else mentioned fencing. Thank you very much for meeting me and talking about it. I know what people think. I know that you people are not interested in large paddocks, but in what the 1958 assessment committee reported.

The Chief gave his own summing up:

What we don't want is to have the twelve acres reduced.

This summary did not satisfy the Chief's critics, and the party activist who was his known friend probed further:

I'm asking about something I don't understand. They say that they are going to reduce the 1958 assessment committee's recommendations. But who attended that meeting?

The planning official answered:

Yes, it was the Chief.

The party activist continued his questioning:

We hear of the agreement. But who agreed with the government?

The planner parried the question:

I don't know. I wasn't there.

Another critic, the Chief's 'uncle' and also a leading party activist, insisted:

You are sent by the government, but you are the government.

The Chief recognised that the line of questioning was directed against him, and answered:

I went to the assessment committee in 1958. Where there is no Council nothing moves [the people of his chiefdom had refused to have a council on the official model, fearing it would be used against them. Later the Chief was able to form such a council, including his 'uncle', the critic and party activist.] If there had been a council, I would have taken two men with me. Don't talk of that now. Some of you were away at the time, working for the Europeans. Some who were here didn't speak up at the time.

There was an uproar, and pandemonium broke out, with various voices shouting:

We're being forced against our will.

The Chief riposted, challenging his critics as mainly labour migrants who had been away in 1958:

We can't wait for boys in town.

His friend and critic drove his questioning home:

How could you agree, when you did not consult the *lubahe*, the court of the Chiefdom?

The Chief's 'uncle' went on to censure the Chief, with great passion and in words beyond anything the Chief was willing to tolerate. He reached his peak by disparaging the Chief for supporting Europeans simply to fight for bread for himself:

What the Chief says does not satisfy us. We think the Chief is supporting Europeans. It shows because he talked alone at the committee. He had not told people. We only saw them coming to castrate us. We did not know what they were talking about. The Chief should agree, for he is fighting for his bread.

At this point the planner's interpreter, a Sindebele speaker not at ease in Kalanga, turned to him to tell him that the Chief would not allow him to translate the last remarks, as an insult. But the planner seemed to get the gist of it, or its intent, and shrugged it off.

The Chief's 'uncle' concluded his remarks:

It disappoints us. Yes, I am disappointed to have to criticise our Chief. He was not chosen by Europeans. When Europeans came, Bango was already here. [The chiefdom predates the colonial era.] And I am disappointed in him.

The Chief replied angrily, claiming that he did have the authority to act on his own, a defence that was soon dismissed:

You should know that when the Chief is chosen, he is for the people [he represents the people]. If I follow that [having to consult first], everything should be refused. How can it work? You say I should tell *you* first?

Another prominent patrikinsman of the Chief interjected:

You ought to say I am still going to tell the people, the men I represent.

Up to this point the Chief's critics had all been at most in their mid-forties, men of his own age or younger, and mainly still labour migrants. But his willingness to claim that he could act on his own provoked his own mother's brother. This authoritative and powerful elder expressed his disapproval in a rhetorical question:

How can you do a thing even in a homestead without telling the people in the homestead?

The Chief's 'uncle' shouted above the muttering:

You are bringing deadly bread now.

Another leader of the protest complained:

We hear now of 1958 and things he did and agreed then. He acted without our knowledge.

The Chief interrupted:

I told them afterwards.

The earlier speaker continued:

Today we hear about it when the country is being split. The Chief will say we despise him, but we obey him. Yet he has not come to his fathers to tell them what has been suggested. If the calf does not suckle from the mother when still allowed to suckle, what will happen? Now we see that the Chief is throwing us away. We don't hate his flesh [him personally], only his law. We know he gets his bread from the Europeans. I don't, so I can say so. He fears he'll lose his job, if he tells us. He doesn't see that he is going to break up the country. The whole truth is that the Chief won't get things done because all of us criticise. The Chief should dream of his deeds every night. When you have all your children under you, why do you throw them away? I'll stop here, but if the Chief does not understand, I'll answer.

In anger and with an open threat against his opponents, the Chief answered:

I thank you for what you have said, that the country has Europeans, for otherwise some of you would have been killed [by the Chief for daring to insult him]. I answered all that I said to the Europeans. I told it all to you. According to one of their laws, there are assessment committees, and if there is no council, the Chief goes to the committee alone, but if there is a council, then two men go for the people.

The Chief's friend among the party activists insisted:

The council is the paddock. If we agree to the council, then we would fall into traps.

The Chief's 'uncle' added:

We are not thankful.

The planning officer tried to conclude with a round of thanks:

Chief Bango and people who have come to discuss this matter, I would like to thank you for coming here and giving me your idea of what you want. These ideas are most important. And the fact that you don't want planning will be put in the report. But what will be done with the plan after that, don't ask me, for I don't know. But I assure you the area will be planned, and all the facts and figures will be put in writing. There'll be no more I was told by so and so, and now so and so says this. The report will be given to your Chief to read. So he'll know what the report says. In fact, he'll know all about it. And I can certainly hope nobody will say we've not been told. With the number of people here there'll be no necessity for such remarks again. Any other developments that take place through me will be passed on to the Chief and to you, unless you want a meeting with me. I'm prepared to come. I don't think I've any more to say. Thank you very much, thank you Chief Bango.

With the meeting virtually over, the Chief tried to extract a concession on the matter that had been the major issue for him. It was to get permission for his people to be allowed to move into the interior of the valley, towards their arable areas, away from the river, and towards the encroaching followers of the next chiefdom. The Chief expressed his own thanks and said:

Thank you very much. The only thing is that some people would like to move to [their] lands to put up their granaries.

The planning officer fobbed the Chief off, by saying:

You're [getting] ahead of me now, but I have to go to Bulawayo in a few days [and can consult about it]. I myself think there's going to be no permission whatsoever.

Following the meeting, the Chief responded to his most openly damning critics by making a political example of them. First, he had them charged under the Law and Order Maintenance Act. Later, he secured the mitigation or suspension of the charges. His outspoken critics had to be wary; he could, if he wished, use the full power of the colonial state against them, but they should know that he did not actually want to do so.

The Chief himself soon found that he had to take a new part in the wider political struggle. At first, however, it seemed as if he would continue to be able to manage the discrepancy between his public co-operation and his private opposition to the state. Shortly before the end of my first visit, Chief Bango was chosen to be a member of the newly established Council of Chiefs. This body was intended to serve the administration as a national alternative to the nationalist leadership in political parties. Despite their strong views about the Chief's political tactics in his competition for territory and followers, district officials thought it wise to strengthen the Chief's position and secure his further co-operation by rewarding him with an increase in his personal allowance. In making a case for that, Native Commissioner Dawson described Bango's leadership in a letter to the Provincial Native Commissioner:

> *Chief Banko Ngugume*
>
> I wish to make the following recommendation:
>
> His personal allowance to be raised from £2 per month to £8 per month bringing his total monthly salary plus allowance up to £25. Banko is our only educated Chief.
>
> He is an ex-schoolteacher and can speak English. He was chosen to be a member of the Chief's Council and will be expected to travel to Salisbury and Bulawayo for meetings of the council. He has to arrange meetings with the other three chiefs of this district and put their views forward at council.
>
> He is a leader of a difficult section who want to have nothing to do with the Land Husbandry Act Unit planning. They took their grazing permits quite well in 1960 but as our destocking orders came to nothing because of the foot and mouth disease, they haven't as yet resisted 'destocking'. Banko tries his best to follow agricultural theory planning and put it over to his people (Native Commissioner, Plumtree 19 September 1961 Ref Per/5/Banko/61).

This view of Chief Bango, that he was doing his loyal best, trying to follow the planning and trying to persuade his people to accept it, did not remain the official assessment for long. Within half a year, Chief Bango had responded to an increasingly more militant mood among his people, the Native Commissioner had changed, and so had the official view of his co-operation. In the later official view, Chief Bango was held to be giving tacit support to threats or acts of civil disobedience, such as threats by some of his people to drive their cattle on to European farms in order to regain their grazing areas. Powell, the new Native Commissioner, wrote to Chief Bango, to put on record a reprimand, threatening to withdraw the whole of Chief Bango's personal allowance and subsidy:

> I am sorry that it is necessary for me to have to write to you a letter of this sort.
>
> I think you are aware that chiefs are expected to co-operate actively with the government. The personal allowance and subsidy paid to a chief is a reward for the assistance and loyalty he gives to the government.

Provision exists for the withdrawal of this subsidy and allowance, if the chief ceases to give active co-operation to the government. I regret to have to say that, during my short period of office here, you do not appear to have co-operated actively with the government. Nor do you appear to have been acting in the best interests of your people.

I hereby warn you that unless there is an immediate and marked change in your attitude I shall be bound to make representation to have your personal allowance and possibly also your subsidy withdrawn.

I think that you are fully aware of the reason for this letter. On a number of occasions you have misrepresented facts to officials. I am also informed that on occasions you misrepresented facts to your own people. There is also the point that I have made a very determined effort to persuade your people to sell as many cattle as possible, because of the very severe drought. In trying to do this I seem to have had no support whatsoever from you, and your own dip tank has had very disappointing entries for sales.

As a member of the Chiefs' Council, you are a person of some standing, and it is very disappointing to find that you are not looking after the interests of your people.

There is another point that I wish to mention. Some of your people have threatened to cut the fences of European farms and to drive their cattle on to these farms. I have been given to understand that you have knowledge of these threats but that you have done nothing to dissuade your people from doing this. As a chief you are expected to control and advise your people and I suggest that you tell your people at once that it would be most unwise to break the law in this way.

I hope that you will take this warning seriously. I have no desire to ask for your allowance and subsidy to be withdrawn but if you carry on as you are doing at present, I shall have no option.

I will be delivering this letter to you in person and if there is anything you do not understand I will be pleased to explain it to you (Native Commissioner, Plumtree, 9 May 1962 per 5/Chief Banko/62).

In fact, it took some eleven years and a number of such political complaints against Chief Bango before his personal allowance and subsidy were withdrawn. But in the face of continuing resistance during the early 1960s, the resettlement scheme for Bango Chiefdom was postponed. Eventually, most of the measures planned under the Land Husbandry Act were abandoned and never implemented at Bango. The administration's retreat was part of its effort to suppress the nationalist movement growing across the country.

But did Chief Bango lose all legitimacy in the eyes of his people, because of his 'co-operation' with the Rhodesians during this period? The evidence I have suggests the opposite: that his actual resistance and opposition to the

Rhodesian state was recognised by many of his people, including his first-born son who became a prominent commander among the guerrillas.

At least from 1976 onwards, Chief Bango gave direct backing to civil disobedience against the Rhodesian regime. He refused to prosecute anyone for non-payment of dues to the local council. He supported the popular refusal to pay school and cattle-dipping fees. At the height of the guerrilla war in 1978, he was taken alive by guerrillas who intended to escort him safely to Botswana. He wrote the following letter to his daughter, Elizabeth, in London, telling about that, in guarded language, after he was recaptured by the Rhodesian Security Forces and placed under protective custody at the District Head-quarters:

> I am now leaving [living] in Plumtree. I am still a life [alive]. I was not killed by the Freedom Fighters.
>
> They abducted me on the 20th of March at 8 a.m. while I was in the field.
>
> They marched me towards Botswana via Brunapeg and Mpoeng's areas. We slept in Brunapeg. They were two armed [guerrillas]. I was having my short [shot] gun with me.
>
> On the 21st of March we came in contact with Security forces, here the firing began, and the Boys retreated. Nobody was hate [hurt] in the contact. I remained covering and I then told the Security men that I have been abducted. I am Chief Bango, and they also told me to cover. I still had my gun with me no bulets [bullets] (Chief Bango, 28 April 1978).

While Chief Bango was under protective custody, the liberation war reached its peak, forcing a new tactic on the part of the Rhodesian regime. The Rhodesians turned to nationalist leaders within the country, above all Bishop Muzorewa of the United African National Council (UANC), who were willing to join a white-dominated government. Their negotiations resulted in an abortive agreement known as the Internal Settlement, under which a show was made of elections in April 1979, despite the intensified guerrilla war. In preparation for the elections at Bango, a district officer held a meeting which was very poorly attended; all the people in the Chief's own section of the chiefdom boycotted it. In his report the district officer gave these opinions:

> If we can get Bango back ... the admin and support could improve drastically. Especily [Especially] during the elections. It appears that some of the locals are scared to come to the polling stations because of the army. They class anyone who wears the camo [camouflage] as army. I believe there has been too much skull bashing in the area and that it would be to our advantage to cut this out as much as possible. I have dispelled this fear. The curfew also seems to be a sore point. They all like the idea of the curfew being from 6 a.m. to 6 p.m. during the election campaign. I told them that if there is a good turn out for the election I would speak to you about keeping the curfew between those times (District Officer, 14/4/70, in SBV2/1).

The District Officer reported that the Chief had considerable support, and that it included the backing of the 'local ANC [African National Congress] man', the local representative of the internal wing (ANCZ) of the nationalists fighting the guerrilla war under Joshua Nkomo's leadership. Who 'the local ANC man' was is important for our understanding of the political strategy Chief Bango pursued. 'The local ANC man' was among the most prominent of the Chief's publicly outspoken critics, who were charged under the Law and Order Maintenance Act in 1961, after their confrontation about the administration's resettlement scheme. This former critic, himself an agnate of the Chief, became one of the Chief's important allies and trusted councillors.

I lack the evidence for a substantial account of Chief Bango's life upon his return. Sadly, I must say more about his brutal death on 12 May 1984. At district headquarters, in the official file for his chiefship (Per/5/Chief Bango), a cable (33/84) from the District Administrator to the Provincial Administrator gave the first government notice:

A report has been received by this office that Chief Bango was assalted [assaulted] and died on Sunday official report to follow.

No further report was filed at district headquarters, other than the following, sent almost a month later by the District Administrator to the Provincial Administrator:

It is with regret that I have to inform you of the death of Chief Ngugana [Ngugama] Bango of Sanzukwi Communal Land who was murdered by dissidents on Saturday the 12th of May 1984 (Per/5/Chief Bango 8 June 1984).

Chief Bango was murdered after independence and, as I explain more fully in Chapter 5, at a time when the notorious Fifth Brigade of the Zimbabwe National Army was still on the rampage, sometimes with the active co-operation of the police. The Fifth Brigade's hunt was for 'dissidents'. Among these 'dissidents' were ex-freedom fighters formerly of ZIPRA, the opposition party's forces, who were suspected of taking up arms again. The phrase 'murdered by dissidents' came to be used by the Fifth Brigade and officials of Zimbabwe in the same way that 'killed in cross-fire' was 'used regularly by the Rhodesian security forces to camouflage the slaughter of civilians during the [liberation] war' (Lawyers Committee for Human Rights, 1986, p. 36). In that year of crop failure, a total blockade was imposed by the Fifth Brigade. It halted the flow of food from the towns and it strangled the countryside throughout the whole of Matabeleland. There was a curfew, harsher, more devastating in terror, even more ruthless in its violation of human rights than the curfew Matabeleland had known under the Smith regime. Chief Bango's people remember that he tried to defend them, that he protested publicly against abuses by soldiers of the Fifth Brigade. Within days of one of his protests, he was found inside his hut, battered to death; his body was stuffed

*3* Chief Jeremiah Ngugama Bango in the colonial regalia

together on his bed. The first person to find him told me that the place was full of soldiers; there were no footprints other than those of soldiers' boots.

Chief Bango's body was taken away for an autopsy. His relatives recovered it, with difficulty, for burial at Bango. Police warned them not to make a complaint, to accept the official version of his murder. Nevertheless, his relatives insisted that I listen to their accounts; they urged me to report the truth of his murder, although they were still wary of themselves being identified by name. According to their accounts, soldiers of the Fifth Brigade claimed a 'dissident', captured at some distance, confessed he had received a gun and ammunition from the Chief. The soldiers accused the Chief of aiding 'dissidents', and used his own shot gun as further proof. (The Zimbabwe Republic Police record for the gun, issued at a time of concern about 'dissidents', associated the Chief with guerrillas:

> ZRP [Zimbabwe Republic Police] police issue voucher for double bar-
> reled 12 bore shot gun weapon purpoted [purported] to be property of
> Chief Bango recovered from guerrilla forces 1978/79 (19/3/81, Per/5/Chief
> Bango).

The Chief's relatives told me the soldiers had beaten him, demanding information about 'dissidents', and ordered him to march to their main camp at Brunapeg, despite his plea that he was too weak for a long march, because he was recovering from surgery. The beatings must have reopened the surgery. The Chief's murder was perceived to be also an attack on the leader of the opposition party, Joshua Nkomo; the Fifth Brigade was said to have intended to kill Nkomo's own Chief, Nkomo having himself been born at Bango. A close relative of the Chief concluded his account by saying, 'He was killed by the government, not by the guerrillas. We hold no truth in our government.'

If in life Chief Bango, having both 'co-operated' and resisted the colonial state, never ceased trying to embody *buxe*, in its richest senses of legitimate public authority over land and people, in death he became an exemplary figure on behalf of his people and their struggles over the land. So brutally murdered, Chief Bango became a figure of martyrdom. Chief Bango has come to embody the suffering of many others at the hands of a merciless force of the post-colonial state, once it turned against former guerrillas and against the people themselves. Their memories about their ordeals during the liberation war and the violence after independence are the subject of Chapter 5, where I return to the significance of Chief Bango's death.

The regulation by the post-colonial state of the chiefly succession roughly followed colonial protocol. Soon after Chief Bango's death, the colonial regalia of chiefly office, known as 'the traditional regalia', a white pith helmet, a Southern Rhodesian badge, a staff, were recalled, to be conferred again at an installation ceremony. Following a year of mourning, an authorised delegation from the chiefdom, testifying to 'a family tree' (the colonial genealogy with current additions) and a history of the chiefdom, reported to district headquarters that family and public meetings had recognised the Chief's first-born son Charles, the former guerrilla commander, as his successor. In turn, district officials forwarded their recommendation, along with the required clearance by the police, for government approval, which was granted, making the official appointment of the new Chief on 8 January 1986.

The installation of Chief Charles Bango on 8 August 1986 was a great public occasion. It was a carry-over from the colonial period, yet in important ways it was quite unlike any colonial installation. Held by the Provincial Governor in the presence of close to a thousand people, it was the first occasion, since the campaign against 'dissidents' had eased or virtually stopped, for the chiefdom to receive numerous senior government officials, party politicians, senators, chiefs and other members of the elite of Matabeleland. It was celebrated with 200 litres of beer donated by the municipal brewery of Bulawayo and game donated by N. A. Greef, the owner of Fairfield Farm and Mavuka Meat Market and a close relative of the chiefdom's late Land Development Officer.

The installation provided a platform, among other things, for dutiful political rhetoric. Such rhetoric avoided comment on the struggle over the land, or it simply called for obedience to the law, stressing the fulfilment of public duty, in the face of the post-independence violence that had threatened to tear the country apart. Most strikingly, the dutiful political rhetoric of the installation was free of direct, open reference to the martyrdom of Chief Bango himself. In a brief appeal for peace and an end to violence in his own home area, Joshua Nkomo, the leader of the opposition party (ZAPU), spoke against 'dissidents' and urged 'that people should co-operate with the law enforcement agencies' (Senior Administrative Officer, Plumtree, 19/8/86, Per/5/Chief Bango). Nkomo made his appeal in accord with negotiations, resumed in late 1985, for unity between the opposition and the ruling parties, for the sake of a one-party state.

The Provincial Governor's speech, recorded in a draft text, is worth quoting entirely, no less for what it left unsaid as for what it said. Some of the draft text was based on the history given by the Bango delegation to their district's Senior Administrative Officer. The text is the draft prepared for the Provincial Governor by the district administrator:

Personal Name: Charles Bango Dube

The Traditional Name [Bango]: a Kalanga word meaning dry wood. The Chief himself is of a famous Nyubi family, being descended of Tshilisamulo. Bango the dry wood who is the most senior chief of the Nyubis in the Matobo Hills. Nyubi people settled in the Matobo Hills area long before the arrival of Mzilikazi, the king of the Ndebele, even well before the Swazis. Second Chief was Nimahamingotshylise. Third Chief Tshilase of the most senior house. Fourth Chief was Kangangwani. Habangana became regent when Nsimbi was still not of the age for chieftainship. Habangana died, his young brother Gulumbalayi had to act in his place for Nsimbi for a very short time. Tawunhla was regent, when Nsimbi became of age, he took over the chieftainship and died in 1924. Following upon the death of Nsimbi, Mbubi was made regent acting for Ngugana the late Chief whose son Charles is being installed today. Following the death of Mbubi in 1937, Luposva was made regent and noted [sic] between 1937 to 1953. Later in years the Bango people settled at a place called Mabunga at the source of Semakwe [Semokwe] River. The notorious Land App. [Apportionment] Act forced the Bango people to split in 1938—main groups with the Chief went to settle in the south of Plumtree the present Sanzukwe Communal Land an area of 46,000 hectares. The other group went to settle in what is now Semokwe Communal Land in the Matobo District. This group is presently headed by Headman Mgulatshani born of Sikafu under Chief Bango Ngugana.

Development Projects—The late Chief Ngugana initiated some grazing schemes in the area and was instrumental in the formation of Bango collective Farming Co-operative. Charles is a keen farmer in deeds not words. Chief Bango had two headmen, one Matenga in Mambale area Sanzukwe Communal Land and the other Mgulatshani in the Semokwe Communal Land in Matobo and has a supporting force of 83 kraal heads in the Sanzukwe Communal Land in Bulilimamangwe [District]. For the chief to discharge his duties correctly and effectively he must be one with the people. The people must give him maximum support and together with the Councillors Communal, VIDCO [Village Development Committee] Chairman, etc. develop the area. Thank you (Per/3/Bango Chieftainship, Draft Speech, Bango Chieftainship).

In content, this draft speech exemplified an official proclamation on orderly practice, regular succession from father to son, apart from the odd caretaker as a temporary stand-in. It could have been made at any time, for the succession of Charles Bango to his father's office. It invoked a traditional past, recalled the reigns of past chiefs and regents, including some of their headmen, and briefly mentioned the late Chief's part in the making of his chiefdom, in particular his contribution to 'development projects'. It called for unity between the people and the Chief in the fulfilment of their duties and for the sake of developing the chiefdom. The closest it came to a hint of conflict was a mere mention of 'the notorious Land Apportionment Act' as a colonial cause of dislocation, dividing the chiefdom between two districts. What it disregarded totally was the terror and the violence which, however much it had eased, no one present could have forgotten. The young Chief was 'a keen farmer'; his leading role as a freedom fighter for ZIPRA, the opposition party's guerrilla force was passed over in silence. There was no place in the draft text or in the rest of the political rhetoric at the installation for talk about the debt of the state to the people, about the impact of their civil disobedience against the colonial state, about their heroic efforts as freedom fighters, about their suffering and deaths as civilian victims of war, or about their sacrifices in the struggle over and for their land.

But what did the people themselves have to say about such matters, and how did they talk about them in accounts of their lives apart from official occasions? The rest of this book answers that and other questions of family history in the light, mainly of the memories of Lupondo's family, their kin and neighbours.

# 2

# Living with Europeans in our Country: Tobela Reflects

Talk about living with Europeans was common in casual conversation at Bango. Members of Lupondo's family and other Kalanga at Bango often exchanged and savoured their observations about Europeans as officials, traders, missionaries and employers in domestic and other services. During my first fieldwork, the one among Lupondo's close relatives who had the most to say about Europeans, their political cunning, their promises and practices and their plans for Africans, was Lupondo's cousin Tobela.

Tobela had first-hand knowledge of Europeans, from the turn of the century onwards, that was by far the richest compared to that of any of the other close relatives. One basis for this was in Tobela's long work career, including some seventeen years as a government clerk. Another was his achievement of political prominence at Bango, such that for some time no important delegation from the chiefdom to the district or provincial headquarters would have been complete without him. Tobela brought a very distinctive perspective of his own to bear on that rich knowledge, which he deployed in conversation with considerable rhetorical skill. His experience of a large number of court cases, being an administrative headman or *sebuku* and one of the Chief's principal counsellors, had given him the opportunity of honing the arts of arguing a case while spinning an anecdote to a persuasive point.

Although in his late sixties or very early seventies, Tobela had the bearing of a man at the height of his power. If his broad-brimmed, felt hat with the faded, brown satin band, which he kept at a rakish angle, was long past its best days, there was still the semblance about him of the 'smart', 'modern' man of his youth. He usually wore a shirt that was clean and ironed, and trousers which were neatly patched together from different pairs. Robust, self-assertive and still sustaining a well-deserved reputation for being proud, even arrogant—a reputation rumoured to have a dark side to it in many notorious accusations of witchcraft—he was actively in command of his own family's major assets, including his large herds. To be fierce in his own defence was a lesson he had learned as a herdboy living away from Kalanga and among Ndebele, who had treated him at first as an inferior and a retainer or servant. His boast, made to me with a characteristically roguish laugh, was that he had returned home to beat other Kalanga boys by fighting with a stick in the Ndebele way. Indeed, as his cousin Lupondo remarked, disapprovingly, carrying a stick, even at a funeral, was a hallmark of Tobela's throughout his life. Once he took me round the hamlets of his 'administrative village', the cluster of homesteads and hamlets over which he had responsibility for tax and public affairs, and concluded the tour with a lordly, sweeping gesture, and the remark, 'These are my "retainers" [balanda].'

Tobela was one of the pioneers of a long-term trend in labour migration from his chiefdom. His succession of jobs in towns and on a farm, from his teens to his late twenties, took him from kitchen boy to cook. The sequence he recalled half a century later was: first, from 1912 to 1913, working within his own country to the closest big town, Bulawayo; then, from 1913 to 1915, outside the country to the distant city of Johannesburg; next in 1916, to a farm near home at Marulla; later, from 1918 to 1919, back to Bulawayo; and finally from 1920 to 1921, back to Johannesburg. Young workers from Lupondo's family and many of their neighbours largely followed his lead until the third succeeding generation. His migration, and theirs in turn, was usually seasonal, tied to the aim of coming home to plough in good years; and he kept to domestic service, which they extended to restaurants and related service industries. What he and they deliberately avoided was mine work. 'We don't go into burrows', a son of Lupondo told me. Going down into the mines was fit for animals, not for them.

Becoming literate and learning to speak English facilitated the new pattern of labour migration which Tobela pioneered. Tobela, like many other Kalanga, had a very high estimation of the schooling he got from missionaries, particularly from John Whiteside. Contemporary letters by John Whiteside and other London Missionary Society missionaries record the great eagerness of Kalanga for schooling, and the difficulties due, as G. J. Wilkerson wrote, to 'the constant moving of the people, partly through the increase of rent, partly through the white farmer requiring the land for himself' (29/1/1911, Fig Tree Siding, L.M.S. Archives). Tobela told me that he went to primary school with two Kalanga who later continued their studies at the L.M.S. Bible School at Tiger Kloof in South Africa, Chief Malaba and the father of Joshua Nkomo, but Tobela's own father refused to let him go with them. 'He said it would mean I would get married too late.' Tobela's memory from 1909 of the attendance at Tiger Kloof by Reverend Mongwa Tjuma, one of the first Kalanga missionaries and the father of my assistant, fits the contemporary report by Superintendent Richard C. Williams, 31/–/1909 in the L.M.S. Archives. It was characteristic of Tobela, the once long-serving clerk responsible for numbers, that he wanted the dates he gave me to be accurate, which they were, so far as I have been able to check.

Tobela married his first wife in 1918, while still a labour migrant, but did not become a polygynist until he returned from town permanently and took up a new, rural job—clerk of the dip tank for cattle. For that job literacy mattered, but it came to him, in good measure, because he was a close and favourite affine of the Chief. The pay Tobela received was less than for the town job he left. His gain was in various advantages other than gross income. Holding the status of a petty official of the administration in his chiefdom made him a 'gate-keeper' in some relations between European officials and Africans. Moreover, his monthly wage, which went from one pound ten shillings in 1921 to three pounds two shillings and six pence in 1938, was secure; and it meant that he usually had ready cash for taxes and school fees, without interruption or much need to sell his livestock excessively, until he resigned in his late forties. Consequently, he was able to marry three more wives, provide for many dependents, educate several of his children beyond primary school standards (none of Lupondo's children had reached beyond the primary standard three at the time of my first fieldwork) and, at the same time, build up his personal wealth. Eventually, his political prominence and influence was recognised by the Chief, who made him a councillor of the court and, thus, one of the Chief's four closest advisers.

Tobela recalled:

My wives were four. I had 'grouped' [made a group of] them. The missionary told me, that year we were baptised by John Whiteside, 'No, you should remain with only one wife, according to the way that I baptise you today.' Then we thought about the minds of our fathers, because of this ploughing and because of having to work for the Europeans. We found that one wife cannot manage to plough alone. We had to get her a companion to help her in ploughing. Then we took that in mind and followed it.

Then we went further, and it troubled us. When it comes to ploughing, they do plough for us, and our food is more than that of a person with one wife. A man with one wife is defeated in the year of starvation, because he must eat perhaps five bags [of grain] or six bags. We eat fifteen bags a year, or even twenty, if people are many in that household. But what makes us fritter away money is that one wife has her children, another has her children, each separately. When I pay out money, I don't pay as little as another person. Some money goes to the mother, some to her children. When they go to school, one has her school fees and the other has her school fees. And the money comes from me only. This troubles me very much.

The thing we were warned about by the missionaries is this we see today [the burden of having several wives and maintaining their children]. For I cannot do it, when I am not working myself. How much of it can I do? There will be words, 'My child is hated. Why was she not bought a new dress?' Yet, I have got enough money for dresses for only two children; and for those other two of the other households I have no money. Then it will be said that 'My children are hated just as I, their mother, am hated.' Yet, you love her, she is your wife, and she gives you food. Eh, I am talking, Dapiwa. [He swore by the name of his sister.] I am conversing with you; I am teaching you, and you are a teacher, you [turning to my assistant].

In our conversations Tobela tried to explain at length the difficulty, even the impossibility, of striking a balance between the households of his family, so that their many needs and claims could be met fairly. Tobela's eldest son had returned, permanently, from labour migration in Johannesburg, and become a wage earner at home, teaching at the local school, roughly at the same time as Tobela had retired from his own rural job at the dip tank.

Such co-ordination by father and son of their careers as rural wage earners might have meant increasing prosperity for Tobela's family as a whole, particularly since Tobela eventually got his son-in-law his old job of dip clerk. But quarrels broke out; the eldest son, who transferred to a school outside the chiefdom, deserted his wife, and tried to avoid providing for her, and even for their children. Tobela complained, in his least charitable moods, that all that bound his son was his interest as the primary heir of Tobela's large herds. 'What holds is the property I have, and the cattle I have in the pen.' Tobela feared that some of his children would suffer and fail to get the same benefits as the others had; and envy would fester with hatred in his family. Only the children of his first wife had reached maturity while he still had his cash income from a rural job. They should have been the ones to help him provide for their juniors, thus repaying their father, now that they were comparatively well educated and able to earn better wages than most. But these favoured children of his first wife, Tobela had occasion to know, would reject obligations, especially towards others who were not their own mother's children.

These considerations, and others bound to them, were grave enough in themselves. But even more grievous, Tobela feared, was the danger that they would be made much worse by further taxes and government restrictions expected to cut back the permitted holdings of land and cattle. This danger had a long history, he saw. As some historians have shown, around the turn of the century, white employers' demands for more cheap labour increased. In response, the colonial administration introduced the early taxation measures Tobela described. The administration's intent was to meet the employers' demands by compelling Africans to work for wages (Gann, 1965, pp. 175–6). Tobela himself viewed the present pressure and the latest measures for 'Land Husbandry' in the light of one past step after another in a gradual yet relentless history of encroachment. There was a long-term strategy of domination which he discerned, and it was implemented through cunning tactics, each one seemingly small and innocent in itself.

From the very beginning of my fieldwork, and I was introduced to Tobela on virtually my first day at Bango, I was drawn into long conversations with him, in which he was the main talker, expounding his views and experiences at length, and I the listener, asking questions to raise a general topic or for clarification but otherwise responding for the sake of mutual understanding in the flow of his speeches. The edited quotations I give from these sessions at his hamlet are from my tape recordings. The fact that I was tape recording was, if anything, an incentive for Tobela; he wanted people in other countries to realise how the local Europeans were treating Africans. When it came to more personal matters, before pouring forth he would sometimes caution me not to let others hear, and I would reassure him that I would not give their own names, when I published the book about them. My assistant served as interpreter, at first, although we eventually had sessions without him, when I became proficient enough in Kalanga, and then we also had many casual conversations, which I did not tape record. Unlike some members of Lupondo's family, who grew more or less cordial, as I explain in a later chapter, Tobela remained willing and eager to talk with me throughout my fieldwork. I found it easy, fruitful and always heartening to spend much time visiting him, based as I was nearby, within a couple of miles, at the hamlet of his cousin Lupondo.

### TOBELA RECALLS

The following are Tobela's reminiscences about living with Europeans:

About our living with Europeans in this country of ours? We can really recall that, and from the year the train came here [in 1897], from the time of that war [1896], and even from the year the Europeans came into this country.

### Taxes and the Influx of Europeans

They were saying, when all the men had been counted, that we should pay a tax of ten shillings. After that, wives were counted, and the word was a man with two wives will pay a tax of one pound and ten shillings. That was the counting of the people's wives to this day.

It went on like that. Later, the dogs had rabies, it was said. 'Now work on dogs and buy mouth bits [muzzles] for your dogs for sixpence.' We bought them, put them into the dogs' mouths, and then the dogs went to pick faeces.

During those days, Thomas, the Native Commissioner, said 'Dogs are distressing us, and people are not eating well. Dogs covered all over in children's faeces come to people. This is distressing. Those bits of iron [the muzzles] weren't good enough.' We said, 'Alright, we have seen it.' They said, 'Come, we shall prepare some good ones for you for a shilling.'

Do you see that we started with a sixpence, and then came to a shilling!

Still at a shilling, we were told we should buy neck collars for the dogs. Those were for two and six. Hau! We bought those collars. Then still there, we heard, 'What now? A dog itself should be five shillings.'

We killed the dogs, and no one remained with a dog. Only the Chief had a dog, for he was earning money, merely a pound in those days. Yes, there was but one dog in those days, at our Chief's, a dog called Bulongo. We spent about three or four years, I think, and found that it was bad in the hamlets, that people could not live like that. So dogs had to be bought for the hamlets, and once bought, they were five shillings forever. Many people had dogs, and they had to pay five shillings, five shillings, five shillings. Later, we found they [the Europeans] had turned about and were saying, 'No, a dog should be ten shillings.' We have paid that tax of ten shillings up to this very day.

Eventually, they came to cattle, saying, 'You should buy dips for cattle, and get a lot of money for them. Your meat will go to England and to any other parts of the world where they need it, because you have bought the dip for the cattle.' And again, 'A person's cattle will fetch a high price.'

People made a collection a pound, a pound each man. At my place we dug out two dips, paid for by the men in our country of Bango. Then when we had done that, we paid tax for the cattle. Next they said, 'Sixpence, sixpence. This money will be used to buy medicine that will be put into the water. This sixpence will be for the wages of the dip attendant who keeps the record.' I was a dip attendant during those days.

For about seven years, I think, we worked that way, working alone under our Native Commissioner, Mr Luning. There were no Europeans with us. After seven years we found them saying, 'No, it is not right that the money should be kept by you black people. You blacks will steal the money when you are there. The collection must be taken by Mr Dawes, a European, once a Constable.'

So we worked with Dawes, the collector, who sent the money to the Native Commissioner, until they hired one called Mr Ingraham, Ma-tanda, and in turn we worked with him until the doctors were hired. Now the Europeans were many. There was no black person who then kept the cattle money, they [the Europeans] collected the money themselves.

They were hiring each other, the doctors and the supervisors. They took the money for the cattle, the dip attendant merely counted, one, two, three, four, until he finished the numbers and put each down in the name of so-and-so. Those others, the Europeans, came to collect the money from that person. And you got just enough money for the month.

In those days, when we were working, we worked hard, yet we got no money, a mere pound a month. It went on further, until I, the old dip attendant, was getting two pounds, ten shillings and the newcomers were getting thirty shillings. And today, as the work is growing and going forward, the dip attendants are getting up to five pounds. I am the one who lifted up the work, but today there is no one who knows me.

### The Census and Early Missionaries

We first played with girls before the first census, before we had taken registration certificates. When the first census was taken, we were also counted. Policemen who travelled on foot, went about lifting up our loinskin pelts. They'd say, 'This one can climb up an ant heap.' Then we were taken to be counted and given registration certificates. That is what used to happen to us. When they said, 'This one can climb up an ant heap', what did they mean? They meant that we had become men, and as they lifted our skin pelts to see our testicles, they said that we were able to go with women. They used to do that to us. We took our registration certificates that way; it was just for the census.

The missionaries came in 1907 bringing school. 'School, school, school, learn', people said, we were taught to read from card one to card twenty two. We read those cards until we finished them.

Reverend Tjuma [the father of my assistant, Timon Mongwa, and one of the earliest Kalanga to attend the London Missionary Society's Bible School at Tiger Kloof] returned to us, wearing a tie when he came from Tiger Kloof. His tie was knotted this way and ours that way. We were not putting on this kind of shoes, for walking on thorns [sandals made from old rubber tires]. We wore real shoes, we were with those of [he named various friends]. Ah, those days are passed. Is it now? No, it's not today. It was 1909.

We were 'gentlemen' [in English] then. When we went along, a European police constable came mounted on a horse. He said, 'Take off your hats.' We said, 'How is that? A European is saying, "Take off your hats."' We pulled off our hats, and we had parted our hair. 'Ah father, father, father, ah.' He came after us. He was using a stick as he went.

[The European was abusing them for taking on the airs of Europeans by wearing hats and parting their hair, and what astonished them was that one European beat them for what—wearing hats—other Europeans, the missionaries, had taught them to do.]

There were then no bicycles. There were no things [motorbikes and cars] then. Only horses. All these things were not then.

In 1912 a white man [the L.M.S. missionary], John Whiteside, told us that, 'We are teaching you. You should study hard. You'll see the white men who will be coming from behind there. They will come flying like birds; yes, flying.' We said, 'Why, Missionary?' 'It's name is Hellplane', he said, 'Hellplane.' 'How, is it so? Will they fly?' He was really telling the truth, that European.

In 1911 he told us, 'There is a star that will arrive [Hailey's Comet]. It will set at dawn. For such a star, you should pray hard. If it meets with the sun, it will break and you will all die.' On the day he said, we saw. By the way, was it in May? If I'm not mistaken it was in May or June. Anyhow, it was long ago in 1911 that we saw that star. Those of us who were told came out and shouted in the middle of the hamlet, at that time when it was still a big one. At night, we found a huge line, a star that had a tail from there to over there. It stayed there for days, that star. Oh, maybe it was telling of these things we see now. We do not know. In that year the star remained there and remained there, until it went to die.

We found that the teachers in Bulawayo were better than our first ones. We had to read the primer, and I read it in Bulawayo, until I was in Standard One. We stayed in Bulawayo and only came home for vacations. I was able to speak English, but the others [at home] were not.

## From Kitchen Boy to Dip Clerk

At the Europeans', in Bulawayo, I worked as a kitchen boy and went to the eight o'clock school in the evening until it finished at ten. We stayed and stayed living like that, and then I was working for whites and no longer learning. I got as far as Standard One, no further, and then worked for myself, under the whites.

Today the children we send to school to be educated come from work, from the Europeans, and the money is theirs. Long ago when we went to work, before we had wives, we would bring the money to father. All the money we had got would be brought before him. Then we'd be given some, 'With this money go and buy your clothes.' Once I was earning five shillings a month, and the money was taken from me. I worked for four months and came with twelve shillings. The rest of the money I used for buying clothes. A vest was one and six, a pair of trousers one and six, a pair of shorts that stop so far, all that was three shillings. And some other money I brought, too, was used by my father to buy a goat from Bulawayo that he lent in trust to Ndodlane who lived nearby, almost in the same hamlet. He bought it from one kraal and it was kept in another kraal. When I grew up, I collected ten plus five goats, fifteen goats altogether. Among them were two he-goats I used to pay Kesbaum's tax.

It was after I had taken a wife that my father told me, 'Your goat is there at Ndodlane, the one I bought with the money you earned. Go and say they should show you the goat.' Truly, they showed me fifteen goats.

As the days passed, we married our wives. But the missionaries said we should not have married without Christian rites. They turned us out of their church, because they said we had broken their rule by not marrying in church. 'And also your membership cards show a lot of debts, [they said]'. We had to pay twelve shillings for our membership cards. So they turned us out saying, 'You took wives and did not marry in church and your membership cards don't show any money in them.' We stayed and stayed with our wives still attending church, but not being members. Later on we took more wives. I married three other wives besides my first wife.

It was in 1921 that I first began to work as a dipping tank clerk. Chief Bango said, 'Since you have the eyes which can see [the capacity to look after something and also the ability to read and write], you ought to be counting the number of cattle at the dipping tank. You can record the money paid by people, and then send it to the authorities in Plumtree.' So as a dipping tank clerk I began collecting tax money from the people in 1922 and sending it to the Native Commissioner in Plumtree. Called Nswo Nswo [a poisonous plant which is blinding if it gets into the eyes], that Native Commissioner would use the money to buy arsenic and bring it to the dipping tank [for purposes of treating the cattle]. I worked that way, collecting money from the people and sending it to the government, until veterinary surgeons came to work among the people. I would get only one pound for my pay. Oh yes, I really worked for those people! They then hired Mr Honey, who was responsible for testing the amount of arsenic in the dipping tank. I worked with him until he grew too old, and left the job. Another one came, and I worked with him, until he, too, went away. Again another one came, I worked with him until he also went away. They then gave me a white man called 'Ndozo' [elder's staff] and said, 'Now the money will be collected by this white man, you, being an African, will not collect it now.' So Ndozo began collecting the money.

In fact, we collected the money together, but it was taken by Mr Ndozo. I was then paid one pound ten shillings. I worked with that man until he died. Another one called Matanda came, and I worked with him, till 1938, when I said, 'Ah, I'm tired, I'm now stopping work.' I told them that cycling to Plumtree was too strenuous, and was ruining me, and that they should give me a place near my home so that I would not have to do much cycling. I asked them to give me a light job to do, and told them that I had worked for them for many years, but nobody paid attention to what I said.

[Tobela's long career as dip clerk was associated by many of his neighbours with powers of sorcery. His cousin Lupondo told me this story explaining why no outsider could keep the job, why it had to go to Tobela's son-in-law:

Once a man was sent to be the dip clerk. The European at Plumtree told him, 'Go to the hamlet of Lupondo. You should not go to Bango, you go and stay there.' I saw him coming and I said, 'Hey, don't you go to the Chief's.' He said, 'No, it was said I should not go there, I should stay here.' 'Is it so?' 'Yes.' 'Have you spoken to the Chief?' 'Yes, I have.' 'Is it Luposva [the Chief]?' 'Yes. I have already given Lupsova the letter written for me.' I said, 'It is all right.' He lived here in this hut of mine. I told him that 'You should not drink beer too much, if you go drinking beer, you see, the people who have been dip attendants want to kill you. Don't you know that their souls grieve that you have come from there to be a dip clerk?'

Isn't it that you know, Mabuyani [the ethnographer] that Tobela was the dip clerk? [Yes, and now his wife-receiver is the dip clerk.] Yes, he [Tobela] is the one who put him in the job, and he is the one who 'put for him' [put poison against an outsider]. I said to him [the dip clerk], 'Hey, you should not be drinking in villages. People will do you evil.'

Whom was I telling? He was a person of beer, and he drank going here and there. He had fallen in love with one over there. Yes, there at Gwiba [Tobela's wife-receiver]. He was always [in Sindebele] 'dancing back and forth' there. 'Ah, hey, you man, you will be injured.' 'Ah, you are now injured. Why are you so white? What makes you so?' I asked him. He said, 'No, I am ill, my stomach is not living with me.' And they were really going at night, he did not sleep here, here, here. [He held his stomach.] It was hot like fire.

Ah, I went to tell Luposva, and he told the Europeans, too. Oh, he did not last out many days, maybe five. Even those who say they know [diviners and healers], no [there was nothing they could do]. He was a sister's child of Mbaya. He said, 'I'll go to Mbaya, maybe he will know something.' I saw a person then coming to say the person is no longer there; that he was dead. We then carried him to the Mission, where he was buried. Here only someone who is strong, very strong can enter the work at the dip tank. If you are just a small person and he says, 'You enter here, then you just enter.' You see this [dip attendant] I think his *ndzimu* [divinity, and by innuendo, familiar for sorcery], ah, well I think maybe he is just a wife-receiver. Sometimes his eyes become very sore, and they amaze people. [Red eyes are associated with a sorcerer; here Lupondo insinuates, they are associated with a son-in-law who, in sorcery, does the bidding of his father-in-law, Tobela.] Can you see the people of this place coming in there? Even there at Plumtree, we hear people saying, 'The dip of Bango is not entered by a person.' You will be throwing yourself into trouble.]

### The Appeal to Arms and the Lasting Policy of Inequality

I recall, too, the time in the days when our Native Commissioner was Mr Posselt that we, the Chief and the administrative headmen, went to Plumtree and were told, 'You people, Chief and the rest of the group, you should pray hard. The war of the Germans, Hitler's war has broken out.' Ah, when we heard that this war is so hard! He said, 'In this war, there is no one who is going to remain behind, if the Europeans say this war should be fought. The whole nation is going to die; that will be the end of the world.'

We had children at school, and when we heard that, we said, 'We will take them.' 'You are going to take them?' Native Commissioner Posselt said. 'Into which cave will you put them? In this war there is no one who will remain. There is no cave in which to hide. Just live. Where they will die, they will have died. And where you will die, you will have died, too. But one thing for you is to pray hard to God, so that the rulers understand each other. They make the war severe!'

Truly, we went there and saw those at school and told them what we had been told by our Nkhosi, the Native Commissioner. We returned, came here, and stayed, timidly. Hitler's war was fought and it was terrible. Some time later, we were told, 'No, Hitler's war has ended. Hitler has run off. It is not known where he is.' Thus, it ended.

Of our people, many died who had gone there, at that war. Yes, many Africans died at that war. At last we heard it had ended, and some came back. We heard then that there are wars and wars.

They were fighting for this country, and when our rulers, the whites, fight, they also invite [koka] us to join in this, their helping party. But when we come back and some of the blacks have died there, the whites come and give some farms to their own people as pensions for having been to war. As for us blacks, no, we are given that little money which is the money of nothing. That is really your money. The guns we used at war are taken away from us. It is said, 'You are going to shoot animals with them. That is not wanted. You are just ordinary people, you are not now known as soldiers.' It is [done by] those white men who are rearing us. But they are ours. They are our rulers; they came to our country, but with wisdom, great wisdom surpassing ours, wisdom that conquers ours. Yes, *their* wisdom. What we fight about now is that after they have invited us to their helping party and we come, they do not make us equal with their own people.

### Evictions and the Promise of Permanence on the Land

From the time [at the beginning of the colonial period towards the end of the nineteenth century], when we lived at Marulla, we were pushed, bit by bit. The train dropped donkeys, taken off at Marulla, in April, when the sorghum was ripe. The sorghum was really white, and I think it was in April. Then the schools had not yet come into our country. [It was close to the turn of the century.] The donkeys ate in the fields until they finished the grain. People went to tell Thomas, who was ruling in those days [as Native Commissioner]. 'Remove from the way of the train. Go far off. Do not live near the train', he said. None of us who came had grain, but we had to go to live there at the mountains.

[Tobela spoke then about living with the first Europeans, and earliest of all, one called Kesbaum Teit, who claimed to own farms and introduced field taxes paid in cash or kind (see his remarks in Chapter 1).]

Someone with two bags would complete all his field tax. Part of the money went to the government for the head tax, and part to Kesbaum [their first farmer] for the farm where we were ploughing. As they collected it, they counted the people; and if they counted houses and found one without an owner, ah, you had to say 'This is the house of so-and-so . . .' If you had no money, you would pay in grain; if no grain you could pay in a blanket, a kaross, a dassey skin or the skin of any animal you had.

[Tobela's following remarks are quoted in Chapter 1. First he gave his account of change in the farms, the greater competition with Africans for grazing and the increased pressure to dispossess them as 'squatters'. Then he recalled the people's resistance, their attempt to complain to the government about their eviction by the farmer at Nswebetani.]

When we went to report to the Government, to our Nkhosi, the Native Commissioner [about the farmer at Nswebetani who drove them off], he said, 'Run off and leave the farms people have bought. I have no power over a person who has bought one for himself.' We removed until we came here to the area they called Groot Fontein. We stayed a mere few days, and then they said, 'You should pay tax for it, ten shillings.' We paid ten shillings and ten shillings.

I was a *sebuku*, 'headman of the kraal' [in English] when the Native Commissioner came and placed us here. He said, 'Chief—and it was then Luposva in those days—you will not pay tax. But all the other people will have to pay a tax of ten shillings for this land.' That was said by the Nkhosi, our magistrate at Plumtree. I then answered, myself Tobela, 'What about me, Nkhosi?' 'No,' he said, 'you will also pay tax.' I said, 'As I am a headman, how can I pay tax?' 'No, we shall only free the Chief, not the headman.' We started to pay tax here in 1939.

One year we found our Native Commissioner, or rather the Assistant Native Commissioner, Mr R. Cockcroft whom we called Ngada Dziya-chukana [the hops, left over from beer, soften and wear each other out]. He said, 'I think here, where you are living, you'll always pay your tax and in years to come this land will be given to you as your own land.' We said, 'We thank the Nkhosi.' And then, the following day, he left the job, I can't remember when [Cockroft was transferred].

And after a few years we heard, 'No, turn and go back to Lupane.' And now, ah, we were the fathers in this country. Our fathers were no longer alive, and we had become the fathers then. Ah, it grieved us, it really pained us. In came Mafohlele, Mr Posselt. And he put us, '*Chuchu majaxa*' 'Hop to it, lads. You have lived in this country. Now this country is for farms. The government has given you lands on the other side of the farms at Lupane.'

We thought, as men still able to talk to their Nkhosi, we thought, 'How can they kill us, when we have done nothing? What wrong have we done? We have no fault, no [court] case.'

[We said,] 'We did not bring ourselves here, Nkhosi. We came by your word, pushing ourselves by your word. We were still controlled. Now that we are near the Ngwato, and you tell us to go to the other side of the railroad. It is very hard, heavy for us.'

[He answered,] 'The case [against you] is not mine. It is the government that talks like this, saying it is an area for farms and it will be bought.'

Show us one who is greater than you,' we said, 'We will talk to him.' We had gone to him at our office at Plumtree, and when we got there he nearly refused, 'There is nothing that I can advise you so that you can go to so and so.'

We were four men and we questioned him. We asked, 'Nkhosi, should we turn back, with the burdens? We will have to go past the ruined sites from which you chased us away.' He said, 'It is the truth. The government says so.' 'No, we are asking, Nkhosi, for the way [permission] to talk to your senior who gives us such work.' 'I permit you to go to Bulawayo to the Provincial Native Commissioner', he replied. And truly we got up and went, being Grey's late father, who was Chief Luposva, Mfundisi, Maohoma, and myself Tobela, four men.

At Bulawayo, we found he had sent a report about us, 'Four people of Bango are coming to talk to you about settlement in the country.' We were taken into the office to talk to the Native Commissioner, who asked, 'No, what has happened?'

We gave our own report, 'Nkhosi, we are tired of burdens. These burdens are the limit. They are to the very end of the country, to the Tswana. We removed from Marulla, when we were driven by the farms. We removed until we came to the River Shashi, along the land of the Ngwato. Now we are down there. We find our Nkhosi says the Government said we should go back with our burden, jump over our ruined sites and go to Lupane. It is heavy for us, crushed as we have been under these loads. But, Nkhosi, how big is our fault that it cannot be met when all those faults can be met?'

Then the Provincial Native Commissioner lit his cigarette. He smoked and faced this side and that, and at last, he said, 'Oh, is it that?' We said, 'Yes, it is, Nkhosi of the men. The men of Bango have sent us to come and ask about this fault [case]. How have we wronged in the country of the government? We are at the Ngwato [territory then in the Bechuanaland Protectorate].

He went on writing and writing in his book. He said, 'Yes, I hear the men of Bango. As I hear the case, you will be told when you will be at the Matoppos [in the headquarters of the next district] . . . I do not see that you can be so troubled. We do not know your case [fault].' That was the Provincial Native Commissioner. 'The country is yours. You will get it because you were driven from Marulla till you came to the Ngwato. When it is said turn back, I do not see that it will not fit. But go to the Matoppos, there you will be given the truth.' We came out and said, 'Nkhosi [Chief, in Sindebele] of the men.' And he touched that wire [sent a cable] telling the one at the Matoppos.

We were in a car, the late Maohoma's, and we drove until we came to the Matoppos at Fort Usher, where we found them already waiting for us. He had touched the wire. Upon our arrival, they announced, 'Bango', and we went in, the four of us. They were saying, 'What has happened?' 'Nkhosi, we have failed', we said. 'The burdens have killed us. Today the Government tells us to go back with our burdens to where we came from. Yet, the case is unknown to us. What kind of case have we that we have not met?'

We heard the Native Commissioner saying, 'No, men of Bango. Calm your hearts. The Government has agreed as from today. It says you will live in that country, the name of which will be [in English] "Native Special Area". Go and tell the children to calm their hearts. You will live in that country forever. You will not have to go where they thought you were to go. You have reported yourselves, and there is no case now. Go, and when you get there, live there; the country is yours. Bango, go.'

We said [the praises] 'Father of men, bringer of the news, the sun that can be seen in the ears of the elephant.' We were thanking, when we came out of the office of Fort Usher.

On our arrival home, we found beer brewed for us, and people ululating, saying, 'You are bare [white and pure, a congratulation on being past a dangerous transition] for the country. The country has been given to us. We shall not remove from it tomorrow.'

Then it was said for that ten shillings we had been paying in tax, we have been given this country.

So, we were given 'Native Special Area'. But soon they went to cut, and said, 'You of Bango, you stop as far as Sanzukwe [River], and the other side of Sanzukwe will be for Chief Tjitji, and this side will be for Bango.' One European, come from Bulawayo, tied a rope to a tree as far as that and then he cut it with a knife in the middle. He said, 'You of Bango, cross and go to your home.' We were then at the bridge of the Sanzukwi. Very much did we cross and go there. What shocks us today is that this country is now full of those Tjitji people. And we of this home are without places.

If I am bothered by white ants or may have seen something bad here, and I want to remove, I am not allowed to go even as far as that [nearby]. The country is controlled that way. It shocks us, for in our place of the

Black people, if you found that the hamlet was ruined, you could remove and go elsewhere, as you liked.

Now they are again cutting this country and saying, 'Where will the cattle graze?' Yet we have none of this [difficulty] for the cattle, for they are ours. We have a time on earth; cattle die, and those that remain, remain, for they are destocked by God. God cuts them down. In a year when the rains have not fallen, cattle die; and God makes the rains to fall, and they reproduce again. There is just one thing that shocks us here. Are the white rulers troubled? Yet, in the destocking of God there was no trouble and there was no one who did not know where his wealth [stock] fed and how much his children ate. They say our cattle are still going to be destocked. Again! Hau! Even though we have been given the country, again they come and cut down our fields; and some children are not given fields. This makes us feel very much pain.

We have followed our rulers very much, but the thing that they have really troubled us with is destocking the cattle, our cattle. When you have given a head of cattle to your child, they say, 'No, don't give your child a head of cattle.' 'Hey, if we give the children we bear our own cattle, what's wrong with that? What is the trouble there?' They say, 'No, you have too many cattle, the cattle are to be destocked.' If you have two tens, they take one ten and leave you only one. But you have many children, and your children must plough with these cattle and get milk from them, too. If you are left with ten, the milk will not be enough to feed the children, and the cattle will not be enough for ploughing. Then we say, 'What shall we do, since we are defeated? Oh, just to follow, when we do not agree? We have to agree in bondage.' And we are forced into what we do not want, though the things are ours.

When they tell us, they say, 'When we do this, it is because we find that otherwise your cattle will die of hunger.' We then say, 'If they die of hunger, it doesn't matter. After they die, we'll buy some others; they are our cattle.' We find they object, 'No, in the country where you live, there must only graze so many cattle.' We still say, 'The cattle are ours, and not yours. You, Nkhosi, why are you pained about our things?' They object and say, 'It is our wish that is done. It is not the preference of the retainer [nlanda] that is done [the master decides].' All right, we agreed.

And they follow us now. We find that the books [the official registers of owners with authorised cattle holdings] are torn from the children to whom we had given the cattle. Some women fail to get cattle, their children are denied cattle, their books are taken away, and they are told they should come to the sale. At the sale a head of cattle gets a paltry two pounds ten shillings, three pounds ten shillings, four to five pounds. There is no money for those who have been destocked. They [the

Europeans] were eating them, doing it this way. You looked carefully and said, 'What shall we do when they are our seniors?'

Again and again, in recent years, we have heard that now the fields are to be cut down. We have said, 'The fields, Nkhosi, how will they be cut down? We have children and wives, and were married by you, and we agreed to pay for them. You know that each wife has her children. How is it that now you cut the fields?' They said, 'No, we shall make it equal. One wife will be given four acres, and the other three acres.' 'Hey, how will it be all right when the wife bears children? How would it be if you cut us men so that we no longer conceive children, instead of cutting down the fields, the food of the children, after we have begot them? Leave us that we plough our fields. The lazy ones will not plough; those who are industrious will plough.'

The Europeans are objecting. They say the country is theirs, and there is no one in the middle; what they say should be done. We live so in this country of ours, that was taken from us when the Europeans came. We are troubled, we are burnt by fire. Fire has been [set] kindled against us. Yet there is no case against us. Ah, you will make me 'killed' by the Europeans, there they are stopping there.

[Pointing to an official's Land Rover parked in the distance, Tobela smiled, he relished his banter with me about the danger in such talk about Europeans in my presence. But curious about what the Land Development Officer was doing, he brought the conversation to a close and left me. When we resumed our conversation, ten days later, he returned to the subject eagerly, for as he often told me, he wanted people of other countries to know what Europeans were doing in the land of Kalanga. Government control of land and settlement was very much in his mind, because it was the day before the confrontation between the planning official and the fathers of the chiefdom.]

What I see is this: we have a law in our country, given to us by the Native Commissioner, that people who have no fields are now to be allocated fields. The people of our place, the Kalanga, say, 'We cannot be allocated fields. We give fields to our children naturally.' This grieves the Black because, a person having a field should give to his children from its head from in front of it. Being 'allocated' confuses us. For these wise people our rulers, came here and found us begetting children and giving them fields by ourselves. What do they see about our children not getting enough fields? It is as if we ourselves are not the ones who cry the country is too small.

Of course, we cry about this country, we cry that it is small; we cry about these farms here that we had to leave, at the railway line where we were pushed, from where all the lands have been bought. We are pushed here to the boundary of the Ngwato, and then it was said that our children were going to be given fields. That shocks us.

We had thought that, since the government is our Nkhosi, when he sees that the Black people are many, he should destroy some farms. For the country is not small for those who bought it. In our life of old, we said, 'The country is for Mwali [God Above]; it is not finished by a person.' But today those who rear us object and say, 'You will finish the land.' They don't think the country is finished by them, because they have money, and go about buying land. One person buys a hundred miles, or even, I think, a thousand miles. One of their persons only.

Yes, that is what troubles us very much. Then they say we have no lands, and the children are to have a portion of the lands you already plough and you'll have to eat from that. Yes! Yet, that child of yours is grown up and will take his own wife and beget his own children. That is what makes 'the acres' [areas of fields under government control, measured and limited], and they cut them in halves, little by little. This means we have to eat everything in summer, and in winter we will have nothing to put in the granaries and nothing to set aside for a year of starvation. We live by ploughing large fields because [Ndzimu] God chooses what he wills. By Ndzimu [God] we mean Mwali, Mwali himself.

So, I find that the thing that troubles the Kalanga is only this one thing. They are troubled by being apportioned and allocated. They say it breaks their bones. They cannot know how to plough if a person is to be given a field by one who doesn't live here, a person who only comes to see the country then says 'You should all plough at one place.'

Yet, it is not like that. In the days when we were just born, we found that our fathers would give a son a nearby field once he had taken his wife so that when the son would go to the Europeans to work there would be someone to look after it. But now when he has been given somewhere else, who can look after that field? At the Europeans' we were working for money to buy clothes, for they [the Europeans] are the ones who brought them with them.

In our life of long ago, children were given fields by their fathers. There was no one who would come from way over there to give a field to a child of someone else. Today it is said, 'My child will be given lands somewhere.' It will be shocking when he has gone to work for Europeans and the birds of God come. Who will drive away the birds from his field? That is where it will shock. And it will be shocking when the cattle are lost, and they come into his field, and that child is sick, sleeping in the house. Who will take the cattle out of the field?

Jealousy and malice, that was started by God. Someone may find those [cattle] in and leave them there, so that he [the cattle owner] becomes his retainer [because of the debt owed for the damage to crops done by the cattle]. Is this a lie? I find it so. Mainly, we find that a person himself must be given a field by his father, near his father's field. He knows that when he will be ill, I will go and look after his crops in his fields. And if he ploughs carelessly, he'll be seen by his father, for his father was taught how to plough.

Naturally, when God began the world, we did not find there was one who was taught how to till. People came with the knowledge of tilling the earth. I, as I am, I was never taught how to till by a stranger, I was taught by my father. He would say, 'Go this way', when we were still using hoes for cultivating, and then he would say, 'Now cultivate' and then you'd cultivate. When the Europeans came, they gave us these ploughs of theirs. They came and taught us how to plough with the ploughs of oxen. We ploughed with them, and now we know how to plough with them. There is nothing about that which troubles us.

The one thing that does trouble us is that the children we beget will be allocated fields, allocated by another person [an outsider], one who is an Nkhosi [an official] and who does not live with us. The Nkhosi does not know where it is good for ploughing. That must be known by the person who stays with the child. Who should know that my child should not plough on a rocky or stony place? A place with many bumps, and where crops do not grow, we know it, we Kalanga. That is what we have always seen.

That is the only thing we shall be meeting for tomorrow, when the Nkhosi [official] says we shall meet on Tuesday. What day? Yes, on the 19th we shall meet the Nkhosi at the bridge which is just being built, the new bridge. They gave us that thought, but we do not know what will be done to us. If they say we should follow the law of the Nkhosi, we shall follow only because we are sheep, being driven. We cannot refuse, for we have not got the power. We shall follow not because it is our liking, but we shall follow in the way it is with a person driving his cattle and dropping them into a gully that they must just fall into, where they know there is danger.

# 3

# Nostalgia, Quarrel Stories, and Cautionary Moments: Grandparents Recall

Far reaching as the impact of Europeans was upon Lupondo's family, it was, in a sense, secondary for many of the older family members, at least in their own perception. Some, including Lupondo himself and his brother's wife Baka Chedza, had never worked for Europeans or lived in towns. On the whole, the older members of Lupondo's family were more inward-looking than Tobela, even more concerned with past events within their own family. Nevertheless, or perhaps for that very reason, family members gave me very different kinds of accounts when I asked them to look back upon their lives. They held quite unlike images of themselves, used contrasting kinds of narrative genre, traced substantially distinct histories, and placed themselves diversely within the family. In the background of their accounts, and resonating through them, was a pool of personal gossip, stories, names, nicknames, representations of character which made up a whole world of family knowledge.

In Lupondo's family quarrelling between wives as mothers was continual from the very start. Important as this fact in itself was for the growth of the family, the reconstruction of the fact in tales of explanation is even more important for locating the life histories in a context of personal discourse. Family members looked, above all, to a *source* in the previous generation for the present. When it came to trust or mistrust, amity or hostility between sons, a partisan version of the history of mothers as wives gave that source. Thus from one viewpoint the source of rivalry between Lupondo's sons, Buka and Dzilo, was the fact that Buka's mother was denied the position of senior wife. She was courted first, and became pregnant before Dzilo's mother married but Dzilo's mother took precedence, nevertheless, becoming the senior wife. From the ensuing struggle between the mothers came the hostility between the sons, family members explained. Such explanations through accounts of the past were part of a growing and inclusive personal discourse, registered in the familiar names and the well-known stories of family members.

The names Lupondo's wives gave their children were an open register of a disagreeable truth of the family's history, open that is to members of the family

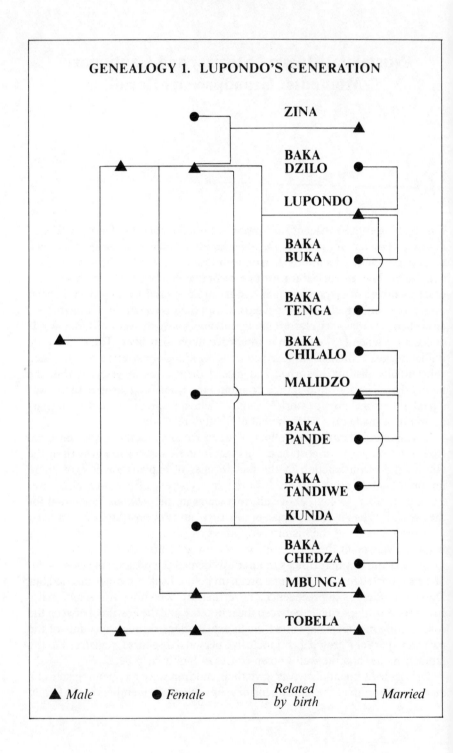

**GENEALOGY 1.  LUPONDO'S GENERATION**

ZINA

BAKA
DZILO

LUPONDO

BAKA
BUKA

BAKA
TENGA

BAKA
CHILALO

MALIDZO

BAKA
PANDE

BAKA
TANDIWE

KUNDA

BAKA
CHEDZA

MBUNGA

TOBELA

▲ *Male*          ● *Female*          *Related by birth*          *Married*

Table 1. *Names and birth dates of Lupondo's Children*

| Senior Wife | Second Wife | Third Wife |
|---|---|---|
| 1. 'You rejected us' b. 1909 female | 1. 'The hamlet is mine' b. 1909 male | 1. 'We wander' b. 1934 male |
| 2. 'You should be polite' b. 1910 male | 2. 'Despised' b. 1910 male | 2. 'Give thanks' b. 1936 female |
| 3. 'You provoked fights' b. 1914 male | 3. 'We lived as your mere hide' b. 1914 male | 3. 'What have I done?' b. 1938 female |
| 4. 'Don't fight' b. 1922 female | 4. 'You make us vomit' b. 1917 | 4. 'You pursue us' b. 1940 female |
|  | 5. 'I am a wasted gourd' (kicked around) b. 1924 male | 5, 6 and 7 named in another hamlet |
|  | 6. 'You are bad' b. 1927 female |  |

themselves. An outsider might not catch the full significance of the names, because abbreviated forms were used, ordinarily, for some of the names, and nicknames for others. But within Lupondo's family 'the names speak', as one son's wife pointed out to me, when she drew my attention to the recriminations and counter-recriminations expressed in the series of names. Table 1 is a translation of the full names of the children born while Lupondo's three wives lived together in a single hamlet (the list excludes the children of inherited wives).

Each era of the family had its quarrelsome personal names and around them family members created an ever-growing repertoire of quarrel stories. In narrating them, members of the family often whispered a formula as an opening disclaimer. 'Sh, sh, don't say I was the one who told you, but . . .' or 'Ah, can this be told?' The quarrel stories were told from different perspectives of course, but it was in the light of some quarrel story that everyone in the family understood how and why family members lived where they did, and with which neighbours as friends and allies. The quarrel stories were as much a force in creating the very tissue of family life as they were an expression of it. However the family might develop, in response to conflicting efforts by its members, it was caught in the very fine webs of quarrel stories, woven and rewoven in each generation around one misunderstanding after another.

It is because of the very great importance of the quarrel stories that I see them as a key to understanding the art of personal narrative used by family members, at least in peacetime and before the guerrilla war. Taking the quarrel stories as a key to differences in narrative genre and regarding the narrator's self-placement towards quarrel stories, I find it useful to recognise four contrasting kinds of genre. These are the four which encompass the life histories I elicited from Lupondo's family in peacetime:

| Attitude to quarrel stories | Self-Placement | Genre |
| --- | --- | --- |
| Engagement | Central | Heroic adventure |
|  | Peripheral (witness) | Cautionary realism |
| Disengagement |  |  |
|    Total avoidance | Central (heroine) | Romance |
|    Partial avoidance | Ambiguous | Nostalgia |

To disclose the family discourse in and through these genres of personal
narrative, I begin in this chapter by considering the accounts of elders,
Lupondo and his brother's wife Baka Chedza. Their accounts exemplify,
respectively, the genres of nostalgia and cautionary realism. In the next
chapter come accounts from the next generation, from three of Lupondo's
sons, Dzilo, Mfila and Buka, and Buka's wife. I give my interpretation first,
followed by the text of the life history, and then after showing how it exempli-
fies a genre, I typify the genre in general terms.

Nostalgia mixed with malicious spite and resentment coloured Lupondo's
stories about his family and himself. The bygone days at their old home had
been much better, in his nostalgic memories, than the present. The one
remaining haven of the good times was the remote hamlet of his third and last
wife, the darling of his old age. Lupondo yearned, in his mid to late seventies,
for the peaceful days, so long gone, when wives were dutiful and obedient, and
a husband could blissfully go off to a beer drink, meet his girlfriend, stay away
for the night, and not hear a murmur of complaint from anyone. Sons who now
neglect him had cared for him and clothed him from their earnings at work in
South Africa, in those better times. All that had been spoiled by wives; the
greatest destroyers were the widows of brothers and the wives of sons.

Lupondo told me his life history, squatting beside his fire at his forecourt in
the front of his hamlet. The place, like the posture, was his favourite, and after
finding him there, I too would come to warm myself by his fire. Our conversations rarely went beyond greetings, comments about the weather, very brief
bits of news, and occasionally caustic remarks when the news did not please
him. Even when others joined us and the conversation flowed more freely, he
preferred to listen, often somewhat quizzically or irritably, I sensed. If usually
passive in communication and more on the way of being an ancestor than an
active, or still very influential elder, he was physically alert, lean, a fast walker
who took pride in showing children how to herd goats carefully. His hands
were restless, seemingly most at ease when busy softening a skin. He dressed
usually in a loinskin, a rather frayed shirt, and a hat of worn felt, except on
visits to his third and favourite wife, when he sported her sons' gifts of
fashionable wear from Johannesburg. In responding to my request for a
recorded interview, late in my first visit, he gave me the impression that he

spoke reluctantly, that he simply had neither time nor patience to keep on talking at length with me or any one else, or so I felt. I continued to warm myself by his fire and chat casually, but never dared attempt a second long interview.

Mixed as Lupondo's nostalgia was in the life history he recounted, it had bite and purpose within the context of our communication. Lupondo's motivation in telling me about his family's past was not disinterested autobiography, if there is such a thing. He wanted me to see certain people in a much worse light. His most revealing stories, intended to prejudice me, targeted his resentment and malice against the people I openly regarded as my very good friends, among them his cousin Tobela, his son Dzilo and others. He knew I had heard versions of events from wives and widows he himself disliked, and the desire to contradict them spurred him on the most.

What Lupondo glossed somewhat defensively in his nostalgia was a truth widely recognised among other members of the family. It was the disagreeable truth about how the family came to be what it was, about how splits developed, and different sides were drawn, such as in the rivalry and hostility between Lupondo's leading sons, Buka and Dzilo. I urged Lupondo's cousin Tobela to tell me about that and he agreed very reluctantly, more so than in speaking on almost any other subject:

Ah, this cannot be told by a person. It grieves to think about it. For that is what is in their hearts. It is that. And it is because the mothers of these boys [Dzilo and Buka] did not see eye to eye. They were always grabbing each other about and always fighting. They were fighting for that way [seniority] I was talking about. Ah, you'll make me talk carelessly. You are not good. You keep your thing [tape recorder] closed, and don't open it at Lupondo's.

I promised not to play it back at Lupondo's but to record for writing it in my book, and Tobela continued:

If you open this, and they hear it, and I'm the one talking, they can hate me. They'll say I am the one who goes about telling people that the one who came first is this one [Buka's mother]. They do not want it to be heard that Buka's mother came first to Lupondo. Most of them say it should be said it is Dzilo's mother who came first. But in those days they did that [made Buka's mother junior] because she was a Mlilo [Ndebele by descent], and so they sent her back, and said they would not have a Mlilo senior wife. They wanted one who was a Kalanga. It was Chief Bango saying that.

If there is one thing that everyone in Lupondo's family agreed upon, it was that the mother of Dzilo was virtually always a powerful force to be contended with in the family. Her outstanding ability to produce crops and to have herds that increased her wealth was much remarked upon, sometimes as proof of her evil powers of sorcery. Still strong and energetic in her early seventies, she had a well-deserved reputation for asserting herself, for pride in her position of seniority, for her caustic tongue and her fierce temper, in the past at least, all too easily unleashed when she got drunk on beer. Lupondo had come to realise that he could not leave her until she died, notwithstanding his yearning to live with his third and favourite wife. It is one limitation of my account of the family that for various reasons I was not able to get her to tell her own life story, and I have had to reconstruct her early part in family events from other eye witnesses.

Few elders with whom I talked, men and women both within and outside Lupondo's family, gave a view of polygyny that was other than ironic or bitterly jaundiced. As Tobela put it, making sure that some of his harangue was loud enough to be heard well by one of his wives:

When I was first married, my wife obeyed me very much, for she was still alone. She obeyed me. Whatever I said should be done would be done. Always. It would be done. When I took a second wife, what I said was done; yes, it was done. Then, when I took the third wife, what I said would be done, but sometimes there were things that would be done secretly, and hidden away from me. What I said was no truth; I no longer had power, recognised in my name.

They were many then. They wanted to have their own small court [like the forum of men] and began joining together, without me. I objected. I began beating, those days. I was not alone among our Kalanga people. Anyone who had many wives was like that. Then came a law of Europeans which said, 'Eh, do you beat wives? You'll be arrested. A wifebeater will be sent to jail.' So we stopped it. Now the wives have gone even further out of bounds. They do what they like, not what their husbands like. All because of the Europeans' law that a wife must not be beaten! Long ago we were beating, and they feared to be beaten. A wife would not do bad things. Even when it came to drinking beer, she would not return home after sunset. Now you may see a wife returning at twelve o'clock or eleven at night. She does what she likes, and you fail to have anything you can do to her, because she relies on reporting you, and then having you arrested. And husbands, too, fear to be sent to jail.

Given his nostalgia, Lupondo had good reason to dwell on the evils of wives and widows. At the peak of his career as a polygynist, late in the 1930s, Lupondo took charge of seven married women. Three were his wives; another three, widows inherited from his late brother Malidzo; the seventh, the wife of his brother Kunda, who virtually abandoned his family during an eight year absence working in Johannesburg. The younger widows were at most in their twenties, keen to have more children by a virile man, and unwilling to submit easily to a much older man like Lupondo. Lupondo was verging on his sixties;

he was seen to cut a poor figure in comparison to his much younger brother Malidzo. Unlike Lupondo, Malidzo was very sociable ('a man of people', as Kalanga say) and active in church; he read the Bible, and used to 'swank' (the English word which Kalanga borrow to mean 'to dress smartly and strut like a cock'). The widows glorifying Malidzo as their dead husband disdained Lupondo.

As the oldest of the widows, Baka Chilalo, put it,

> Could we have to cry for an old man? Ours used to 'swank'. He was one of the lads. At this time of night, you would hear girls knocking at his door. He would get his children, but he wasn't one for piss [adultery with someone else's wife] like his brother, this one over there. He was a person of people always. When they were not there, his girlfriends were there, but he did not go to the wives of others. And if we had children chatting with us at night, he would simply stand up and go to his own hut. This one wearing loinskins [Lupondo], we wouldn't have admitted him ourselves.

Lupondo's efforts to keep these women in the face of their quarrels, their lovers, and what he saw as their conspiring to gang up against him eventually made him a battered husband. The new and last wife Lupondo took when he was already an elder, became his most beloved of all. That drove his senior wife mad with jealousy, Baka Chilalo told me, remarking that 'polygyny pains'. When Lupondo tried to beat his senior wife with a sjambok, saying 'When I talk she does not hear me, she makes herself out to be my husband', she bit his little finger right to the bone, nearly severing it. It healed, a year later, remaining scarred and deformed. The memory of it—'she got it, chewed it up and crushed it flat'—still made Baka Chilalo laugh at Lupondo and his senior wife more than twenty years later, in 1961.

One of the widows Lupondo inherited, and came to resent and despise, was Baka Tandiwe. Her lover, Mbunga, was also a 'husband', at least nominally, being like Lupondo in Kalanga terms the deceased's 'brother' and in our terms a parallel cousin of the deceased. If tolerant, out of practical necessity, of such a lover 'husband', Lupondo objected to the widow's outrageous demand that he pay five shillings for her sexual favours or be denied his conjugal rights. Having paid at least once, he made the mistake of seeking further satisfaction through a lawsuit, first at her parents' home and eventually at the Chief's court. The scandal left him something of a laughing stock. Unable to make her see reason, as he saw it, he let her go her own way. As a parting shot, his warning was that it was her own fault and that the fault and debt would remain a grudge for the future. Many years later, when his opportunity came, he snubbed her, and tried to get some revenge. Recalling his humiliation at a time when her sons were about to return home to their natal hamlet and thus to him, Lupondo gloated to me spitefully at the prospect of her having to come humbly back with them.

The attraction for the sons was hardly Lupondo himself. More important were the sons' sentiments towards a widow at his hamlet, their mother's wealthy sister Baka Chilalo, and their interests in her property. She was also their father's widow and sonless. The sons looked to Baka Chilalo for help in meeting marriage payments and other debts. She had reared one of them as if he were her own son, with great generosity and affection. This favourite son expected to inherit a sizeable share of her large herd, and while continuing to live with her as a young man during his first fieldwork, he became a magnet drawing the others to him. He told me that even though Lupondo was the one who begot him, Lupondo had never given him anything; that it made his heart ache that Lupondo had never bought him even a khaki shirt to show he was his father; that other men take over the children of a late brother and provide for them all, saying that all these are my children. By the time of my return in 1989, his mother had very much come into her own; the sons had established themselves with her in a substantial hamlet, close to others in Lupondo's family; and the favourite son, a successful labour migrant, was surrounded, in his middle age, by his wife, numerous children and grandchildren.

Lupondo's own career as a *sebuku*, or administrative village headman, so important for the development of his family, owed much to his having been reared in the Chief's hamlet, and by his mother's sister, the mother of a future chief. In line with the family's use of quarrel stories, his rearing was itself regarded as an attempt to get him at a safe distance from the sorcery of his mother's enemies. If small compared to villages elsewhere, that hamlet was large by Kalanga standards—Lupondo recalled in it the families of a dozen men—and it had a number of people who were eager to link themselves even more closely to the Chief through Lupondo, either by marriage or later by entering his tax register. The scarcity of good arable land near the Chief's hamlet had become pressing by the time Lupondo married his first two wives. Some of his elders began to cultivate on both sides of the river to meet their needs. But Lupondo claimed that he feared to do that himself, and that he preferred to join a hamlet belonging to the Chief's junior patrikin, where there was more arable land. In part his fear was due to the hardship of having to cross the river bearing ploughs and later crops. The Chief and his elders insisted, however, that if Lupondo wanted to leave, he had to go back to his late father's home and become independent in his own hamlet. The Chief's promise was that at home he could have his own 'book' or tax register and an administrative village. But he was not to become someone else's dependent, remain nearby, join their junior and rival patrikinsmen, and strengthen them.

Upon his return home near Nigoba hamlet, Lupondo established his own hamlet. In this way he avoided becoming a follower under his brother Zina, the Nigoba hamlet head. He placed himself close yet far, close enough to influence his brothers and others within a range of neighbourliness and yet far enough to be independent of anyone else's authority. There he was able to help his brothers and others by providing services, such as in ploughing, and goods especially in the form of loans of cattle, in the main his senior wife's cattle. His strategic action won his brothers' loyalty and the loyalty of other unrelated neighbours, for whom he became the *sebuku*, administrative village headman.

Lupondo served as *sebuku* and raised his own large family without either leaving the countryside to work for wages or becoming literate. He had already married two of his wives before it became usual for most young men to spend long periods at work in distant cities. His younger brothers, and later his sons and other dependants, earned cash as labour migrants in domestic service and in unskilled work. But his part in that circulation of workers between town and country was different: the management for the absentees of their affairs at home.

Lupondo managed, sometimes ineptly, sometimes more under the direction of his senior wife and her eldest son than according to his own choosing. His managerial role was costly. He had to make onerous tax payments for his absent sons. For long periods, especially at the beginning of their careers as workers, his sons sent home no remittances from their earnings. Instead, their taxes had to come from the sale of some of the family's rural assets, such as goats and cattle. Like so many others in the countryside, Lupondo and his wives subsidised their sons' labour migration by paying their taxes during their youth.

If the colonial officials intended the taxation to push Africans from the countryside to join the paid labour force in towns and on farms, that was not the actual impact it had on Lupondo's family in particular. Besides siphoning off resources from the countryside, tax payment altered the balance of power within the family, somewhat to Lupondo's disadvantage relative to his wives. The more Lupondo met demands on him as a tax headman and made up the shortfall in one of his households, the more he was outstripped by a wife's accumulation of capital in pigs, livestock and cash. He became the poor husband of some rich wives, and at least one very poor one. Keeping a balance between them eventually became more than he could manage. He simply could not continue to juggle the family's resources or borrow successfully from one household for the sake of another. His errors of judgement plagued him. Quarrels multiplied.

In at least one instance, he took the risk of acting behind his senior wife's back. Without her permission, he sold a cow they had jointly bought as a calf, for the sake of another wife's sons. His senior wife's permission was needed but knowing he could not get it, he simply went ahead without it. The affair, much fought over at the time, continued to live in quarrel stories, raked up and much talked about many years later. Late in his middle age, and not long after moving to the Sanzukwe Special Native Area, Lupondo found it best to resign his tax headmanship in favour of his senior son, Dzilo. That was the price exacted by his senior and richest wife for helping, through this son, to pay for the other sons' taxes.

In commenting upon Lupondo's life history as nostalgic narrative, I have not dwelt upon the actual changes that, in some fundamental ways from Lupondo's perspective, did mark the passing of the good old days. In one such change, which spread throughout Bango chiefdom, the countryside lost to the town in a competition for male labour. The change swept away a basic prerogative in the services commanded by a 'Father' or head of the family from his dependants as a whole. No longer did family and hamlet members give their labour to work the family head's fields on occasions called *hunde*. *Hunde* or tributary labour was simply not performed. The change was introduced by the next generation after Lupondo's. That was the first generation in which it came to be taken for granted, a matter of recognised norm, that men had to go on labour migration. The members of this generation cut the tie between patriarchal authority and command of an entire family's labour.

It might be thought, albeit mistakenly, that such a withdrawal of labour meant the breakdown in patriarchal authority which such changes are sometimes supposed to effect or reflect. Instead of that, later generations knew patriarchal authority very differently. There was a renewed subordination of younger men to their elders, upon whom the younger men were dependent for management of their affairs while absentees at work. As a consequence also, and given an accompanying increase in the importance of women's labour and their new roles in the men's absence, family members could not simply reproduce the family from generation to generation as it had been. They continued to talk about the family head's authority over the members of his hamlet and administrative village as if that were between a 'father' and his 'children'. But in new ways and on new bases, the family members in the second generation had to regenerate, even reinvent, the family head's authority and, along with that, their loyalties and trust or mistrust towards each other. Certain women accumulated capital in herds, and family members had to contend with their growing power as wives and mothers. All of this raises a main concern of my next chapter: family members' accounts of quarrelling and the moral dynamics of the reinvention of loyalty, trust and personal esteem within the family.

The main subjects of this present chapter are the earlier generation of grandparents, Lupondo's own generation: most prominently, Lupondo himself, his wives in order of seniority: Baka Dzilo, Baka Buka, Baka Tenga; his own brother Malidzo and his widows, especially Baka Chilalo; his paternal brother Kunda and his wife Baka Chedza. Their stories, stories by and about them, follow immediately.

I

LUPONDO RECALLS

## Growing up in the Chief's Hamlet

I was taken from my mother and my father by Nsimbi, our Chief's grandfather, when I was about as big as this, about as big as that child [pointing to a toddler playing nearby]. I was taken, and I was reared at the railway line. Saying, 'Raise this child', Nsimbi gave me to his younger brother [Mbubi, a future Chief] who looked after me while he still had only his first wife. Later, he took his second and afterwards, his third. I am the one who went [bumba] courting for him; and I am the one who, while still a boy, escorted the marriage cattle. Yes, escorting them myself. Those wives of Mbubi are my 'mothers' and they looked after me.

[Lupondo went on to give a rather bland chronicle of moves from site to site, identifying the people who made them, particularly his own affines and kin of the Chief, but not volunteering any comment upon them. Once he came to tell about establishing his own hamlet, he became less matter-of-fact, and reported how he was approached by others to become the administrative headman, as if he had no ambition of his own, ambition being a quality that headmen are expected to disown. He was ready to make personal judgements when he took up the issue that still gave him much inner disquiet: the subject of blame for 'scattering and destroying' his hamlet.]

I lived there [in the 1880s] while it was still a very big hamlet, very big before the Europeans came in. Ah no [he exclaimed relishing the memory of the grand hamlet of his childhood]! All the children, we left there, and we crossed over the river to Makwila. The hamlet was still one, the same as we had left it. The men there were many, but some of them I know and remember: Chandiwana, the close kin of [the future Chief] Luposva; Tategulu, the father of Dzilo's mother (Lupondo's first wife); Ndiwenyu, the father of Luposva's mother; Nunyana, a younger brother of Baka Tenga's father [Baka Tenga became Lupondo's third wife], five there and also Kuwanika, the older brother of Tategulu, six men. The younger brothers of Nsimbi, were there, too. I am not counting them. Should I count them? [Yes.] I said the people [men] of the hamlet are this many, six. There was also [the Chief and his brothers] Nsimbi, Mbubi, Nlaxiwa, Buzhvani, Chilume, Keti, they were six. And twelve all together. We came from there, and we settled in one hamlet again like that.

When we separated, Kuwanika crossed to the other side of the Shashani River, while his younger brother, Tategulu, remained on this side at Mabunga. Jani, who came and joined us where we were settled, later separated from us at Mabunga. His younger brother remained this way at Mabunga. We remained so. And we lived and lived. We remained there, living there. We were then Nsimbi, and his younger brothers, and

Gwaladi [the father of Lupondo's second wife] and the younger brother of
Gwaladi, who died, the father of this wife of Mfila [Lupondo's son].

It was one hamlet when we were there. And then Mbaya [a cousin of the
Chief] came from Obodo, finding that our hamlet was as great as from
here to Jobe [three hamlets away]. And they settled there, Mbaya, Siyepe
and then Dabila, all had their hamlet there, far from us but we would see
each other. Next were Tjaloba and Hlokana the older brother of Tjaloba,
they came and made their hamlet in front of ours, and Gwaladi had come
out to make his hamlet there somewhere, too. Those are the people we
grew up with, and they are the ones I know.

### Founding a New Hamlet and Becoming a *Sebuku*

At last I moved from Bango [hamlet], leaving my elders, because I feared
[having to cross] the river, while we were ploughing on its other side. We
were there on that side of it at Mabunga.

'I fear this River Semukwe. This river is troubling me', I said. 'I would
build with those of Mbaya.'

They said, 'No, it is better that you go to your home. You are grown up
and you now have a hamlet. When you leave us, you can't just go and
build somewhere else [in a competing hamlet, rather than in his own].'

Then I removed close to the hamlet of Nigoba [his father's hamlet],
building about as far off as that mopane tree, that was when my father had
died and it was still a big hamlet. Was it a hamlet? No, it was a town! It was
bigger than this one. Was it a hamlet! It was where my younger brother
was living, Malidzo, the husband of this mother, Baka Chilalo.

I came with my two wives and built my small hamlet. We would cook
and eat together in the same plate, my younger brother and I. He, too, had
two wives. I was then given Baka Tenga [Lupondo's third wife] while I
was still in my small hamlet. My 'father' [the heir to his father's name and
position, Zina] was still there. They were many. We lived and lived until
Zina removed to Mambale, where he is today. We remained, and those
with whom he had been living also remained and said, 'You can't come
out. You are the one who will be our *sebuku*.'

'Oh yes?'

'Yes, it is so.'

'Are you now going to follow your *sebuku*?'

'No, we cannot follow him.'

We then left, and came to build at Dziya, having come from that small
hamlet, at that old site. My younger brother [Malidzo] said, 'I will not
remain, I am going into my older brother's.'

And Kunda, too, said, 'I am going into my older brother's.'

I said, 'Is it so, men?'

And also Mfani said, 'I am going into this one. He is a younger brother to my father.'

The father of Mfani had already died before they came out of the old site. Then Mtalaza came in, he was a man of Mbangani. When Mfani built there and Mtalaza built there, I was also here. Now it was my hamlet, alone with my mates [bakwinya], there was no 'ordinary' person [no outsider or newcomer who had not already belonged in the old Nigoba hamlet]. Then also, there were my children and we had our hamlet so. There is no one who later came to us at that hamlet, that hamlet of Nigoba.

When we removed our hamlet, and came here [to Bango chiefdom in the Sanzukwe Special Native Area 'C'], an 'ordinary' person [an outsider] was Kunda, my younger brother.

[Lupondo speaks of Kunda as an 'outsider' at this time because he was a latecomer who found the new hamlet already built. Kunda returned after an eight year absence working in Johannesburg, during which time he virtually abandoned his wife and daughters. They had stayed behind, awaiting his return, when many of their neighbours moved to the Special Native Area.]

My own younger brother died there. So we were myself, and my children, and this man Jole [an unrelated friend, whose daughter married a son of Lupondo's own brother not long after my first fieldwork]. Having refused to have a tax book at his home, he came to me, and became my person, this Jole. I had left him there, and he followed me here. Galani [a friend and affine] who had had his own hamlet with his father far from us, also came to me, building near those huts of Baka Chilalo [the widow of Lupondo's own brother]. When his wife died, he went to Johannesburg, and then came into the huts of the younger sister of Baka Chilalo, Baka Tandiwe. Baka Tandiwe had come, built, and then gone wild and astray and left.

### The Troubles of Wives and Widows

The one who scattered and destroyed was Baka Tandiwe [the junior wife of his younger brother, Malidzo]. I saw this already at the old site. I was seeing her. She was making love to get her son. You see this boy here, Nunguna, this battered one like a wet chicken, that one now at the Europeans? He was begot by Mbunga. Did you see his legs and his eyes? Oh, it is Mbunga, he is not mine. We were still at the old site. His hut, before they left, was over there where [Lupondo's son] Buka's are. I just kept quiet as if I did not see it. What could I do? He [Mbunga] would go [to the widow, Baka Tandiwe]. There was nothing wrong.

She would say I could come in with five shillings. And I did baulk at that.

'Should I pay money? Do you make that one [Mbunga] pay five shillings, too? Does your lover pay five?'

I paid it once. And then I went to Baka Chilalo [the senior wife who was

responsible for her junior co-wives, especially for this one, her younger
sister married in sororate]. I told her, 'Do you see what your "child" is
doing?' 'What does she do? What is she doing that for?'

And the day we went to her home to complain, I mentioned this lover,
'When you go to a wife, does she say you must pay five shillings?' All the
people opened their mouths and said, 'Is it so?' I said, 'Here she is. Ask
her. When I go to her hut, she says I must pay five shillings.' The people
said, 'Yes, the wife-receiver is true. You people with wives, [we ask] if a
wife loses her husband, and she comes to be taken by the brother of the
husband, has she the right to say he should pay money, when he comes
into the hut? Where is that done?' They were just opening their mouths
and saying, 'Ah, ya.'

I said, 'I see that I do not care about her. I did not make love to her, she
came on her own.' She said she did not see it. I said, 'You did not see it. If
Baka Chilalo comes here, can she not speak about it?' And she kept quiet.
That woman she was a crook, a crook, ah.

'I am going', she was saying. I said, 'Go, it is your own fault. Where are
you going to?' She said, 'My husband has died, so I am going. I have
nothing to do with you.'

That one left when we were still at the old site, at Dziya, when we were
yet to come this way. She became tough, when we brought the cattle this
way. We said, 'What about cattle? We are going where people are going
to, and you are becoming hard.' She said, 'I am not going. I do not get
along with this one [Dzilo's mother].' She was telling lies, and she was
really proud.

[The 'lies' Lupondo alludes to were about a quarrel between the widow and
Lupondo's senior wife. The indirectness of his speech had become characteristic, when it came to affairs involving blame against his senior wife.]

When I took our cattle, I left hers. When she remained as we came this
way, she went elsewhere and never returned. She 'hopped about' here and
there, till she got an old man, one she still has, who has had no children
with her. But now where can she go to? The children are now objecting,
and they are coming to their home. She will come here [which, in fact she
did, some time after Lupondo's death]. I told her so when she passed here
on the way to her home. I said, 'You see.' Also at [the locality where
Lupondo's third wife lives] she came to me. She was at Baka Tenga's
[Lupondo's third wife]. She called me, while I was drinking my beer; and
I ignored her and did not go. I just kept on drinking my beer. When I got
there, I found her gone, and she had said we'll see each other at home.

When there was drinking at Nvoni [another hamlet], we went with
Baka Tenga and [a neighbour], and I sent a child, saying, 'Go and call
her.' I called her to where we were drinking beer. She came, we greeted
each other, and she said, 'Is it you who have called me?' I said, 'Yes.' And

I said, 'If you would have come to me there, what would have happened?'
'I feared people.' I said, 'Hey, you come off it.' I told her off. 'You see,
you will come, your children are failing you. Who will you remain with?
Tell me, who will you live with? The children are objecting, and are here
with me. You will come and squat here. You see the mother of that one
from [another hamlet] who removed going there, has she not come back?
She has come.'

The day these children, Malebeswa and the others, take wives, you will
see the mother of Malebeswa coming. You'll see her eyeballs popping
here. Is there anyone who could be worse than she was? A person who had
her heart? Ah, those [lovers] of that one could not be counted; she had too
many [lovers]. She had many men, this Baka Tandiwe. Yes, and this one
of Kunda [Baka Chedza] and Baka Tandiwe were egging each other on.
They liked each other frightfully and 'called' [men] for each other.
Having talked to them [men], they would spend the day, one with hers
and the other with hers.

Do you say she [Baka Chedza] was a good woman? No, she was not.
You hear Kunda [her husband] always squabbling with her. They were
not good, when she was with Baka Tandiwe. She was going with [a
neighbour] Galani [at a time when her husband had abandoned her].
What? They loved each other frightfully, Baka Tandiwe and Baka
Chedza, they were like this [he showed two parallel fingers]. Where they
went, they went together. Or if it was a thing drunk here, then they would
stand and go together. Always.

They came to this one of mine [his third wife, Baka Tenga] while we
were still at Dziya. They wanted to hook her. Baka Tenga refused and
said, 'I do not know this.' They said, 'Ah, she's a dog and she will follow.
What does this dog know?' She said, 'Ay, I never saw this [she does not
know or understand their ways].' If she would have been a person like
that, they would have been three, but that one [Baka Tenga] defeated
them. She refused to go with them. At last we found that they did not get
along with her.

This one! What! If Baka Chilalo [the senior widow of his brother and
sister of Baka Tandiwe) ever went with anyone, it was with me. All these
wives, Buka's mother and Dzilo's mother, hey, no they never did it. But
those two, they were snakes. If anyone with a banjo came here, just a
visitor, and spent the day here and slept here, the following day he would
be loved. Hey, what! That is why she [Baka Chedza] did not get any
children, she got only two. Hey, she is a sorceress. If there would be some
dancing to drums, there is no one who would go, without having gone in
there.

[The contrast Lupondo had in mind was to a time when wives kept to the
right way of long ago, a time of mutual understanding, dutifulness, good order

under the Chief in the hamlet of Lupondo's youth. At that time, wives tended
the head of the hamlet, sent him milk and beer, waited peacefully for an absent
husband, and would come to his hut upon his return to greet him and answer
about their actions. Wives of long ago, unlike present ones, would not ignore a
husband, if he failed to come first to them in their compounds.]

When I was still in Mbubi's hamlet, my wives [the first two] understood
each other. I would go and spend a whole month at my girlfriend's. I did
not hear that when a husband has gone and he returns, he is closed
outside. They were still of long ago. If I would have gone and stayed there,
perhaps as long as three weeks, I'd return, and find them. On my return, I
would go to my hut, the one I had there at Nsimbi's. The old man was
Mbubi, the owner of them. All milked for him. One calabash even of the
beer that would be brewed, would go there. A dish of food would go there.

When I returned home, I would not go to their compounds. I would go
to my hut. To the wives? No. Then I would see what they would do. They
would come in and visit me, and answer. It is only then that I would go to
the compounds. These [wives] of now, if you do that, you cannot be seen.
Those of long ago were very good. They did not curse and fight. No, no,
never. They liked each other very much. At beer parties they would just
drink. To find them fighting? No, no. And when I was away, they
supported each other, and the food went there to the old man [Mbubi].
And a small calabash, if Baka Buka had brewed, went there to the old
man. This Baka Dzilo, too, if she had brewed, would send a small
calabash to the old man. They were 'children' and he would say, 'My
children' to them.

Or if I would have drunk beer, when the people of Nigoba were still up
there, I would sleep there. And I did not hear them saying anything. Can
you do that now? Is it not war? 'He has remained at his concubine's', those
wives of today say. Do you think that long ago it was like this? No, no. It
was not like this.

[Having listened to Lupondo's complaints against the wives of today, I
raised the thorny issue of seniority among his own wives. If it was true that
Buka's mother had been his girlfriend first, how come she became his second
wife? In response, he appealed to the authority of a proverb about adultery. In
applying it to Buka's mother, he did not mean that she was an adulteress in the
usual sense of the word among Kalanga. For a woman to be an adulteress, she
has to be married and have sexual intercourse with a lover, not her husband.
Buka's mother was simply Lupondo's girlfriend; she became pregnant by him
before coming in marriage to his homestead. Lupondo twisted the proverb to
make the point that a woman is not entitled to be a man's senior wife merely
because she sleeps with him.]

Now, you ask about the senior wife. Could that one [Buka's mother] be made senior wife? Ah, ah, ah, do the Kalanga do like that? It is said, 'An adulteress, even if you have her, you can't make her a senior wife.'

I took her [Buka's mother] when I had taken the other one [Dzilo's mother]. No, the Kalanga do not do that. It would be if I had taken her first [that she could be the senior]. This one, Dzilo's mother, when I took her [in marriage] was offered to me while that one was my girlfriend. And then I was given that one [his third wife]. They did not give this one having had marriage offerings *pisa bukwe* [the wife-receivers' donation for the 'stripped', prior to bridewealth]. I then went back and took.

When the mother of this one [Buka] came, she didn't have the hang of ploughing; and the mother of these [Dzilo and his siblings] when she came, she ploughed and ploughed and ploughed. Also, when she was here, she sold and got money and bought cattle. That is when the bags were still bought and sold at the stores [to the European store owners]. At the beginning she bought cattle, and again, till they were four, cows only, bought from people. Buka's mother was there, too, and I was with her. But the cattle liked her [Dzilo's mother]. They reproduced, and reproduced, and reproduced, then she took one and gave it to Galani [a follower recently registered in Lupondo's tax 'book']. She said, 'Galani, look after this cow of mine.' And here it really 'defecated', defecating female ones only. You see him with a pen, it is of those. She did 'beat one on' for him (she gave him one], and the pen became very full. Phew! That cow, when it came and was bought, bore only females, only females. And it was the same with Galani. We found Galani had a pen, too, and a hamlet of his own. Au, how does this cow reproduce?

I have another hamlet [kept by his third wife, Baka Tenga, in another locality]. While this old woman of mine [Dzilo's mother] is still alive, I just stay here. When she dies, I will go there. [Lupondo did that, after her death, and himself died at his third wife's hamlet.] She [Baka Tenga—the third wife] is also my wife, she will be living there, too, for she has her lads. They are now marrying wives, and even [the third son] will be taking a wife.

## Sons and Sons' Wives

[For the sake of encouraging Lupondo to say more, I made what I thought was an innocuous remark to the effect that it was a good thing that even this third son was now taking his wife. My remark elicited a diatribe from Lupondo about how wives make children scorn their father and have so little care for him that they become 'fuckolo', fuck-offs or cast-offs. His dying son, Mfila, and his sons by his favourite wife were the exceptions, and telling about these great comforts to his old age, and the tobacco they brought him, made him withdraw into the pleasure of silence.]

You mention wives! You, Mabuyani [the ethnographer], do you not know that wives spoil the children of a person? They will go to the father, but once they follow their wives, they are 'fuckolo'. The one [Mfila] does not follow the wife. You see them bewitching my child [Mfila]. No, he does not follow the wife. I cannot go a day long in hunger. You hear him saying, 'Has my father eaten?' And these others, like Dzabubu [a beer nickname given Dzilo by the ethnographer] the friend of Mabuyani [the ethnographer], 'he's a mongoose'. No, that year he came from Johannesburg, he gave me an overcoat. And Buka, too, went to Johannesburg, and then I was given an overcoat. But now that they have taken wives, I no longer see it. They brew beer, and they do not give me even a small calabash. All these, including Dzilo, all these and this one who has recently removed [Buka who had just then come to bid farewell], they used to give me a calabash, when I was still looking after my fields here. Now they do not do it.

When it comes to food, the one who is dying [Mfila] he is the one who knows me. And this big one, this big man [Dzilo], if his wife has brewed some beer, can you hear it said, 'Here is a calabash for my father?' I also drink in the kitchen, when they are still sifting it. But if it is for sale, I have to buy with my own money. And this one, this one here, you see them bewitching him saying he gives his father.

And those children, those there [at the third wife's], ah, clothes, I wear and throw them away. Shirts, I wear and throw away. From those two small ones, and that one in Johannesburg. And the eldest sometimes gives me a shirt when he comes home. This year he is in town, but when he returns, he will give me. And that one [a second son] is there, if you hear that he has come down for his holidays and has come to see me, ah with tobacco, I smoke and throw away [he chuckled]. He came, the first time, when the cattle went to the cattleposts and gave me that coat I always wear, that khaki one. Yes, this year I was given a shirt and a coat, only new things. And [a mongoloid son of his brother] was given a shirt, and a pair of trousers by [a young son of his third wife]. We were both given at the same time.

[Lupondo laughed at the ridiculousness of being treated in old age the same as that mongoloid son of his brother, relished the prospect of receiving tobacco, too, then gave a sigh, and sitting back on his haunches, sank into reflection.]

Ah, he [his third son] is a man. Yes, he's a man. The day he comes—ah, tobacco—I don't talk.

## II

### BAKA CHEDZA

In our conversations, Baka Chedza never spoke ill of Lupondo, even though, to me at least, he carped against her. Characteristically modest, her image for her own and her husband's place within the family was an image of usefulness in being junior: 'the lath for the rain drain'. 'By this we mean a child of a junior wife', she explained, and implied that Lupondo was the centre pole, the senior. She praised Lupondo for rescuing her and Kunda her husband from great hardship, although it was actually Lupondo's son Dzilo who won her lasting loyalty by ploughing and saving them from hunger. She recalled insisting that her husband follow Lupondo and separate from another brother, their senior. She saw herself and her husband Kunda as having been in Lupondo's hand, supported under his care.

It 'started from the root', she said, from the fact that while being junior co-wives, Lupondo's mother had been immediately senior to her husband's mother. The sons' mutual understanding, the care of the senior for the junior, the junior's trust and loyalty in return, all had to be understood as growing from generation to generation out of that original source. The present was an effect caused by the past. Hence to know the past down to the circumstantial details of who said what to whom, when and where was to anticipate, to gain forewarning of characteristic actions by family members. What informed Baka Chedza's vision of family life was, above all, a sense of 'starting from the root', a sense of what we might call the historicity of kinship.

Baka Chedza brought that sense to bear while she held to a certain estimation that a person's motivation often remains opaque and that personal knowledge is always limited—'Things of others' compounds, we cannot know them all'. Commenting upon the opaqueness of motivation, she told me,

> If a person has hated you and still hates you, he can never tell you. But it is still there, the reason for hating you. Something grieves him, something that he knows. Anyone, a mere outsider, will be saying 'A person is a person' [he is normal, like anyone else, and not set apart by secret motives]. Yet there is something that he is worrying about. When you meet him, you will just laugh with him, yet his heart is very *tsu*, red and sore. You can end by going to be buried in the soil here, because of a person.

Baka Chedza was born, in the early 1900s, while her mother was still unmarried and at her Ndebele grandfather's hamlet. That is how she came to be reared among Ndebele. But the man whom she spoke of as 'my father who begot me' eventually brought her to live among Kalanga and made formal marriage arrangements for her. She was proud of the fact that a formal arrangement was made for her marriage, she was 'offered', and did not have to elope, as some must because they have become pregnant or their parents object to the marriage.

As one of the few surviving wives of the oldest generation in the family, Baka Chedza had come to play the part of a keeper of memories. She was someone who could remind her husband what had really happened when he was asked as the family's junior elder. Her recollections, which she gave to me when she was in her early fifties, were neither nostalgic nor heroic, certainly not focused on herself as heroine. In her childhood, while she was being reared among Ndebele, her mother's father fought and murdered his first-born son with a chisel. The atrocity was carried out while she watched helplessly. Baka Chedza had to testify against her grandfather first to the police and later in the Native Commissioner's court at district headquarters. The trauma left her with a strong sense of herself as a witness. She told me her version of the family's history, speaking as someone who evidently felt she had to testify, if not always openly or completely, at least realistically and without nostalgia about the quarrels of the people closest to her.

For our understanding of her vision of family life, the quarrels that became the personal vendetta between Lupondo's senior and favourite wives, Baka Dzilo and Baka Tenga, are among the most important. In that personal vendetta a crisis came when Baka Tenga tried to hush up the fact that her daughter Bengani had got pregnant in town. Baka Tenga and her daughter Bengani acted perversely, in Baka Chedza's view. In a life crisis at birth just as at death, they ought to have summoned responsible relatives, the people they were living with, to inform them, to consult them, to get their help in 'working' a way through the crisis. The 'work' had to be collective and public, if it was to accomplish a good purpose. But Baka Tenga acted with her daughter alone and in private isolation. Here much of the point of Baka Chedza's story depends upon understanding the motivation for this action. Even more, what Baka Chedza was doing through her story was defining the way to interpret motivation within the family, and especially between the senior and the favourite wife.

Following Baka Chedza's implicit bias in favour of Baka Dzilo, we can say that Baka Tenga's perverse action was seen to be motivated in part by the moral weakness of her daughter's condition. Baka Tenga was unwilling to give her senior co-wife and others the chance to assert their own moral superiority by expressing their strong disapproval towards her daughter for sexual promiscuousness with miners or other labour migrants in town. Worse still, her daughter could be accused of endangering her own life and her child's by such promiscuousness. Indeed, years later that is what Baka Tenga's brother is supposed to have told her in a quarrel—that Bengani was actually killed in town, having brought her death upon herself.

Baka Chedza implied, however, that there was even more causing Baka Tenga to act as she did, at least as her motivation came to be understood in the family after the action and after Bengani died in pregnancy. Two causes were perceived, immediately a threat made by the senior wife's son Mfila, and even more fundamentally, longstanding grievances over cattle and other goods, involving Lupondo as the husband of the co-wives.

Mfila was said to have made his threat because Bengani had carried letters between a lover and Mfila's wife, during his absence as a labour migrant. Upon discovering that and in a murderous rage, he shouted at Bengani and others among his 'juniors'. Later, after Bengani's death, Baka Tenga flung her version of Mfila's words back at him as a threat that had been fulfilled. She wailed her accusation publicly at the height of the funeral, a time when men are usually more subdued but women often hold nothing back and in their grief wildly scream out blame for killing by sorcery. Having thus accused Mfila and his mother of sorcery, Baka Tenga took her belongings, abandoned the hamlet, and returned to her brother at her original home in a distant locality.

As Baka Chedza recalled, there was a justified mode of vengeance, 'beating on the grave'. It was considered justified because it returned harm to the injurer; the intent was to strike back only upon the sorcerer who was guilty of causing the person in the grave to die. But given the innocence of Baka Dzilo and the culpability of the late Bengani, and Lupondo paid for diviners who confirmed that, such a justified mode of vengeance could not work against Baka Dzilo. Baka Tenga had to have help from some ally in the family still living with Baka Dzilo, in order to strike at her, to claim a life for a life, the life of Baka Dzilo's young first-born daughter for Baka Tenga's own first born. The internal ally had to be close enough to be able to get a dress belonging to Baka Dzilo's daughter and thus her personal dirt for use in killing her by contagious sorcery. Hence Baka Dzilo's daughter's death became an occasion for further suspicion and accusation against an internal member of the family, rather than an outsider alone.

Again, Baka Chedza recalled, family members did not keep to the justified mode of vengeance. Instead, Baka Dzilo acted in a way that was puzzling, burning a fire on a path in the bush and treating her daughter when she was already dead or as good as dead. It made Baka Chedza reflect and ask why Baka Dzilo did that. Although Baka Chedza put the question in a way that implied one answer—for the sake of sorcery in the vendetta against Baka Tenga—her reflection, like her way of speaking about it, was guarded, understated, left implicit. 'No,' Baka Chedza said, 'it ended like that and we looked at it and left it there, too . . . we think it is a thing she did with her child.' What Baka Chedza conveyed, in her loyalty to Baka Dzilo's son Dzilo, was that there are some matters best left alone, not examined too closely, or at least not talked about too openly.

For Baka Chedza the story was about an unremitting and ongoing struggle within the family, not an episode finished in the past, somehow resolved by mere physical separation. In that struggle family members were understood to be motivated to strike against each other by a principle of a life for a life. The powerful assumption was that vengeance had to be sought above all within the family; that 'one is killed by one's own person, not someone coming from afar'.

Baka Chedza's own life had not been an easy one. Never having had sons, she never had daughters-in-law to fetch and carry and ease her domestic burdens. One daughter came home as a divorcee, and indeed was still in the vicinity with her children, grandchildren and great grandchildren nearly thirty years later, but that daughter brought her no great relief. The daughter was lazy, took after her rather feckless father Kunda, and often embroiled Baka Chedza in quarrels with Kunda, who objected to having the daughter's lover coming and going as if he belonged in their huts. It may be, as Lupondo carped against her, branding her a sorceress, that Baka Chedza had had many lovers— her husband, too long away in Johannesburg, had virtually abandoned her during the 1930s. Plump, with bright sparkling eyes, often very jolly, much given to a toothy grin then a rumbling laugh, she still had about her something of what I might call 'a good time girl'. The poverty and hardships she had known had not at all embittered her. She made no complaints on her own behalf against others in her recollections. But being very loyal to her friends, she defended them, and taking her friends' sides, she recounted only certain of the accusations widely believed in the family about blame for illness, death and other affliction.

Baka Chedza's huts were next to my own and that of my assistant. Towards us both, she was most generous, caring and solicitous of our comfort. I felt that she mothered us, as if we were the sons she herself wanted but never had. Once, hearing that our supplies had run short, she presented us with a bucket full to the brim with dried beans, enough to last us months.

In her reminiscences, Baka Chedza dwelt upon agonies, faults and debts, quarrels over bits of property, crises at birth and death. If in a sense a family historian as a keeper of memories, she was not so much interested in evidence as in emotionally charged debris, in fragments of the past as memories or things that still agitate and thus endanger the living. I have said that she mothered my assistant and me, and it may be that her reminiscences were another form of mothering, disclosing moments dangerous for the very reproduction of the family itself.

### BAKA CHEDZA RECALLS

### Being a Witness: A Childhood Trauma

I grew up and was reared at my grandfather's, and while I was there my grandfather murdered his child, his first born, then already a young man. He stabbed him with a chisel, here on the head, his first born, a young man about to grow a beard. That was the time when children did not take wives early. Ah, he was a young lad! And he [grandfather] was then arrested, captured at Mphoengs [near the international border] while crossing to Lulwani. The police of this side caught him and brought him back.

How big was I then? I was as big as Tubu [about five or six]. He returned, and I was the witness to the murder of that child. They took me with my grandmother to Plumtree [the district headquarters]. I was the witness who was to testify, for I had seen the murder, when the sun was here [pointing to the position of the sun in the afternoon]. I had come from herding. My goats were always nearby there. My mother's brother had called me by name saying, 'Come and give me water.'

I was afraid to go to the hut where grandfather was. I feared, for he had in his hands knobkerries and spears, and he was swearing in that hut. I feared to go in, because I thought he would kill me, too. I told my mother's brother while I was outside, 'The water is there in grandmother's house.'

The child came out of his house, took water, and drank. His father was inside. His father had hurled insults and insults at him, making him sleep with his mother, who bore him [in the curses]. He became angry at that, 'My father has long been swearing at me.' Coming out of his house, he had his axe in his hand and his stick. He was armed. 'We shall see each other, father.' But just as he was about to come out of his house, his father was there before him [she pointed to her forehead] and hurled the chisel right at him. He hit and destroyed him there, and he went off forever. I was there. I wept there, seeing him fall. He did not pull the chisel out, he left it there. I cried, 'Ah.'

I ran to a hamlet as far as there, and told them, 'Masapa has been murdered by grandfather.' When he had killed him, he took a knobkerry, and said to him, 'What do you say now, mate?' The father then went into the house of the son and took about ten shillings and some of the son's clothing, something as big as a coat. He put it on, stood up and ran off. He climbed a mountain. Don't you know that mountain, Zamanyoni of Mbijan? We lived near there. He went to live inside Zamanyoni mountain.

There were some of his goats that, in old days, were said to be dedicated for the divinities of the dead in the way of Ndebele. [Such goats were not to be killed merely for food, although her grandfather was about to do just that.] One was a big goat, as big as a calf. People then said, 'Now that this man has become so wild, this child should no longer herd. He may find her in the bush and kill her.'

'The next day the goats were let loose and they returned: the following day they were again let out, and returned. On the third day, when they returned, that goat was not there. He had caught it and dragged it off to the mountain. For water he would go down at night and drink from the Shashani. In the evening, people would see fire shining, twinkle, twinkle, on top of the mountain where he was living. After he had eaten that goat he went to Mphoengs; after he had finished the meat that was helping him [keep alive]. He ran off and went on sleeping in ant-bear holes, for then there were still many lions in this country.

He had a friend of his, a Tswana, a man; and they knew each other. One day, in the morning, when children were still making fire, they saw a man coming. He was very pale, and he had that coat he had slept on in the holes of ant-bears. And children ran off to their father [the Tswana friend], 'We have seen a white man, and we don't know him.' Their father came out. 'How big a person was he?' They said, 'You will see him.' The affair had already been reported, and the police had been sent to search for him. When he got there, the man and he knew each other, and they talked.

'Where are you from?' 'I am from here.' 'Where are you from coming like this?' 'I am from here. You see me here, I am one who has been troubled. My first born has died.' Was it not that he was misleading him? And then he said, 'How did your first born die?' 'I fought with him, and the next day he was dead.' 'Did you just fight with your mouths [arguing with words], or did you take hold of each other with your hands?' 'No, we fought with our mouths and never touched each other. Then the next day he was dead.' 'What had you done to him, you, his father?' 'No, I had done nothing to him.' 'Is it so?' 'Yes.' 'That is alright. Hunger, there is much hunger.' 'Never mind the hunger, I am just passing, I have ten shillings here in my pocket. Could you take it and get me some mealie meal so that I may eat on my way?' 'Is that so?' 'Yes.' 'Alright you may bring it here. I will get you the mealie meal.' He took that money from his friend and went to his compound and said to his wife, 'This man is the one who has been reported and has to be arrested when found, because he is the one who killed the child.' They brought him into a hut and locked it. 'Sit here.' He sat inside; they made food, and brought it to him to eat. Then his friend left and went to the police camp at Mphoengs.

Four police came, two white, two black. They were all on horses, two on each horse. In those days there were no bicycles. They came and opened the door of the house. When he saw the police, he fell faint. They ran to him with water and poured it on him, and he got up. They took him and tied him to the horse, that man. They came when the sun was here [afternoon].

I was already in Plumtree, with grandmother. When they arrived, then the sun was here [pointing to a time much later in the afternoon]. I went to my grandmother and said, 'There is grandfather.' Then grandmother said, 'Did you see him?' 'Yes, he is with white police.' He was then sent to the 'office'. He sat there for a while, then I saw a policeman coming to call me. I went there, grandmother did not go at first. She stayed behind, for I was the one who had seen what had happened. I went with the police.

There I was questioned in Sindebele. 'Do you know this man?' I said, 'Yes.' 'Do you know him?' 'Yes.' 'Who is he?' 'He is grandfather.' 'What is his name?' 'Sifelani.' 'His praise-name?' 'Ndiweni.' 'Do you really know him?' I said, 'I know him very well, he is my grandfather who reared me.' 'Is it so?' 'Yes.' 'And you, old man, do you know this child?' 'No, I do not know her, but I seem to recognise her.' 'Whom does she look like?' 'Ah, ah, ah, she looks like my grandchild.' (Baka Chedza reported his speech in Sindebele.] Then it was said, 'Come out, and you child, go to the compound.' Then I went out. We slept in the compound.

The next day we were called, and I was asked again. 'You child, are you telling the truth when you say you know this old man?' I said, 'I know him very well, not a little. For he is my grandfather who reared me. My mother had been taken off like a captive. She was hauled from her mother, when she was still young, and she was brought up by this old man, until she bore me. But he killed the child while I watched him.' That chisel was there too, just leaning against the wall. It had a note on it, that chisel he used to kill the child.

We had his case in Plumtree for how many days? For so many, ah, three days. On the first day we talked, and it failed us; and then they said it must be taken to the High Court in town.

We had to take a train on Friday. I went with my grandmother and that policeman who had come to take me. When we got there, we were sent to the High Court in town. The European Native Commissioner then was Thomas. You know him don't you? [Yes.] That one of Plumtree? [Yes.] The first one who spoke Sindebele, he is the one who had questioned me in Sindebele. He asked me, and I answered him in Sindebele. 'Did you really see? Were you there?' 'Yes, I saw the murder of this child. And it is I who went to tell the people that the child had been murdered by his father.' 'Is it so?' 'Yes.' 'Is it the truth? Do you know this man?' 'I know him very, very well. He is my grandfather who reared me, while I was growing from just this to be as I am now.'

We entered the High Court on Wednesday and went until we come to Friday and Saturday the sixth, and on the seventh day, the High Court was closed. The man was 'condemned to death'.

[The phrase Baka Chedza used for 'condemned to death' was literally 'charged for a pole'. It is a phrase meaning 'to be tortured to death', borrowed from Ndebele, who supposedly would have tied a condemned man to a pole and then smeared him with fat so that ants would torture him to death.]

He was to live, and be fed, then be killed. The case ended. For being a witness, I was given ten shillings. I came with that when grandmother was along too. Though he was 'charged for a pole', he was never killed. No, he just died. He died alone in jail, when he was overcome by anxiety.

I came to live with grandmother. We left when she went to Antelope Mine. She fell in love with a miner at Antelope Mine, and we went to Gwanda, while we were still children, going with that miner of grandmother's. [She laughed at the ridiculousness of her grandmother running away with her lover.] The miner worked there, and afterwards he came back to Antelope Mine. My father who begot me heard that, 'The child has come back.' My mother heard this too. So father came to take me from Antelope Mine. I came here, when he took me forever, to this country of the Kalanga.

I never returned to my grandmother, and I do not know if she stayed there. She may have died. I never went to see her. And her children that she had left, I never went back to see them. I came to stay here forever. I grew up here, and here I was ululated for [by women celebrating her first menstruation].

### Marrying into the Great Hamlet of Lupondo's Father

[Baka Chedza went on to tell of her experience of being 'offered' in marriage, an arrangement of great importance for Lupondo's family since it was the formal offering of a senior wife, Baka Dzilo, that gave her precedence over her juniors. 'Offering' in marriage was an elaborate affair of numerous transactions, costly, time consuming, highly public, and very prestigious. Two sides, wife-receivers and wife-givers, made the transactions, which were initiated by intermediaries.]

[To begin with the *dombo*, either a man or woman as intermediary, would be sent as a relative to the guardian of the prospective wife. This opening phase was spoken of as 'scraping fire' [*pala moto*] or 'begging fire' [*kumbila moto*]. It was an indirect approach in that the intermediary had to go first to the woman's 'junior father', her father's younger brother or his other junior yet responsible patrikinsman. In his turn, the 'junior father' carried the proposal to her father or guardian.]

[To consider the proposal further, the father or guardian had to summon a meeting of the bride's close paternal and maternal kin. Given the approval of the meeting, the wife-receiver's intermediary, the *dombo*, would be told, 'We of ... and of ... [naming the wife-givers and the wife-receivers] should visit one another.' In response, the prospective groom would come courting.]

[Eventually, the wife-givers would send a woman who, as their intermediary (*mbvana*), conveyed their demands for various marriage payments, such as *misa bukwe*, the conjugal payments, *malobola*, the paternity payments, *mari ye makukuta*, money for skins which the wife-receivers should soften (nowadays a woven store-bought blanket), and so forth. The wife-givers' woman intermediary would be treated lavishly upon her arrival among the wife-receivers during a feast of 'thanking' (*misa bukwe*). A goat would be slaughtered; and a head of cattle, *ngombe ya bokuku*, the beast of the mothers-in-law, would be designated and shown to her.]

[In their turn, the wife-receivers would visit the wife-givers, bearing a basketful of the meat from the feast of thanking, and also a blanket (instead of the money for skins). The following phase would be *luba*, the bride's first stay at her marital home, when she would come bringing her first basket of stamped grain. During this stay, she performed various services for all the men and all the women of her husband's hamlet, services for which she was rewarded, usually with gifts of money. Later, she would return to her parents' home to await the night phase of *bomba*, during which, while her parents slept, her husband would come to take her to his home. Eventually, after holding a feast in her absence for neighbours in a wide vicinity, her parents and the neighbours would send her numerous baskets of stamped sorghum and millet, at least one basket per household and altogether sometimes as much as several two hundred pound sacks. Not all of these phases were observed in every formalised marriage, of course, but even nowadays most are regarded as orthodox for a formally arranged marriage, virtually unheard of as that now is.]

Still a girl, I was married, before I was pregnant. I came to *luba* [on her first visit]. We would get up at night, go with a child of my father, the one with whom we did the bride-service. We would draw water, moving alongside the houses of the women to give it to them. At night! The hamlet of Nigoba started from there [pointing to the end of this hamlet] and stopped as far as Siya [two hamlets away]. It was all one hamlet [perhaps two or three times its present size). We would put the pots by the doors, then fill them. By the men's houses, too, we would come and put water at night. We would be given grain to stamp until the sun rose, for we were the brides. After stamping, we would go for wood. In the evening, we would make a big fire, and from it, set fires by the houses of all the elders. We kept on making fire, till we had gone through the hamlet. And again we would go, when the people went to chat and visit, so that they would find fire burning [on the hearths], when they went to their huts. Only then would we ourselves go to sleep. That is what I saw.

[Baka Chedza laughed at the memory of being a bride at everyone's service.] This stamping, while a bride, no, you would never stop, and you would never breathe, 'hah, hah'. [She demonstrated, gasping heavily.] You would stamp, while you were quiet, until the grain was ready, and you would go on stamping until the grain would spill out of the stamping block, until someone would come with money to stop you. [She laughed again at the ordeal.] That is what I saw in my growth, starting from when I was just there.

[She indicated enough above the ground for a child of about six, and was referring back to having told us about her rearing and the trauma of watching the murder of her mother's brother by her grandfather].

Do you remember the year of the influenza [1919]? Don't you know it? When the influenza said 'One' [began] in this country of the Kalanga, it started with me at Nigoba, when I had gone to do bride-service. For the whole day I was sick. I suffered from headache. The next day I was lying flat, then our father [her father-in-law], our father who begot Kunda [her husband] said to my mother-in-law, 'My child, I see this illness swells on the child of other people. Go along with this child, send her home, for I see the days are so many since she came. This illness is spreading in this country; it may be too heavy.' Then she got up very early in the morning. We went along, and when I felt tired, I sat down; and when she felt tired, she, too, sat down. We went in this way until we came home, and I fell down flat. My mother-in-law said, 'I left at home, when it was just like this. I must go home. This illness has spread too far.' My father thanked her very much and said, 'You have done very well, Moyo [person of a Heart clan]. Here, too, we see that the disease has spread.'

I became ill, until they overturned the stamping blocks [a sign of domestic disorder, of sadness, of not eating, see Werbner, 1989, p. 89, on this practice in domestic possession]. I remained there, until I recovered. When I was well, my parents said, 'The child left her husband's, when she had not finished her work. She must go back.' I said, 'No, I just cannot go back. How can I go when the sickness is still so great? It will come on me again.' Father insisted that I go back, but I said no, and remained at home, until the sickness stopped. Then I went back to my basket [of grain], which I had left when I was a bride, and I 'took the womb' of Chedza [became pregnant].

Everything in that hamlet of Nigoba, I saw. And also the wives of the hamlet, the wives of Zina's father [the hamlet head], were five, and Zina himself [a paternal brother of Lupondo] had four wives. Malidzo [Lupondo's full brother] had two wives, and so too did Lupondo, who had been living at his senior mother's place at Bango. Later, he crossed the Semukwe River and came to settle near Zina. But all these children of his he begot at Bango. No child of his was born at Nigoba. He was living at his senior mother's.

## Lupondo: From Rearing to Headmanship

Yes, Lupondo grew up, reared by his senior mother at Bango, until he married while he was at Bango. Malidzo, Lupondo's younger brother, was the one who stayed with their mother at their home, at Nigoba. She had had her children dying, they were being finished off, until she had this Lupondo. So he had to flee [from Nigoba hamlet where his mother feared sorcery], for it was said, 'He had better go and live somewhere at his senior mother's, at his mother's sister's.'

At first, while Lupondo was still living at Bango, from time to time, when others went to plough [hunde the tributary labour for a 'father' or senior elder at the head of a hamlet], Lupondo's children would come to herd for them. Then Malidzo was ploughing with Baka Chilalo at the fields, when she was still the only wife. When it was Malidzo's turn, Lupondo would send some boys to herd at the turn of their junior father here at Nigoba. When it was someone else's turn, they would go back home. We were in one hamlet with Malidzo, when Lupondo left Bango.

'Well,' he said, 'I am now going to my home, I have been raised, I am grown up, and I have my children now. I must go back to my home.' Then he came, and built at the back, outside our hamlet, when we were still in one place with Zina's people, before they went to Mambale [in the Special Native Area 'C']. Saying, 'I cannot come into the hamlet of other people; the hamlet has grown old,' Lupondo came and built outside there with his wives.

[Baka Chedza went on to tell of a quarrel over cattle between her husband Kunda and his senior brother Zina. The cattle in dispute were brought in marriage payments for her sister-in-law. Kunda, being the bride's only full brother, had a right to them. But they were received and then kept by his paternal brother Zina, the heir to their father's name and position. Kunda's claims had been met already, Zina insisted, because at Kunda's marriage, their father paid an amount equal to the total later received for Kunda's sister. The upshot of the quarrel was the impoverishment of Kunda. Zina took away other cattle, belonging to their father's estate, which he had allowed Kunda to have for ploughing.]

While my husband was at Nigoba, he fought with his brother [Zina], who took cattle from him. Lupondo objected, 'No, this one [Kunda] is a child of my father, he cannot lose.' He then took cows as many as this [two], and said, 'Kunda, plough.' Besides these cattle, Kunda had two; and altogether they were four oxen. He said, 'Plough, but when they go to the *hunde* [the tributory labour] of Zina, you must not go with my oxen; they should not plough the *hunde* for Zina. Zina is fighting with you. Your wife should go with a hoe to finish up unploughed parts.'

The children, this Chedza (her first-born daughter], and this Dzilo when still a boy, would remain ploughing. I would leave when I had enspanned the oxen for them, and I would go to the *hunde* of Zina, to hoe there. In the evening I would tell them to outspan the oxen for grazing. When I would come from there, I would meet my children carrying their seed and coming home.

When Zina left [late in the 1930s] for Mambale [in the Sanzukwe Special Native Area 'C'], he said, 'Why has it come about that Kunda remains with Lupondo? He should have come with me so that I make him my 'servant' [*tshicaka*—in Sindebele].' I said [to Kunda], when I was there, 'If you want to go with the child of your father, go. I am not going. I am not going to be the servant of the wives of another person. I am going to stay here. I am going to stay with this one in whose hand I have always been. He is the one who has held me by the hand.' It failed like that.

Up to this day, you see us supporting each other so much. It started from the root, from, well, the mother of Lupondo and the mother of Kunda who were senior and junior wives; they are the ones who followed each other. I mean they were 'mistress' [*batezi*] and 'little bride'

[*nlongwana*]. There was also the 'great wife' [*bawosi*]; and these were the
ones who followed each other after her. As you see me, living like this, I
am in the hand of Lupondo's mother. For Kunda's mother was the
younger and junior wife to Lupondo's mother.

## The Lath for the Rain Drain

I, as I am, say 'There is a lath for the rain drain.' [The understood contrast
in this image of the hut, used for the family in their hamlet, is between the
centre pole, for the senior, and the lath, for the junior.] By this we mean a
child of a junior wife, and not the child of the senior wife. I, as I am, I am
'the lath for the rain drain' in the hamlet of Nigoba. Oh, if they may go to
sow their first seed, I cannot be worried, if I do not go the same day. Or if I
do not go to sow the seeds, I do not mind. They may be the first, I 'avoid'
going to sow seeds before them. I am lesser than they are. If the seniors go
to plough and sow all their seeds, I do not care. I cannot complain that
they have ploughed before me. I am a 'young one'. It goes like that, Dube
[addressing me by the Zebra totem]. I am a 'lath for the rain drain' in the
hamlet of Nigoba.

When Zina's people removed to Mambale, we also moved to come
together with Lupondo. Then Lupondo was there with his younger
brothers, Malidzo and Kunda, and their sister's daughter. She is the one
whose brother has died this year at Zina's. We stayed there, and then
Malidzo too left us. When Malidzo died, people said, 'The people of
Bango are leaving; they are leaving for Elephant Fell [their new place in
the Sanzukwe Special Native Area 'C'].

## The Death of Lupondo's Own Brother Malidzo

The way it was, when people still lived and it was talked about, when
Malidzo was ill, he would have swollen legs. His legs would swell and then
the swelling would go down. Those who talked about it said, 'This child
Malidzo has suffered from the sorcery of [a neighbour] Baka Chileba, the
mother of Baka Siya [still living in a nearby hamlet], the mother of this
very Baka Siya.' I heard this, too, when I was just coming [in marriage]
because it spread out. It was said, 'There is a woman at Nigoba, she is
called Baka Chileba. She does not have to practice sorcery, all she has to
do is command, saying "one" [begin], inside in the hamlet.' It was said
she bewitched Malidzo's feet, so that she might sleep with him. The child
[Malidzo] said, 'I cannot sleep with such a big woman.' Then she beat a
finger at him, saying [threateningly] 'You hate me. You have always hated
me.' Or when they drank beer she would start up, 'Malidzo hates me. He
does not see me with an eye.' 'Hating you? Why should I hate you, when
you are my mother?' 'No, you have always hated me.' That is where the
death of Malidzo started, until he died.

I heard them talking about it, when I came there. For when they talk about a thing, and you have ears for hearing, then you hear that it is told like this and this. That is where I heard, 'Is it not that Malidzo dies and is dying for this talk!'

Malidzo died not in the hamlet but when we had taken him to the field, so that he would come out, on the advice of a diviner: 'You had better take him out so that he is beaten by the air.' He was taken out and a shelter made for him there, in our fields. It was spring, and I can say people had not yet said. 'These melons which fall first can be picked.' The day he died a *manje* [the small plant not yet ripe] of a water melon was brought to him. He said, 'Give me a watermelon, I am going to die having tasted only a watermelon.' It was brought for him by his wife, this Baka Chilalo. That watermelon, not yet ripe, having barely fallen a day or so before, was cut for him, when he was still lying there, on the ground in the shelter. He took a piece of it and bit it. And we saw, 'Ah.'

I was there. The sun was like this. I saw the hand, living; and it fell down. I saw the person go. I said to Baka Chilalo, 'There is nothing.' Baka Chilalo had gone to boil some water. I came out of the thicket and said, 'Baka Chilalo there is nothing there.' At sunset, the oxen were enspanned to carry him from the shelter and bring him home.

While we remained eating the first fruits, he was gone, a person no longer there. He was taken by the feet. His feet started in that way when he was a boy and they were like that when he got married. He went to the Europeans at the hospitals, they failed; he went to the Africans, they too failed. I can say that is the thing I saw, Dube [calling the anthropologist Zebra, the totem of his adopted clan which was the Chief's].

Malidzo had no cattle of his own, but he kept cattle belonging to his brother, Zina. And on that day, a day after Malidzo died, Zina came and collected all of those cattle. He did not leave even one. The person who had cattle was Baka Chilalo [his wife], but Malidzo died without any, even his children did not get any 'tears'. Baka Chilalo remained ploughing with her own cattle and herding them.

[Tears of the dead are shed by the living, when they cry in mourning. Yet the tears are of the dead, physically embodied in all the goods and livestock that come from them to the living. The 'tears' Baka Chedza referred to were cattle from Malidzo's father's estate, which were awarded but never given, because the senior son Zina confiscated the whole estate.]

When Malidzo's father died, each son was awarded 'cattle of tears'. Ndapama, Mpondo, Lupondo, Malidzo, Kunda, all were awarded 'cattle of tears'. You know that beer of inheritance is brewed, then the people have to distribute the things. Such cattle were left by the father of Zina. Zina went off with the cattle that had been given to his juniors. He ate them, taking them from Lupondo and Kunda. But Malidzo was stubborn, he grabbed hold of it, and said, 'I was also born. I will not do it like others who say, when their cattle are taken, "It is his affair".'

[Their phrase implied, 'Let him suffer the consequences'. That might be the wrath of the divinities of the dead in retribution.]

Malidzo took them by force; and it happened that he then became a weakling, always ill, he could not walk for two days. And that Zina, who is at Mambale, was installed to be father [in succession to his own father], only for the divinities of the dead. When he saw Malidzo falling down, and buried, on that very day—not as we have buried Mfila so that it is now a week—when Malidzo had been buried just the day before, Zina went to call the Ndebele of Mlotcwa with whom we lived. They came and bought those cattle. He took six cattle, not leaving even one so that it would remain for a child of Malidzo. That old man at Mambale [Zina] took them and sold all of them. The only cattle that remained are Baka Chilalo's and later her junior co-wife bought hers. Malidzo, as he was, had no cattle. No, I cannot tell lies, I saw this thing with my own eyes. I did not see him with cattle.

If a person has hated you and still hates you, he can never tell you. But it is still there, the reason for hating you. Something grieves him, something that he knows. Anyone, a mere outsider, will be saying 'A person is a person' [he seems normal to the outsider, but actually is someone who has secret motives]. Yet there is something that he is worrying about. When you meet him, you will just laugh with him, yet his heart is very *tsu*, red and sore. You can end by going to be buried in the soil here, because of a person.' So it was with Dzilo's mother [Lupondo's senior wife] and her 'little husband' [Malidzo]. No, they did not see each other. And, too, the little husband was mad. If she would talk aside [provocatively], the little husband would beat her. Yes, Malidzo really beat her when she talked aside.

[Others, including Malidzo's own wife Baka Chilalo, blamed Malidzo's death, if not his original trouble with his feet, on Dzilo's mother's sorcery. But Baka Chedza denied having heard that, and was reluctant to admit openly that there was any truth in accusations against Dzilo's mother. Malidzo's widow herself told me that her husband 'died for a scotch cart'. She traced his death to a quarrel over it between her husband and Dzilo's mother that eventually involved Lupondo's sons, as Baka Chedza explains later. Baka Chedza and the widow Baka Chilalo took opposite views on Dzilo's mother's sorcery in accord with their taking opposite sides in the rivalry between Lupondo's leading sons, Baka Chadza being more for Dzilo and Baka Chilalo more for Buka.]

## The Separation of Malidzo's Widows and Children

Malidzo had this many wives, three. Baka Chilalo is the senior wife, followed by Baka Pande, and Baka Pande followed by Baka Tandiwe, a younger sister of Baka Chilalo; they are the children of one man. And then, when Malidzo had died, these two wives [the second and third] fought bearing a grudge against each other, they alone. Their elder said, 'So, my juniors, if you fight over this grudge while you are alone and have no husband, what has happened? You have no husband, your husband is dead.' She found that one was saying, 'My junior goes about telling people that I am going to buy some medicine to kill her. Why is she staying here? Even when I talk to someone she complains, why should I even talk to those people.' Then she said, 'My juniors, can you do that and afford it?'

One day, when Baka Chilalo was 'still sitting' [biding her time] she found that her juniors had grabbed each other with their hands which 'eat' porridge.

[Their hands, in domestic peace, were for nurture, even sharing food from the same plate.]

'My juniors, why did you fight?'

'No, I cannot go on living here the way I have been living here. This co-wife of mine is driving me away; she says I should go.'

'As you see, I cannot hold you. I cannot stop you; I am not a man. If you see where you can go, you may go, because you have your "parents" [senior patrikin]. I, Baka Chilalo, as I am, I have no parents. Can I take these children and go to Mpati? There at Wangu? Can I afford that? No, I am going to remain here. You will see for yourselves. As you have said, you are young and cannot live without husbands. You may go where you like.' Then those juniors went.

Baka Pande left with three children of Malidzo, one a girl, another, a girl, and one a boy. At his home, she got the fourth, and then that boy died. There remained two girls and the one that was still sucking. We said we had seen them. We heard what about? We heard that the child of Bambuya had died, and then another boy died. We stayed and stayed: and at last she had her friend, her Chindoga, this one who begot the child called Jega. He had fallen in love with this junior wife of Baka Chilalo; he was the one who was giving her those children. One was buried here. They came to cradle and cuddle, and the child was rotting with boils, though just born and only one month old. It was buried here in this hamlet. She had come when the sun was here, saying she was going to the hospital in Mphoengs. The child died that day and the next day we went to bury it.

They went back to wipe off their hands, and stayed and stayed, and then she became pregnant again. Once she gave birth, the same thing happened. And they ended by just living only. That friend of hers who was giving her children later died also. She just stayed, not bearing children, and said, 'I have grown old.' She lived with her children. I can say the children of Baka Pande who died are four. The children of Malidzo who died are four; there remained two girls and one boy. This very year, now, this year of these crops, the first born called Penda died, the one born when the mother was awakened [into the cult of demonic possession, see Werbner, 1989, Chapter 2]. He left behind two children, only those. Only two, one girl, who has married, and one boy, a policeman, remain, five of them went down. Those are the children of Malidzo who have remained.

Baka Tandiwe, Malidzo's junior wife after Baka Pande, gave birth to Tandiwe, Malebeswa and Wobunga. Those are the children of this place, three. Then, she started there at Degetshu, and she got a boy, who died when he was this big. Now she is a person who is just living there at Degetshu. She has no child there, the children belong here at Nigoba only.

Baka Chilalo, as she is like this, she gave birth to Chilalo and then Nzana; and there are two wombs [pregnancies] that miscarried, and she stopped like that. I myself had no miscarriages. I bore these two children of mine and then I just stayed; I never had a third pregnancy. I bore Chedza and Mbamba, girls following each other, and I just stayed.

Yes, we were friends together, Baka Tandiwe and I. I was the senior. But in friendship, Baka Tandiwe and I were friends. Younger though she was, she knew me very well. She knew that I was her senior, and I knew that she was my junior. Baka Tenga [Lupondo's third wife] did not want to listen to us. Yet she is an infant. She was not my agemate. She was not even an agemate of Baka Tadiwe. Why should I mention myself, when I am the mother?

[Baka Chedza was both older and a first wife, albeit of a younger brother to Lupondo.]

Then it happened that Baka Tenga went to inform the husband [Lupondo as the husband, who succeeded his brother Malidzo], telling him that Baka Tandiwe 'goes' with [is sleeping with] Mbunga. Malidzo had died. Baka Tandiwe had been offered to Malidzo having already given birth to Tandiwe, while still a girl at her home. Her boyfriend made her pregnant at her home, and then she was given to Malidzo, for she was 'going to hold the hand of her elder'.

[Her elder sister, Malidzo's first wife, was then barren; the younger sister married in sororate, which the phrase in quotation describes.]

Malidzo died leaving Tandiwe still suckling. Malebeswa [the first son] was still to be fathered by Lupondo, and Wobunga [another son] by Mbunga.

Before Baka Tandiwe left, Dzilo's mother [the first wife of Lupondo] scolded her. 'Why should you run about, when you came to your elder sister?' Today you are running to the enclosures of Mbunga, where are you from, and where are you going to? It is the enclosure of another cooking place there.

And Baka Tandiwe said, 'Why should I be sitting [doing nothing]? Should I just sit? Have I a husband? I have no husband.' [Her husband's successor, Lupondo, was as good as no husband, when it came to having children.]

'You say you have no husband. What about this Malebeswa [the son fathered by Lupondo], who begot him? Today you say you have no husband. Who begot Malebeswa? Did you conceive him with a stump? Is it that the people of Mbunga, people you've only known today, will make you a wife? Go then, remove from here and go to those of Mbunga.'

When she left she said, 'I fought with Dzilo's mother. I have been chased away by Dzilo's mother, and the people are also saying I am making love with Mbunga.' 'Even so, are you not making love with Mbunga? Haven't you got a child with him? And again, they will influence you that you should go to such and such a place. When you remove, we shall find you in front and take you from there.' And today they are falling on their backs and saying 'I am not taking a person with fits.' They have been crooks and tricked her there again.

### The Quarrels and Bereavement of Lupondo's Beloved Wife

Baka Tenga, Lupondo's [third wife] wife, came in marriage from Jela when we were at Nigoba, at Dziya not at Bango. She was given to Lupondo by her father. She was holding her child, a toddler called Bengani, who died here and sleeps at the ant heap. She was the first born of Baka Tenga and was followed by Tenga.

It happened the way it happened to [my grandchild] when she left school. Baka Cheka [a neighbour] stood up and said, 'Ah, do not take a child and make her like the hillbillies who do not send children to school. Take a child. You see us; we have educated Cheka, who is now working in town. Now that your child has left school, take her to school in town.' Baka Tenga talked with this Baka Cheka and her husband at her enclosure, and the child went off to town to stay with Cheka. There, Cheka saw the child always coming at night. 'Hey, this child, how is she working then?' Cheka asked, 'Hey, Bengani, you have got used to the town, when you do not know it. Where are you all the time that you come at night?'

When the child heard Cheka saying so, '*Phe*,' she tied up [her things], went off [in a huff] to a sister of Makanda, Chileka, and stayed there, not working. She did the same trick at Chileka's, and Chileka said, 'Ah this child.' When Chileka went to work and then returned she would find, ah, the house was full of men. Chileka looked at it and said, 'Ah this child is going to put me into danger and bring me trouble.' 'You child, it's better for you to go home, since you do not find any work. Go home.' Then, of course, Bengani came home, and she was already pregnant.

She came and stayed here for a few days, and we heard people spreading rumours about, 'Bengani looks as if she is pregnant.' She sat there with her mother and father at their hut. At last, a word came out saying, 'Why is it that a child is to come like this, when she is not asked from where she got this load?'

It was then that the mother of the child [Baka Tenga] said, 'Never, a person should never, never ask my child. I will heap abuse on that person, and I'll make her know.' And that child, too, said, 'And also that little woman who will be sent to come and ask me, I'll be abusive and shock her.' They stayed like that, Baka Tenga and her husband [Lupondo]; and the pregnancy of the child grew on. It was not known who was the 'owner of the womb' [the father], whether from this place or not.

It stayed so until the womb [the pregnancy] was mature, when the days had come. We were carrying the crops, and we had already reaped them. She was with her mother and that old woman [the grandmother] who had been called for the pregnancy of the child.

We here were not told anything. No, we would get up, yoke the oxen, and go with the sledges to carry the crops. When we had unyoked the oxen, they [Baka Tenga and her daughter] remained here. They spent the day, struggling vainly, making efforts to no avail, for the child was having labour pains. And the people here in the hamlet were not told!

The child remained for three days. We were told on the fourth day, when they had seen that the pregnancy now was overwhelming and grieving them. At last, the mother of Baka Tenga said, 'It is long since I came here and I am now three days here, and I have not seen anyone of the Nigoba people saying "What is it?" or coming. Did you tell the people that the child is having trouble in her belly?' Baka Tenga said, 'No, I did not tell them.' 'Ah, having not told the people in the hamlet, how can you work on it [treat the difficulty in the pregnancy], now that it is failing?'

While at the threshing place, we saw a child coming, 'It was said that I should come and tell you that Bengani is having pain in her belly.' 'Having pain in labour?' 'Yes.' Immediately, we returned to the fields to carry the load, unyoked the cattle, came home and cooked, and then went there.

We found the child. Ah, people were going about vainly. I do not know whether it was a pregnancy by the mine workers. People do not give birth in huts, so she was carried and sent down to the soil pits; and a shelter was made for her out there. She slept there, to no avail. She was again brought into Baka Jeremiah's hut, that kitchen before it had been roofed. She was put in it, and it was still to no avail. That time the pregnancy of the child was somewhere at the chest, not down here, but here at the heart.

'People, you should have gone to Tanai [a nearby diviner and healer]'—
because there were no hospitals then and the town was far. 'You should
have gone to Tanai, he is the one who helps people, and those who have
been helped by Tanai are alive.' The mother of the child said, 'No, Tanai
has many cripples, too many cripples.' And the child had the pregnancy,
until at last the child was taken by the womb. She died like that, full
bellied.

They took her, to bury her; and when they had done that, and when
Baka Tenga was wailing [at the height of the funeral] she said, 'Where
about? My child has been killed, Mfila [the younger son of her senior
co-wife] has killed my child, and done it with his mother.' He had said, 'I
am going to kill and kill even the chickens.' 'When I said it, to whom was I
telling it', Mfila answered. 'Should I have neglected to warn my juniors?
Who are the people who are taking letters and giving them to my wife?
Should I not have warned them saying I would beat them? Is it by this that
I killed her?'. Then Tenga tied them [her things] up and went off [to a
distant neighbourhood] saying, 'My child has been killed by Dzilo's
mother and Mfila'.

### Cattle and the Vendetta of the Favourite and the Senior Wives

Do you see the many oxen in Mfila's pen? They are his mother's cattle,
born by her cow from her brother, which came to be milked for the
children, when we were still at the old sites. When I came in marriage, I
found them already there, having come from her home. And the father of
Dzilo's mother said before he died, 'You see, you juniors, when I am dead
you should not go to collect that cow. You must not go to collect those
cattle. They are tears. She will see me there, too. You may take all these
cattle here and share these here.' That is how the cow of Baka Dzilo
remained, it remained and it reproduced, it excreted the whole pen. Then
Dzilo's mother bought hers, too. When she had bought that one, it too
had many calves, so Lupondo sold one to the junior wife [Baka Tenga],
but without telling Dzilo's mother. He meant to give her back a calf, when
it had given calves.

Dzilo's mother complained, 'How is it that you did not talk to me about
it, though we paid for it together?' He found then that it was hard. They
were fighting, so that it was said, 'Dzilo's mother has a thirst [is greedy].'
It was the junior wife who said, 'I cannot agree [to just give it up], when I
have bought a head of cattle from the old man. And yet Dzilo's mother
says that they bought it together.' It was hard. Then the old man went to
show Baka Tenga that head of cattle at Dudwane. And the senior [wife]
refused the cattle. Whether Baka Tenga went to collect or sold there, I do
not know. But even to this day the talking continues and has not stopped
about it.

After Baka Tenga went away [to live at her brother's home], the old man [Lupondo] here was selling cattle and sending money there so that she could go and hunt for diviners to kill Dzilo's mother because 'She is the one who killed my child.' When it got to diviners, they saw nothing and said, 'You, you may say I should work on these people, but there is nothing that I see. There is nothing that I see; they did nothing. The child was killed by her burden that came from very far, not from the hamlet here. You say I should work, but there is nothing that I can do. You will be wasting your money.' And Baka Tenga said, 'Just work.' 'Even if I may work, there is nothing that I can do. There is nothing that I can see.' 'Just work. What I want is that name for her [Baka] "Mother of"—just as I was said to be "Mother of". I was called Baka Bengani [Mother of Bengani], and that has ended. I want that name, Baka Matilela [Mother of Matilela, the name then used for Dzilo's mother] to end too.' The diviner said, 'You are going to work, for you know I have not got medicines that I can just waste. I want my money. I don't see that this person got to that place you are talking of. She did not get there.'

I think Baka Bengani finished the world. It was not that she wanted the grave. No, she wanted dirt of Matilela [for sorcery though contagious magic], to get the people quickly to do wrong. 'You who are living with her, get it for me.' So, she went about saying that, 'That name Baka Matilela should end just as mine, Baka Bengani, has ended.' And it ended so.

When Baka Tenga left, she went over there to Jela, to live with her brother, saying 'I have suffered sorcery by a senior wife, by Baka Dzilo.' Yet the child [Bengani] refused to go to school, left here and went to work in town. And when she got there she courted Zezuru [Shona] from whom she got pregnant; and that is the pregnancy she died with. Then the mother of the child said 'I have suffered sorcery by a senior wife.' They [Baka Bengani and Dzilo's mother] fought and fought very badly, so much so that they could not step on each other's blankets. Nor would they drink water from each other. They hunted doctors for [magic or sorcery against] each other. If it had really been true that Dzilo's mother killed the child of the junior wife, they should have died and even the chickens should have died. There was nothing good in that. It was seen that she did not do it, that thing.

When those were grieving in their huts, they went to trap the first born of Dzilo's mother, Matilela. They went hunting for her, getting her dress to trap her and working on it with a doctor. They went to harm her maliciously, even though she was not the one who did it. They went to look for her so that such a child should die having gone into her blankets forever. And she died like that. When she was menstruating, she died like that, when they had trapped. She died, and is lying here.

Baka Tenga worked, saying, 'Dzilo's mother is the one who killed my child.' Yet her child had gone to get pregnant from mine workers. And the parcels that came to that child, she did not show them to people. She took them herself. It came out now when she was quarrelling with her brother, just now.

[Her brother said,] 'Is that what you left the Nigoba hamlet for? You were saying your child had been killed by a wife of Nigoba. Yet you have come to destroy my hamlet with your silliness. And your child came with her pregnancy from the mines. She was killed there in town. Today you are destroying my hamlet.' Yes, they are fighting there; she is fighting with her own brother, the child of her mother.

### The Aggression and Bereavement of Lupondo's Senior Wife

Long ago, Dzilo's mother would not get up and go, if there was beer like this. Now she drinks beer and goes without talking too much. That time, when we were still at the old sites, if she drank beer, there would be nothing good; to her junior wife there would be nothing good or to the wives of her husband's brother. They always lived like that. These people of the younger brother were always quiet and others would say, 'Do not follow up this person who is babbling and speaking freely after her. Let her babble alone and then she'll talk until she becomes quiet, seeing that others do not answer her.'

When that child of hers, Matilela, died, she was taken from Patzwa [at the mother's brother's] already dying. Mlilo [a healer and diviner] was called; he tried and failed. One day when we got up and went to the fields on this path here, early in the morning, 'Hey, what about those who have made fire on the path here? What is the fire for?' It was just a small fireplace, and then the fire remained as charcoal there until it was just spread apart. In the middle of the path! We came along that path and said, 'Hey, who made this fire here at night? And there are some footprints here.' We then went to the fields, and next day we heard that the child had died. We heard that it was Dzilo's mother who had made the fire and spent the night treating her daughter there.

Why had she gone to treat her there? Why did she treat her, when the child was dead? Why did she do that at the bush? If she would have done that and the child would have lived that would have been better. But now that the child is dead, for what was she treating her there? [The answer implied is that Dzilo's mother was doing that for sorcery, to harm her enemy, Baka Tenga.] No, it ended like that and we looked at it and left it there, too. I do not know whether the mother's brother of the child went to hear what had eaten the child, I do not know. Things of others' compounds, we cannot know them all. I never heard even whether they went to a diviner or not about Matilela's death. But [Dzilo's mother] she is rich, she has her cattle. Yet she did not say, 'I have been bereaved of my child, and you brothers go, take this money, and go and hear what has eaten your sister.' No, it ended like that, we think it is a thing she did with her child.

We people when we think of the death of Matilela, we see it is the war of Dzilo's mother, Mfila [her son], and Baka Tenga. Baka Tenga's daughter Bengani also died in pregnancy, and it is so that the death of Matilela came.

### The Current Aftermath of the Senior Wife's Quarrels

The talk [dispute] about these things is still on today. Yes, when Mfila went to Johannesburg a wife of Mpalo [a neighbour] was there, and she said, 'Tata Lufu [Mfila], your wife is courting another.' He said, 'Who is my wife?' 'Ah, there at home, how many wives do you have?' Ah, as you know, when a man is told a thing, do you think that he can laugh? That wife of Mpalo told it all. Mfila came back home, arriving here early in the morning, and he had a big knobkerry, one as big as this [quite large]. He found Jena had been born; he had left his wife pregnant and on his return found she had given birth to that child. But he refused to 'lick marula' saying the child was not his.

[The reunion of husband and wife through 'licking marula' implied a ritual acknowledgement of the child by the father. It was done by husband and wife before resuming sexual relations. What is licked is figuratively, not literally marula fruit; it is a preparation of herbs and body wastes.]

He was taking it from the words of Mpalo's wife, yet he had left Baka Lufu [his wife] pregnant, and her pregnancy was big enough so that she remained to give birth to that child. When letters were written telling him that 'Your wife has given birth' he had already heard the words of Mpalo's wife. 'I am not the one who conceived this child', he said. He came very early, that boy, I do not know where he slept, and he was holding his knobkerry. It was a great noise.

While Malidzo was alive, he and Lupondo bought their scotch cart and paid for it together. I never heard the noise about it then. The noise about the scotch cart came when Malidzo was dead and when the scotch cart, too, was already a dead, useless thing, having only wheels left. Then Dzilo and Mfila, his brother who had just died, said, 'How would it be if we repaired the scotch cart and use it?' And one [Buka, their brother] took out a word, he did not take it before their eyes, he took it out to any person [outsiders, such as Tobela, Lupondo's cousin] 'We shall see the one who is going to use this scotch cart. The one who is going to repair it will send it to be repaired. That is the one who'll send it for repairs, but we will all use it.' That was Buka saying so. At last, it was said that the scotch cart should be left alone, and Lupondo took his wheels, selling them to Mzola; they were still new and had been repaired. The planks of the box are these that are separated. Some of them are used for doors and others for scraping on top. That is when Dzilo's mother went to buy this scotch cart, with her own money.

You know that when people came to Elephant Fell [in the Sanzukwe Native Area], I remained for a while and didn't come here quickly. [The reason was that she had been abandoned by her husband.] I came after they had been ploughing here perhaps as much as five years. It was the year Buka [Lupondo's eldest son] also came home from Johannesburg with his wife, the one called Ma Dube. I came and ploughed this field at the red soil, for the first time. Buka was shown his field at the same time that they showed me mine at the sweet reeds, over there.

We had unyoked the cattle and were sitting there, Tata Chedza [her husband Kunda], a sister's child who has now followed her mother to town, and I. We saw Buka coming from this side. He sat down, we greeted each other, and Buka began to speak to Kunda, 'Old man, you see me coming here. I have come to ask. I am asking how many are the cattle of my father here. I do not know them, because it is long since I went to the Europeans.' He answered, 'No, I do not know, I cannot be sure about anything here. What I know is the cattle that came from the old site. I know the cattle of Dzilo's mother. Of the old man, I know only one head of cattle, which is said to have come from Patzwa, that one he worked with a scotch cart when the people of Patzwa were removing to come this way. That is the cow I know, that black cow. That one there is the offspring of it. Its mother was caught by a hyena, and the offspring remained.'

'I simply wanted knowledge,' Buka answered, 'since now we are children, and we are many, and there are also boys. Tomorrow the old man will take cattle and give them to the other, or send them to that junior house.' Tata Chedza said, 'No, no, there are no cattle that I know my son. I cannot tell lies to you. I am also just arriving, I have been eight years, too, in Johannesburg I cannot know.' 'No, old man, I was merely asking only.' 'Is that so?' 'Yes.' And he said, 'You may ask from your brothers.' He said, 'No, I cannot ask my brothers. I wanted to hear it from you.' Ta Chedza refused like that.

It went on till people lived here for some time and Buka came to quarrel with that wife of his from Johannesburg. He was now courting elsewhere. He wanted to divorce Ma Dube and take Ma Nkomo. They came and built huts there [pointing to the other end of the hamlet]. When those people of Ntolo came and built their huts, Buka had no space; he had only one hut and lacked a space to build more, and so they put him over here. It was said, 'Come this way.' Then Buka built here. This scotch cart is the one from the marriage payment for Matilela, this one who is sleeping at the ant hill. She was the first born of Lupondo [by his senior wife] followed by Dzilo.

Lupondo took out a head of cattle from Patzwa [his senior wife's natal home] for that scotch cart. That head of cattle, a bull, was a marriage payment, the 'wetting of the mouths' from Patzwa [from Dzilo's mother's natal home]. It came as a calf, this 'wetting of the mouths', and they said, 'It is a fine calf, and it is better that we make it a bull.' And truly it did remain and grew up to be a big bull. And then he said, 'It is better that I sell it and buy a scotch cart.' They bought that scotch cart when we were at the old site, and they used it. It was used by Buka himself.

Buka would carry watermelons to town, when his father's younger brother [Malidzo] was ill and no longer driving it. Buka went on doing that until he went to Johannesburg, and they stayed on, then moved and came here with that scotch cart. They moved with it and came here, till it died here. I do not know whether they talked about it before I came. I can say that they talked about it, because when it became old there, it had no owner who could say, 'How would it be if we make a collection to repair this scotch cart which we'll be using.' Such a person was lacking, until it fell into decay.

It was when it was dead that this one [Mfila] and his older brother [Dzilo], said, 'How would it be if we repair this scotch cart for ourselves? Let's send it to be repaired so that it may be alright.' And those who heard when it was talked, passed the word that, 'The one who is to send it to the repairers, should know we are going to use it together, because it is our father's. It was bought by father.' When the others heard the word coming out like that, they said, 'There is no help in our doing such a thing, better we talk to our mother and buy our own, that will be called ours. Let us leave this one.' And they left that scotch cart and it remained so. All the planks fell away and were finished, until it only had wheels, and the wheels were sold by the old man, Lupondo, to the child of Muzola, over the river.

Dzilo's mother sold her cattle to buy this scotch cart. And the scotch cart came and we said, 'It has been said that the scotch cart is the mother's and has been bought by Dzilo's mother.' 'It is so?' 'Yes.' 'Well, we shall also hire it and use it.' Perhaps people were grieved that the old man said the cattle belong to Dzilo's mother and also that he takes out money and cattle, adding on to that of his other children. Nevertheless, the cattle are Dzilo's mother's. The old man has not a piece in it. He has nothing to do with it. This old man was given a head of cattle, and he had the cattle of Buzhvani. I think it is said, 'There are three, this is the mother, these are the offspring.' Those are the cattle of the old man. All that pen you see of over there, they are the cattle of the old lady. You see the cattle coming out there, all those cattle are Dzilo's mother's. The person who has the cattle of his own power is Dzilo. He bought them. In his pen, Dzilo has none of his mother's cattle. No, no, he has not got them. For this child that has

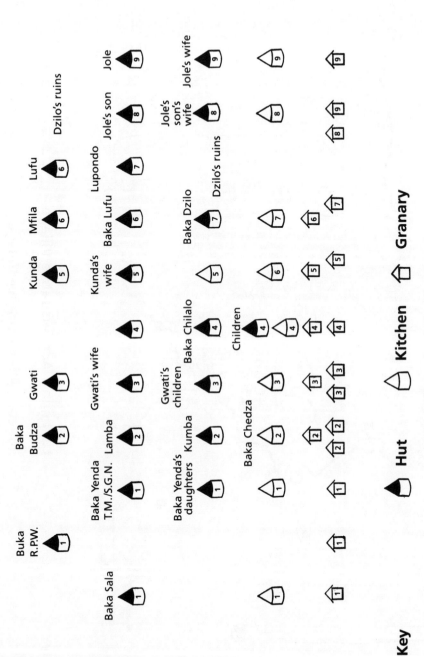

*Map 3* Plan of Lupondo's hamlet, 1961

**Key**   ◀ **Hut**   ◁ **Kitchen**   ⌂ **Granary**

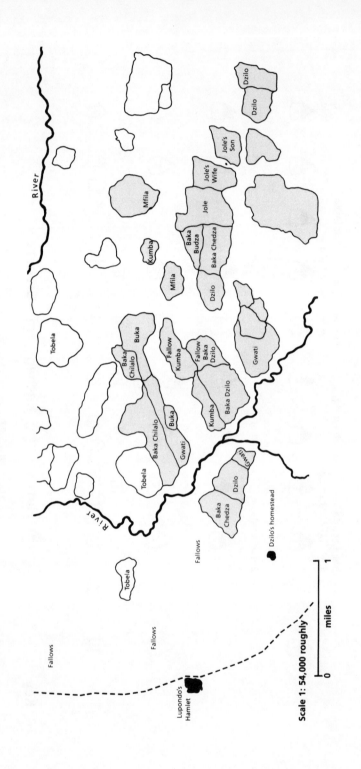

Key

▬ Lupondo's Administrative Village    – – – Track

◌ Tobela's Administrative Village

*Map 4* Fields of Lupondo's family, 1961

Scale 1: 54,000 roughly

0    miles    1

just died [Mfila] I think they are not as many as that one's [Dzilo's]. The mother's are the most here. It is like that.

## THE ACCOUNTS OF LUPONDO AND BAKA CHEDZA IN RETROSPECT

The history of a family, seen from within, can never be a single account. Family members invariably develop very different ways of knowing and telling about their lives. The accounts by Lupondo and Baka Chedza, although overlapping in some aspects, highlight two of the genres of personal narrative that we find in the same family.

As exemplified in Lupondo's life history, the genre of nostalgia turns on the moral opposition between past and present. What the narrator tells about is not so much a continuing series of moments, but a radical and irreversible break, from the good to the bad. The quarrel stories come from the break. The narrator, characteristically reaching a sense of loss in old age, indulges in nostalgia and longs for bygone times when he was once central in the life around him.

In a second genre, as used by Baka Chedza, the narrator regards one life crisis after another, seeing each as a cautionary moment. Recalled, it is a moment that still warns of the dangers in interpersonal relations, dangers to the very reproduction of the family itself. The agonies of birth and death, the ordeals of inheritance and marriage, the struggles in passing sentimental and highly valued bits of property from generation to generation, all these are grist for memory that mills them finely into the cautionary moments of a family account. The very fineness of the memory, the circumstantial details of who said what to whom, when and where, is a hallmark of truth, at least for an insider. To the outsider, bewildered by the sheer pettiness of the family events, it seems an obsession with circumstances for their own sake.

An insider looking backwards upon cautionary moments engages with the future as much as with the past. The interest is in the ongoing anticipation of life crises still to come; it is in being forewarned and being able to give forewarning. The narration pre-empts the future.

Around family members lies the debris of the past, the souvenirs of people and the actual remains of goods, but that debris is not inert, merely waiting to be dug up by the ethnographer as a would-be archaeologist of everyday life. Instead, family members have to defend themselves against the active force of their debris, because recognising the debris for what it is evokes passion and emotions in the present. The family debris is internalised in the current knowledge and expectations that family members have of each other. They can reconstitute the debris in a whole kaleidoscope of different ways. But what they cannot do is simply ignore it.

# 4

## Justification, Rivalry and Romance: Moral Argument in the Second Generation

Lupondo's sons told me their life histories in the context of a moral argument about past rights and wrongs. At the heart of it was their awareness that they had reached a crisis of maturity, that they had to take charge in splitting the family, that soon sons of different mothers would no longer live together, that some if not all would become heads of their own homesteads. Roughly a year earlier, Lupondo's senior son, Dzilo, had felt forced to make the first move, when he built his homestead alone nearby. Next, towards the end of my visit, came his rival, Buka, still within the neighbourhood. Others followed their example within a few years after my visit, until the split was complete and the old hamlet abandoned. By the time of my return, nearly thirty years later, the offspring of Lupondo and his brothers had spread their homesteads through-out much of a neighbourhood between their original site near the river to the east and their fields in the valley to the west. They had become one of the largest and most prominent families in their part of the chiefdom; and at a major feast for a young bride, a daughter of Lupondo's son Gwati, they mobilised the rest of that part of the chiefdom, nearly ninety households, to donate baskets of millet flour, altogether over six hundred pounds, as a bridal gift.

The generation of Lupondo's sons, the first to reach maturity and middle age in the Sanzukwe Special Native Area, brought the family through a major change, making it more dispersed in small homesteads and yet more stable as a whole within a neighbourhood. Lupondo's own generation had moved from place to place, sometimes because of internal quarrels and other personal reasons, sometimes also under outside pressure, from farmers or the colonial state. It was the period when white farmers backed by the colonial state appropriated their land and dispossessed them, making their land virtually free of 'squatters' or tenants. It was also the period when men younger than Lupondo himself began to spend long stretches, even years at a stint, as labour migrants in distant towns and cities, leaving their wives and children behind in the care of others. Lupondo's generation had grown up at a time, so they

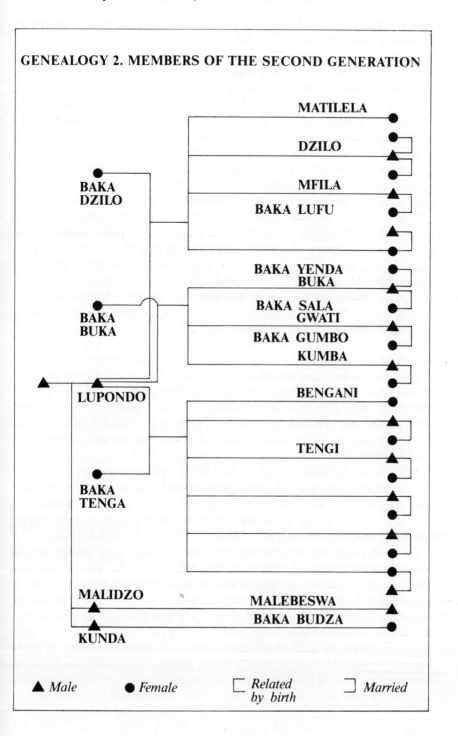

GENEALOGY 2. MEMBERS OF THE SECOND GENERATION

remembered, when the largest hamlets had as much as a dozen married men including some strangers as retainers of the hamlet head. Large hamlets became fewer, smaller, more restricted to the family of the hamlet head, during the maturity of Lupondo's generation. To have a large hamlet and to keep its members together became an increasingly more difficult accomplishment and, as a consequence, all the more a proof of the prominence of the hamlet head's family, of their ability to mobilise in support of each other, and of their considerable resources in cattle and land.

Having grown up in such a hamlet before coming to the Sanzukwe Special Native Area, Lupondo's sons managed to maintain it for the first two decades after their arrival. They made their hamlet the largest in their part of the chiefdom, and they kept their family together up to a peak of development. But they did so in the face of an increasingly more general trend towards the separation of homesteads and an end to large hamlets. By 1960, virtually all the other families in their section of the chiefdom had divided at an earlier stage in their development. What had become usual was for brothers to gain their independence and live apart by their mid-fifties, having reached an age when, no longer labour migrants, they had adult and married children and were themselves on the verge of elderhood. At the upper limit, which included a very small minority of elders, no more than a pair of brothers managed to keep together through their elderhood; in no case did several brothers do so, requiring one brother to be in immediate authority over them all.

Yet, if usual and long anticipated, the split in Lupondo's family was none the less traumatic, disturbing, a cause of much anguish and uncertainty. No one in Lupondo's family took the emerging split as a matter of course, as if it were natural and unavoidable. Everyone, even those expressing relief that at last they would live by themselves, saw it as an injury to the family which was a matter of blame.

But who was to blame? And for what? Were they to scatter into many small homesteads or to try to live together in a few, and how far apart? It is because they had wrestled with these questions and argued about the answers in everyday life over a long period that Lupondo's sons told life histories characterised by much moral reflection, pious rhetoric and self-justification.

Before the split, family members had felt themselves to be under a certain moral pressure because of the very strong obligations that kin have while living together. They had to share food at various times, to give and receive in many casual ways. If they did not, and often even when they did, they had to hear complaints, inescapably niggling complaints, about failures to co-operate and make fair returns for past help. They could hardly avoid turning to some family members for neighbourly exchanges of domestic goods and services, like the pooling of labour, especially female labour, for burdensome domestic tasks such as brewing beer. Each time they abandoned agreements for working and sharing together or when they preferred arrangements with outsiders, they

had to make excuses about acting under duress. Whoever initiated such a
change had to convince himself and others that it was right to divide and
discriminate, to refuse some in the family what should otherwise have been due
them morally: co-operation, reciprocity, trust.

In accomplishing the split, family members remolded their everyday involvement in each other's affairs. They did put physical and social distances
between themselves, but these distances were not great. Virtually all of the
family went, at first, to new sites in the immediate neighbourhood, though not
next to each other. Still being agricultural neighbours, with long-term interests
in producing upon adjacent fields, they continued to live close enough to make
effective claims of many kinds upon each other. In doing so, they renegotiated
a moral order within the family. Many of them acted as if they anticipated
living most of their lives in the midst of the family, if not exclusively so. Their
anticipation, arising in a context of wider insecurity about land, proved true in
actuality in good measure because of the serious risks and restrictions on the
land under the colonial state. Hence it is their sense of enduring prospects
within the family, kinship in the long-term, which we must keep in mind
reading the moral argument Lupondo's sons carried forward in their life
histories. They were about to divide, but not to cut themselves off from the
family, or from the fine personal judgements members of the family made
about their actions.

My recording of Lupondo's sons' life histories was itself shaped by the moral
argument going on among them. Buka, Lupondo's eldest son and the first born
of his second wife, told me his life history early in my first visit. It was at the
beginning of December 1960, a couple of months after my arrival in Lupondo's hamlet, and at a time when Buka hoped, and tried to impress others,
that I would help him to become a *sebuku*, administrative headman, and make
his cause my own. After all, I had come to know him first, before his brothers,
through the Chief, and had then elicited an invitation from him, for myself and
my assistant, to live in his huts. Not surprisingly, Buka's brothers were wary of
me at first. Partly as a consequence, I had to wait for most of a year before I
could ask his senior brother and rival Dzilo for his life history. My rapport with
Dzilo and his younger brother Mfila developed gradually and somewhat at the
expense of rapport with Buka. Buka was sensitive to gossip against him; he
knew, and remarked himself, that it was said that he could never live with
anyone else; and he was very concerned that family members not be able to say
he and I had quarrelled and were no longer on good terms with each other.
Nevertheless, the more I spent time with his brothers and became a friend of
Dzilo's, whose ebullient company I much enjoyed, the less approachable Buka
became, although he generously let us continue to live in his huts even after he
himself left the hamlet and needed our hut poles and doors for building.

Each of the leading rivals among Lupondo's sons, Buka and Dzilo, had a
keen sense of wrongs done to him, and a tale of grievances. But Buka was the

more embittered of the two. From childhood onwards, according to his own account, he had suffered from his father's mistreatment of his mother. Furthermore, in so far as he had prospered, he claimed, it was through his own efforts, since his father had failed to provide for him and had never given him cattle. Faced with hardship, he turned to divination to find out the cause of his own and his mother's miserable lot. He blamed it upon the sorcery of his mother's senior co-wife, Baka Dzilo. The outcome was that he stood aside from the common plate with his paternal brothers, out of fear of sorcery and death in it. Similarly, once he realised that he had squandered ten years, with little or no savings from labour migration, he returned to Johannesburg with a definite target in mind, to earn enough cash to buy cattle so his mother could live well. Indeed, he portrayed himself as a paragon of filial devotion towards his mother. Although Buka did not comment upon it himself, it is striking that in his own marriages he reversed his father's discrimination. Whereas his father mistreated his beloved girlfriend, Buka's mother, by making her into a junior wife, and favoured the senior wife over the junior, Buka himself did the opposite, at the expense of his senior wife. He indulged his junior wife as his favourite, giving her seniority in all but name.

As for personal ambition, he denied he had any desire to take what was not his. If leadership and office did fall to him, it would be because that belonged to him. Thus he insisted that his paternal brothers had suffered misfortune due to their own adultery and other wrongs, and not to any fault or sorcery of his. Throughout his account, he drew invidious comparisons with others, by implication especially his rival Dzilo, while, at the same time, he protested that he himself innocently endured the slander and malicious gossip of those whom he had never wronged.

Unlike Buka, who regarded himself as someone vilified unfairly by so much gossip and backbiting, Dzilo represented himself as basking in the good words of the people around him. 'Ah, the "wind" [mhepo, soul] I was born with is good. I became good. In this hamlet you can never hear them talking bad of me. They all say "Tata Tembanyana" [Little Father of Temba, his first-born]', Dzilo said, uttering a diminutive form of his own name in a tender and affectionate manner. If an enemy hated him, he asserted proudly, it was because of his ability to capture loyalty and win people away from that enemy.

In gossip, Buka was often caricatured by members of the family as 'a man of wives', whereas the very sociable Dzilo was 'a man of people'. With Buka's caricature went much sarcastic comment, deriding him for spending a great deal of time at his favourite wife's compound, where he was unmistakably most at ease. Buka so preferred the company of his wives, especially his favourite one, that with the exception of his father's cousin Tobela, he rarely visited other men in the vicinity to join their entertainment and add to their sociability. Dzilo was the convivial opposite, and passed endless time with neighbours, drinking, loafing and joking boisterously.

The nickname which stuck to Buka, behind his back, was 'Forker', 'the one who accompanies you on one path and then branches off to go by himself'. It was a nickname which defined in an exaggerated form much of what family members took to be a characteristic difference between the brothers. Both were politically ambitious men in their very early fifties, with two wives and almost a dozen children, although Buka, until almost the end of my first stay, had had no sons by his present wives. Buka, who had divorced or deserted at least four wives, was considered by many family members to be the more erratic and unreliable, closed and devious; and Dzilo, the more prosperous and stable, open and straightforward. Buka was mimicked for being a mumbler and a mutterer, Dzilo for his infectious whoop of delight, which usually resounded when he was drunk and on his way to a liaison. I myself gave him a nickname, Dzabube, which became a favourite in the family, I found on my return visit. The nickname was the sound of his whoop; when he made it, he would beat his chest with both hands in something of a mating call.

In addition, in a further caricature, some members of the family spoke of Buka as 'a man of the town'. More than once, over his long and relatively successful career as a labour migrant (in turn, a kitchen boy in Bulawayo; then in Johannesburg, a kitchen boy, a cook, a floor sander until his mid-forties), he had spent stretches of four or five years away at work in Johannesburg, not coming home for a visit; and in one ten-year period, he visited merely at Christmastime. He brought his town wife home, but could not keep her in the countryside. Their childless marriage ended in separation within less than a year, much to his regret, upon her return to Johannesburg—she was unwilling to accept polygyny. A literate man, who if given the chance would have continued in primary school beyond the second grade or Standard Two, he made no secret of the fact that he relished town life more than living in the countryside.

Again, in sharp contrast, Dzilo had the opposite preference. Town, he once told me, made his head ache. As a lad, he ran away from school before learning to read and became a herd boy on farms near Bulawayo. Although he had once stayed in Johannesburg without coming home for some three years, he kept his adult career as a labour migrant relatively short, ending it in his mid-thirties. Apart from a brief job as a house boy, most of his work was hard physical labour, much more poorly paid than Buka's jobs in domestic service and in a factory, although Dzilo saved more than Buka. Despite all that, however, Dzilo was actually at a greater advantage when it came to interests spanning town and country. This advantage came from Dzilo's enduring friendship with a cousin of the Chief, a former union leader who had become a sophisticated entrepreneur, the owner of a large store, a petrol station, and other businesses in a township of Bulawayo in addition to hundreds of cattle in the Sanzukwe Special Native Area. His great esteem for Dzilo, which was widely recognised, influenced local support for Dzilo. In turn, Dzilo's co-operation was known to be most important in enabling the entrepreneur to manage the rural sector of his enterprises, with only occasional visits to the chiefdom.

Buka, too, had his allies, of course. Among them, not surprisingly, were opponents or rivals of this entrepreneur, including the Chief himself and Lupondo's cousin Tobela. Some seven years after Buka retired from labour migration, his friendship with the Chief brought him the kind of advantage in the countryside that Tobela had had in the previous generation, namely a steady cash income from one of the very few paid jobs available at home. The job the Chief got him, at a pay of seven pounds ten shillings a month, was that of watchman of the newly built pump for watering cattle.

Dzilo, who was a very powerful, big man, physically as well as socially, had won the reputation of being 'a man of co-operative work parties'. Much of the time his clothes, especially a much favoured undershirt which he often wore without a covering shirt, were dishevelled, even sloppy, from his chores. He boasted to me, with good cause, 'If you see people jealous of me, it's because before their very eyes I worked, and I took away people from them.' By contrast, Buka, a dapper little man, wiry but not powerful, very rarely took part in co-operative labour on other people's fields. When he did mobilise co-operative work parties of his own, they were always lesser occasions than Dzilo's. Fewer people, less representative of a wide vicinity, came to work for Buka. His cash income, which made him rely less on his crops—indeed, he bought far more grain than anyone else in Lupondo's family during my first year's stay with the family—also eased the pressure on him to extend help and in turn be helped by his neighbours. He had long been a more progressive farmer, proud of past prizes won for improved farming, so that he cultivated smaller fields more intensively than Dzilo. Furthermore, he resorted more to cash transactions and would hire labour to do work which Dzilo would do himself or co-operatively, on a reciprocal basis.

Compared to Dzilo's large herd of cattle, at the time of my fieldwork, Buka's was smaller, about twenty-three head. It was also less his to dispose of, a fact that diminished his public stature. Nearly all of his herd, apart from three or four beasts, as was widely known in the family, belonged to Buka's senior wife. Buka had begun to save for investment in livestock only towards the end of his career as a labour migrant; and then he retired from working in town years after Dzilo, and as an older man. Dzilo had been prudently saving at the same time that Buka had been consuming his earnings, or spending them, on his visits from town, in displays of generosity and numerous gifts to kin and friends. Dzilo had come to be known as the kind of man who 'has his own power', as Baka Chedza put it, insisting that now Dzilo had only his own cattle in his pen. Moreover, the fact that in the past, during the minority or youth of his younger brother Mfila, Dzilo had a large herd to manage for his mother, along with his own investments, meant that he was able to provide benefits needed by kin and friends, without an expenditure like Buka's. Dzilo had durable, productive resources which he lent or gave in trust, for example the plough team he lent Baka Chedza. All of that invidious comparison enhanced the moral basis of Dzilo's leadership of Lupondo's family and administrative village, the acceptance that his authority ought to have been greater than Buka's, because Dzilo fulfilled roles so crucial for the viability of the family as a whole, for neighbourliness, and for the productive interdependence of neighbours.

At the same time, Buka found himself in the predicament of a person whose moral worth was seen as deteriorating. Such moral deterioration, at least of his perceived character, went hand in glove with change in his career as a labour migrant, and it was in good measure a construction that family members put on that change.

No longer the labour migrant, coming home briefly to shower his kin with gifts, Buka was no longer known, in moral terms, to be the same very kind, open-handed benefactor that he had been seen to be in the past. His second wife, much blamed for sorcery, was identified with the period of his perceived moral deterioration. As the period of his permanent settlement at home, it was actually the period in his life when he had to adjust to staying in the countryside and supporting his family from his land, livestock and other rural resources. He married her in 1953, the year after he retired from labour migration, which was also the year after his mother died. His efforts to increase his immediate family, marry two wives and sustain them without a labour migrant's cash income made him seem to be a different person in the following years.

In addition, what had not much concerned Buka at a distance, during his absence as a labour migrant, namely Dzilo's authority in the position of acting head of the family, came to be something hard to bear close by and in day-to-day deference. Once home, he found himself smarting in resentment, privately if not publicly, at being displaced from a position he came to regard as rightfully his own. The perception other family members had of his resentment made them reconstruct his former character as if he had become, or worse still, perhaps always was, someone subversive of the established order in the family.

Besides this connection to labour migration, to the end of a career, there was also a connection between the construction or destruction of Buka's character within Lupondo's family and the dislocation from European farms. Buka came home to quite a different context of moral argument than the one he knew when starting his long absences as a labour migrant. The need to move to the Sanzukwe Special Native Area brought together, as neighbours, people who had long been separated from each other, but who had once been immediately involved in each other's affairs and who could rake up old scandal. Tobela and Lupondo's family were such neighbours. Tobela claimed that he was a witness to the very beginning of the dispute over the seniority of Buka's mother and thus Buka himself; that he was the herdboy who accompanied her bridewealth

cattle; that Lupondo's father had meant her to be senior but had been persuaded otherwise by the Chief; that rightfully Dzilo should have been junior to
Buka. Against that, members of Lupondo's family, including Dzilo himself
and his brother Mfila, complained that when Tobela and Dzilo came to be
neighbouring administrative headmen, Tobela began to envy Dzilo; the envy
being that the younger man, a 'small boy' relative to Tobela in Kalanga terms,
should surpass his elder in local prominence.

In that new context of moral argument and invidious comparison, it may be
that Tobela fanned Buka's growing resentment, for reasons of his own, including personal complaints against Dzilo. But whether or not that was
actually true, it was believed to be so by most of Lupondo's family. They
complained that Tobela, when drunk, would 'spread dirt', raking up the old
scandal about the displacement of Buka's mother and, in turn, Buka himself
from seniority. In taking up that 'dirt' and allying himself with Tobela, Buka
was thus seen to be the kind of insider who subverts from within the family in
collusion with an outsider, that kind of insider being the one who resorts to
sorcery.

Buka's brothers, along with some other family members, found that they
had to account for what they saw as a change in Buka. Before his favourite wife
came, he had seemed to them, at least in retrospect, to have been one kind of
person, generous, kind, fair, without discrimination. Afterwards, he turned
for the worse, and became the antisocial opposite. He got that 'mhepo', that
'wind', as Kalanga say alluding by their stress on that, in an idiom of indirect
speech, to that soul or character which is antisocial and bent upon sorcery. But
had he had that antisocial mhepo, 'wind', soul, or character all along? Most
thought, no; but some thought, yes.

Reflecting upon the change in Buka from the earlier days, Dzilo's younger
brother, Mfila, said:

> And [before leaving their old home outside the Special Native Area] there
> was no one thinking that he [Buka] could do this. I do not know the
> mhepo, 'wind', of people. I may say, 'He does not think of this.' Yet, he
> was born thinking like that, one who has such a heart. Some people are
> seen from the beginning that they got up being like that. Another person
> lives, and after he gets from the ground, he is seen not to be the one
> [another lives and it is seen later that he was not the one he should be].
> And you can see a person, that his 'wind,' ah it is standing like this, huh,
> huh [he expressed his disapproval].
>
> At our old sites, we did not know of this thing. We began to know it just
> now when this fight arose. We heard Tobela saying, 'This one's mother
> [Buka's mother] was the beloved one and the mother of those [the mother
> of Dzilo and Mfila] was offered [in marriage]. Yes, it was Tobela who was
> the one saying that the mother of Buka was the beloved one and our
> mother was offered.

You do know about the offering of long ago, don't you? [I answered, 'Yes'.] Well, our mother was offered to father, and she was the one who became the senior wife. The other was just being courted [by Lupondo]. Then it was spread widely, and they [Tobela and Buka] put this dirt about. I do not know how many years it has been going on, but it began when we were here. Buka was one who had been staying at the Europeans, and I can't remember when he came back, maybe it was sometime after 1940. But it was when he came from the Europeans that Buka began this dirt and began working with Tobela.

Long ago it was not there. I learned it from people saying it now, I did not know it before. We thought, 'Why didn't they tell us?' We should have been told that since she [Buka's mother] was courted by him, she was the senior.

We had worked and worked, and we were 'eaten' in Johannesburg [stayed too long]. I am the one who came with his [Buka's] goods. I was pulling him saying 'Let's go home now.' I came with the goods, myself. It was when we were still living at the old site. I found that here there were still only cattle posts. I think it was in 1939. I took Gwati [Buka's full brother] and we went to Francistown to take the boxes [of the returning labour migrant's goods], and I came home with his help. Then we went there [to the old site], the cattle were here, and in 1939 and 1940 people ploughed here. That is when Buka came.

Before that, he came and went back, came and went back; and there was still none of this dirt. And long ago we were not living with Tobela. Say we were living here, then he would be at [a locality about six miles away]. At our old sites, they had been at Lukerere, and we were in Smith Block.

Baka Chedza's daughter, Baka Budza, put the alternative view, that there was an actual change in *mhepo*, speaking about Buka:

From his beginning, no one was as good as he was. He had much kindness. He was the one who would know and look after any visitor who came. But then after his mother died [in 1952], we thought he was buying his charms [to send lightning and occult attack] from Tobela. Before that he was living well with his brothers. Once he bought those things of his, he no longer had peaceful harmony and mutual understanding with the others. He became a person of wives only. Now he too is surprised by what has happened to him.

Long ago, he got on well with everyone, without exception, even with all of his mothers. And when he would come back from the Europeans, each of his mothers who would come to see him would go back carrying something in her hand. He was a person who did not know that, 'Ah, this one is really my mother, and that one not'. Ah, no! Now he has his own hamlet. But all along he did not have that *mhepo*, that wind, that kind of character. Now he says that the position of *sebuku* was given to an idiot, it wants a clever man. Now everything he does is strong [and well] at the junior wife, everything starts for her first. Even now when they are building, hers is first. The senior one's house has not even got the supporting poles, and her granary has not yet been started.

Buka's amity with his brothers soured, the more his friendship with Tobela bloomed. Buka helped Tobela's wives and, in turn, relied upon help from them rather than his brothers' wives. This change, too, was one that family members had to account for in terms of morality, character and motivation. The explanation most widely accepted was temptation: Buka gave in to lust and greed for another man's wife. He pursued his friendship with Tobela to cover up his continuing adultery with one of Tobela's wives; so that Tobela 'would not see him properly at the wife', Baka Chedza's daughter told me, for as a friend of Tobela's, Buka helped, shared beer, and spent much time with Tobela's wife, all without arousing Tobela's suspicion. When I asked Lupondo about that friendship, he said, 'Buka and Tobela, well, they "eat each other's wives".' I expressed astonishment that an elder like Tobela could come to the wives of a younger man like Buka. 'No,' Lupondo continued, 'even if he [Tobela] does not eat, this one [Buka] does eat', and he laughed in delight at the cuckolding of so proud a man as Tobela:

He [Buka] eats that red one, the junior wife. What are you telling me? For beer they are called, those of Tobela [Tobela and his wives were always invited to a free drink of Buka's beer, before it was sold to the public]. He cannot drink it alone. If he [Buka] has a small helping party of his alone, he goes to call those of Tobela. They have their wives.

In the same vein, Mfila told me:

If you are a fool, and you go with a friend, he will enter from behind [commit adultery behind your back], so there at Tobela, Buka is the one who goes in. Even today, if you look at those boys who tend the donkeys, you will see by their ears that it is Buka. [Buka's own ears were somewhat pointed, like theirs.]

Mfila too laughed at Buka's cunning in cuckolding Tobela.

If Buka had detractors of his moral character, he also had defenders. The argument around him, in which he actively mobilised his defence, could not be one-sided. Because of having been reared first in the compound of his mother's brother then in that of Malidzo, his father's full younger brother, Buka had ties of rearing to women confidants who, as elders, were assertive, relatively rich and influential, especially in making moral evaluations through gossip. The most important of these women was Baka Chilalo, Malidzo's widow. Baka Chilalo still blamed Dzilo's mother for her husband's death, decades afterwards. Baka Chilalo's fields were next to Buka's within a common fence, which made regular co-operation easy. She was constantly consulted by Buka as his confidant, and she defended Buka's reputation, after Dzilo's brother, Mfila died, having had epileptic fits, towards the end of my first visit. Dzilo, his mother and his mother's brother, who went to a diviner together, leaked an accusation through gossip, blaming Mfila's death on Buka's sorcery. In Buka's defence and in the confidence of my hut, Baka Chilalo raised her hands as if making horns above her head, and swore to me by her cattle:

> They are playing about with Buka. The old man, my husband, was a person who looked after boys, and when Buka was in my compound, he went to school and became a person of the church. No matter how sour and bitter it is [about the death of Mfila], you can hear me say, 'A person of the church? He killed him? What was he killing him for, when it is his mother who was courted first and then taken out?'

Right was on Buka's side, Baka Chilalo insisted, so that he had no need to resort to sorcery.

Over the past two decades, because Dzilo was recognised to be the senior son, his father's official successor as administrative headman, and thus the one who stood for the unity of the family as a whole, Buka was the rival who had had to take step after step, sometimes years apart, to push the split forward. First, he withdrew from commensality with all the brothers. Then he got his full brothers to keep their cattle penned and herded apart from those of his paternal brothers. Next he abandoned the family's threshing grounds for a place of his own where his threshing was done separately. At each move towards separation and against existing joint arrangements, he found occasion to blame the mother of his rival Dzilo for a further act of sorcery.

Again and again, Buka prevailed on Kumba and Gwati, his full brothers, through appeals to their moral sentiments. Trying to get them to side with him against a common enemy, he divined repeatedly that his rival Dzilo's mother had been maliciously inflicting harm upon their mother and them in order to put herself and her sons at a greater advantage. He never confronted Dzilo's mother or her sons directly or openly by making accusations at a public seance. He went to divine alone, or with his own brothers and wives. The closest he came to a public demonstration was an occasion for vengeance magic, roughly in 1955. At that time, he summoned the Chief and prominent elders to witness an apparently dangerous trespass; he claimed that in grain trampled at his threshing ground there were traces of an ant-bear, the outlines of a sorcerer's familiar. At the Chief's command, the grain was magically protected. In this way, vengeance was threatened against a would-be sorcerer, but the suspect was not publicly exposed.

The campaign against Baka Dzilo got some support within her own compound, from the wife of her son Mfila, with whom she was living. Mfila had married in 1943 against his mother's wishes. She did not want her son to marry the close relative of her co-wife, Baka Buka, with whom she had quarrelled over so many years. Yet in Kalanga terms, it was a culturally preferred marriage, of the kind that followed an established direction of exchange between affines, one side as wife-givers (*bakalabgwa*), the other as wife-receivers (*bakwaxa*). By taking his wife from the same 'house' as his father had in marrying Baka Buka, Mfila was seen to be one of the wife-receivers, who comes to his wife-givers, once again for a wife. Mfila's marriage to a cross-cousin of Buka's fitted and indeed grew out of his own ease and amity with Buka and his brothers, at that time, although it ran against the old hostility between his mother and Buka's. Mfila had herded with Buka's brothers, kept in touch with Buka while at work, persuaded him to come home, and been himself on the best of terms with the other brothers. In the face of his mother's objections, Mfila brought his wife home by stealth, as she told me, in response to my intentionally polite remark that Baka Dzilo often seemed like such a quiet person:

> You see her to be a quiet person, but the way I see her, well, we gag on each other. Her son took where she did not want him to take and then he held on with a hard head [obstinately]. So how could she get on well with the wife then? I was taken while she was away, having gone to town to have her eyes treated. She found me at home. Sometimes, when she would get drunk, she would still say it out, 'I did not want you to take from this house.' Then if we would be sitting together one would look this way, and the other that way [casting angry looks over the shoulder]. The next day I can complain that 'This is why things happened as they have'. When I gave birth to that child [who died in 1957], she did not come to hold the child while it was alive. She held the child for me only when it was brought to the grave. Well, the wind [*mhepo*] of a person reveals itself. It is seen by what it does.

I was told that Mfila's wife blamed her mother-in-law, Baka Dzilo, for her child's death, although in talking about it to me she put her accusation in an idiom of allusion, indirection and implicit suggestion.

Much resistance from Buka's brothers, Kumba and Gwati, muted his own campaign against Baka Dzilo. Buka was constrained to keep his accusations concealed in gossip by the fact that his brothers were very markedly reluctant to give him their wholehearted support. Buka's brothers saw him to be pursuing interests somewhat opposed to or in competition with theirs and those of their own elementary families. I heard them grumble among themselves about his inconsiderateness and self-seeking. When he sold a black bull which was a server of their herd, they gossiped that he did so with the deliberate intent to begrudge them an increase in their cattle.

Buka's brothers seemed noticeably less at ease with him than with their paternal brothers, Dzilo and Mfila. Each of Buka's brothers had benefited and been helped by Dzilo and Mfila in the sharing of food or in co-operative labour. Dzilo and his wives had looked after Kumba when his wife deserted him, and were continuing to do so. Mfila and Gwati shared a common threshing ground; their wives helped each other in onerous domestic labour, such as in the brewing of beer. While Buka had long been absent as a labour migrant, his full brothers had worked out a basis for trust and interdependence with their paternal half-brothers. In the light of actual practice in kinship, the true fulfilment of 'brotherhood', they found a moral defence against Buka's appeal to their loyalty as sons of the same mother, against their greater friendship with the other sons of their father: they put the blame for sorcery on Buka's favourite wife.

During my first visit, one brother, Gwati, occasionally accompanied by the other, Kumba, consulted diviners several times about the cause of the sickness of Gwati's wife and children. The reported conclusions condemned Buka's favourite wife repeatedly; her sorcery was the suspected cause. During the roughly seven years of her marriage, she had become embroiled in a series of squabbles with Dzilo's wives, and despite the fact that she had not herself quarrelled directly with her accusers, Gwati and Kumba, or their wives, they blamed her for the misunderstanding, even hatred, between themselves and their brother Buka. Their accusations responded to accusations that others made, such as Dzilo and Mfila, who blamed Buka for colluding in sorcery with Buka's favourite wife and Tobela. But by making the accusations against Buka's wife and not Buka himself, Gwati and Kumba allowed for the loyalty they owed towards Buka.

In this continuing moral argument within the family, Lupondo's sons drew upon a fund of personal knowledge, attuned to fine, life-long, moral evaluations in gossip about their own deeds or misdeeds. They seemed to know very specifically what was often being said about them in private as well as in public, whether they were told it or could easily guess, and did not need to be told. In Baka Chedza's daughter, Baka Budza, they had in their midst a divorced cousin, a 'sister' in Kalanga terms. Her presence meant they had someone sure of easy access to all of their compounds, who could readily elicit and spread gossip from wife to wife and brother to brother. About this cousin, Buka's own daughter remarked to me, 'She goes all around this hamlet, and she finishes it. She backbites, telling things that cause people to quarrel'.

While raising accusations of blame against others, Lupondo's sons were sensitive, in their self-justification, to family opinions about their own guilt. It was rumoured that Buka had once thrown a plate in anger, injuring his late mother. Buka's response may have reflected guilt, and it was perhaps also defensive in the face of the sorcery accusations against his favourite wife. In accord with such guilt and self-defence, Buka divined repeatedly that there were faults which had aroused divinities as shades of the dead to trouble that wife's children. On one such occasion late in 1961, when his favourite wife had difficulties during labour, Buka divined that the aroused shade was that of his own mother. Throughout this period, however, he continued to raise charges of sorcery against Dzilo's mother.

Similarly, Dzilo's younger brother, Mfila, was much aware that he was considered culpable because of his adultery. As a consequence, when divining about the causes of his illness, he acknowledged his own guilt, admitting that adultery had made him vulnerable to attack. On the other hand, he also blamed Dzilo's rival Buka for sorcery.

Mfila gave me his account of guilt and blame which he confirmed first through divination and later through consulting Zionists in their church:

When we got there [to a distant chiefdom], the old man beat them [divined with bones] three times. He said, 'Yah, boy.' I was with this Lufu [son]. 'Your divinity is strong, the divinity of your grandfather, boy. The illness started on you when you were in the bush. That spear did not want to help you, it wanted to die there in the bush. Then the divinity of Nigoba [his clan ancestor] defeated it.'

Hey! Is that right? I looked at it and said, 'But where is this spear [of sorcery] from?' He beat them, and beat them, and said, 'The spear comes from this that you go with other people's wives. And this spear comes from you, you are killing each other, you.' I said, 'Ay, perhaps this one of the bones is telling lies.' When I went to the Zionists [in their church] they did not hunt for it [they found it without searching]. They said, 'This spear comes from this, that you go with the wife of another man. The spear comes from your hamlet. She was taught, and she agreed. That is how this spear came.'

One day, if I were still drinking beer, well my head is not good, one day, I can beat him [Buka] and go tell him that, 'Do you know that you bewitch?' I stop myself these days, because there is 'respect' [hlonipa, in Sindebele].

I had not had many months there [having been converted to the Zion Christian Church]. I had just recently stayed [at the Church headquarters] when I was told, 'In your hamlet, it is not good. Some of the people you say you are living with are killing you.' It was just a woman, a woman who is a prophet. I don't know, the wives of others—as we are here in this hamlet, if you can hear that I have made love to someone's wife, no! But well, those of the country, I really hurried after them. Dirt here in the hamlet? The wife of a hamlet? No, no.

I have no thirst for other people's things. Even if a person's thing is right here, I have nothing to do with it. I was bad on women; but now even if she is here, I have nothing to do with it. I find her stinking to me. A woman! If I am just sitting, I don't even think, and I do not think of that 'wind' [mhepo]. A woman! When I was still in Johannesburg, I did not want a woman to walk there, then. Now, ah no, since I have entered in this church, I do not know whether I shall ever turn back. I have no issue with them. When I looked at it, I found that it was dirt, rubbish, loathsome.

Mfila was one of the family members who kept alive a memory of past harmony and explained present discord as a break from harmony that was a matter of personal blame:

> We were living together. I had not thought that there is the 'colour bar' [in English] in the world. The colour bar started for me in these years, and I cannot remember when it started. The colour bar I see is that we do not understand one another. I never expected that there would be anyone saying so.

Mfila used 'colour bar' ironically to refer to the depth of misunderstanding and discrimination within the family, and he traced its origins back to the coming of a new wife, Baka Tenga, who was his father's third wife. And in speaking of her as a 'new' wife, Mfila conveyed her special attraction for his father and thus the special treatment she demanded. At first, she sent her sons to be her brother's herd boys. Later, she compelled her husband to let her keep her household's cattle with her brother; she refused to co-operate with her senior co-wife, Mfila's mother, and her children, whom she distrusted.

As Mfila remembered it:

> Those brothers of ours [Baka Tenga's sons] were living at their mother's brother's. These, Gwati, Dzilo, and I were herding. And Buka was at the Europeans [working in town]. We were the ones herding cattle. And we did not know that there were cattle for this one or that one. We were just herding them all.
>
> When the new wife came, it was said, 'There is no one who will look after the other person's cattle.' New children had been borne by the junior wife. 'There is no one to herd the cattle of another, each one should herd hers.' It was just all right. Then colour bar came out when we were here. We are not twenty years here, and it came out here.
>
> Ah, when we came here, we had been living very well, without anything troubling us. And everyone in the country was saying, 'Ah, in the hamlet of Nigoba [Lupondo's clan name], it is really lived.' I do not know what it is that came in, I do not know what it is, 'nit' [in Afrikaans]. Once these people were taken in, ah they are the ones who brought in 'colour bar'. But when it had not happened so, we were living very well.

While Mfila blamed this junior wife, Baka Tenga, for 'colour bar', the beginning of a split in the family, Mfila insisted also that in his youth no one expected Buka to turn to sorcery out of malicious jealousy. Nor did anyone talk about Buka's mother having been displaced from the position of senior wife; all that began when Buka returned from work in town, after the move to the present chiefdom.

A brief incident which occurred in the middle of my first visit, in February 1961, shows how easily the crisis could flare up, then calm down and yet leave the family members still struggling in their moral argument. The incident, if distressing, would ordinarily have been treated as trivial, a household affair and not of consequence for the whole family. A young son of Dzilo's was lost, and not found until late in the night, when his mother discovered him hiding in her granary. Later, a supporter of Buka's, the elderly widow Baka Chilalo, claimed that she had seen the boy eating sweet cane which he had stolen from Gwati's son, and that the boy had hidden merely to avoid being beaten in punishment. The boy's mother screamed hysterically when she found him, until virtually all of the family and various neighbours rushed to Dzilo's hamlet. She harangued them about people who were trying to turn her son into an idiot. She had had to leave Lupondo's hamlet, the hamlet of the Nigoba people, though she had not wanted to, and yet people were still pursuing her with troubles, she complained:

> What is that you want from me? Are you quarrelling about the cattle of your father? Kill me and leave my sons. I know nothing about your cattle. You are stretched out in my hut here, for what have you come? You people of Nigoba are sorcerers. I do not fear to die. Do it, since you have already started.

Her husband Dzilo remained quiet, and his brother Mfila answered her, addressing everyone present:

> No, she should not talk that way. We should call the Zionists [members of the Zion Christian Church to which he belonged; see Werbner, 1989, Chapter 8] here to tell everything to them. If she is just going to say we are sorcerers, then on whose granary was the child found? Is it not hers?

Others agreed, taking up his theme, and Dzilo's wife fell silent.

A Zionist meeting, which attracted a large number of the neighbours within three or four miles of Dzilo's hamlet, was held within a few weeks. The leader of the meeting preached peace, and prayed for healing in the hamlet. He urged Lupondo's family not to search for sorcerers in their midst. According to Dzilo, the Zionists would then have pointed out sorcerers, if the family had chosen to quarrel openly and demanded to know who the sorcerers were. Even if the accusations had become open, however, the Zionists' findings would not have been final. A couple of weeks before the arrival of the Zionists, Buka was visited, from a great distance, by an alien witchdoctor of the Ndebele cult of *sangoma* possession. The *sangoma* was a professional antagonist of the Zionists, and culturally opposed to them also. Buka let it be known that he was ready to be the witchdoctor's client; that he would summon the *sangoma* again, this time for a public dance and a finding of sorcerers. This threat made it seem as if Buka was ready for a major battle of diviners. In the immediate upshot, after the Zionists identified no sorcerer in the hamlet, Buka went about claiming that the result vindicated him and Tobela of wrongful accusations. During the incident, all the brothers proved their mutual unwillingness to force a show-down or a radical rupture in the family as a whole. But whatever else they achieved through the ritual, the brothers did not attempt or manage to reach any lasting reconciliation or resolution of long-term rivalries within the family.

## THE LIFE HISTORIES OF BUKA, BAKA GWILA, AND DZILO

### Buka Recalls

#### Boyhood Escapades

What I shall speak about is this. I shall tell of my birth. I was born at Woloba. We lived in the hamlet of Bango, where I played with my friends Salani, Wilila, Mayedza and Lubahi [kin of his mother and unrelated friends]. We moved from Woloba to Chivuvubge, and still in the hamlet of Bango with my friends, the boys of my home, I herded and played drums and 'choir' [singing in groups that went from hamlet to hamlet at night]. We stole watermelons when we were boys. When we came to a field, we shouted, 'Go out of the field at the other side', so that owner of the field could hear. 'We'll go out of this field through that way.' If the owner was there, he would ask us where we were going. But if nobody came, we knew that no one was there. And if there was no one, we would enter the field, take watermelons, and leave by the other side. Then we would bring the watermelons and return to the goats.

One day when we were herding, we stole some watermelons this way, and we saw a woman called Baka Bakwe coming to us. She beat us and beat us, and beat us. And we ran home and left the goats. And the goats strayed into the fields of other people. When we came home, Tata Mapalani [the Chief and hamlet head] beat us and beat us and beat us. We ran out into the bush, and when it was dark, after they had gone to bed, we came back and hid ourselves in the hut where we slept with the others. The next day he didn't beat us. We opened the goats' pen and went away with the goats again. And on that day they didn't get into anyone's fields. But on another day they did. Father got hold of us and beat us and beat us. Then I ran away. I went to my [maternal] grandfather's to stay. He followed me after some days, and took me back home. After a few days I returned to my grandfather's hamlet. I stayed with grandfather, stayed there, stayed there; and he came and took me back again. I stayed home, and stayed home, and stayed home. And I was becoming more sensible. We herded and did not let the goats stray into people's fields, until I was a man.

We would hold the breasts of the girls, when we were making love to them. [He laughed at the way times have changed.] Long ago when you made love to girls you had to catch the breasts, but now you only use your mouth. But then you used to hold on to the breasts. [He laughed again.]

#### Leaving School and Going to Work

When I was fully grown, I went to work in town, Bulawayo. I went away because I had no clothes. First of all, I went and worked at a farm. Then I came home for a few days, and went to Bulawayo. In town I didn't suffer.

I looked for work and got it. But I was troubled by the man I found working there. He was older than I was, for I was a boy. He woke me up early in the morning, and said that I should make a fire in the kitchen, while he was still in bed. That is how I suffered when I got work. One day the wife of my employer woke up early in the morning and found me making a fire in the kitchen, and she asked me where the cook was. I told her that he was asleep. When he woke up, she asked him why he woke me up to make a fire, while he remained in bed. She told him that it was not my work to make the fire, since I had been hired as a waiter. So one day he beat me when the white people were away. He said I had squealed on him. That is how I suffered.

I lived there for many years; but exactly how long I cannot say. I've forgotten. My mother followed me to town and brought me home, because I no longer wanted to come home. When my mother brought me from town we had left the Bango hamlet and gone to live in Nigoba hamlet where I also had friends. I played and herded with Mapani, Linayi, Bonyo, Makanda, and Mapise [mainly paternal kin].

I grew up as a suffering child. That is because I was not well cared for at home, and there were troubles in my mother's household. Yes, I grew with troubles in my mother's household. Our mother did not live well. She lived a very hard life, because she was given little care by her master.

You ask about the way we lived in our household, and especially about food, well, we had one common plate together with my friends and my father's sons. And we grew up to be young men. But later on I thought that was not good for me. I alone was the first to cut myself off from the plate of the others.

I ate alone. I found that eating in the common plate was not good for me. It was because of the troubles that my mother had, and also because the way she was treated was not a clean way. That is what made me say, 'Oh, I am now following the white man's custom, eating alone in my own plate.' This was because my mother was poorly treated. Father did not treat my mother in a clean way.

There was always trouble, and whenever we went to those who claim that they know, the diviners, they would say that the trouble was in the compound, in the 'Post' [Bango, one of the casts of the divining dice], this means 'in the senior person'.

Later when I had grown up and had become reasonable [a thinking person], I said to myself that even if all the things the diviners say are lies, I will take them as truth, because they all say the same thing. So I said I cannot live in such things, and I put myself apart, and stood aside. The troubles in the compound have not ended up to today. They say that I set myself up to be their better, because I do not mix with others. But I stood aside and left the others in the same condition we were in when we lived long ago.

I had my own place. What made me leave the others was the way we were treated. That is why I left their things. Right up today I have nothing of my father's. I have my own things. Even cattle, I have none of my father's; the cattle I have I bought with my own money. I left all my father's property to my seniors and my elders, for I said I wanted to have things of my own, things that would be called by my name and not by my father's name. Even today I have things of my own power, and not things of anyone else's power.

I went to Usher Institute because I wanted to learn. But father did not have the money to keep me at school. So I had to pay for myself. I studied there, but learned little then. I went to those Salvation Army Missionaries at Usher and stayed there for a year. After that, I realised that I was helpless, for I had no money to buy clothes, and everything. Then I left school and went to Johannesburg, because I had no money to help me in school. So I went to work.

I didn't go to work secretly, I went publicly, and not like other people [he has his brother Dzilo in mind] who went away secretly, without permission from their parents. I went to Johannesburg with some others in 1934, when people used to go on foot, before they boarded a train. It took us 12 days to get to Johannesburg. I did not suffer when we got there, because I found a job as a kitchen boy. Then I left that job and worked six years in a factory using flooring machines. The white man who was the foreman left that job and went to work for Transvaal newspapers in Hook Street near the park station. He took me with him, and I worked for Transvaal newspapers for three years. But when my old employer came from the war, he took me back to his factory, where I worked until today [until returning home]. I didn't suffer in Johannesburg. I led a very decent life. I went with . . . [various neighbours and local men].

### Coming to a Manly Realisation and Returning to Work

I stayed in Johannesburg for ten years, then came home, and found that the people had moved from the place where I had left them near a kopje called Dziya. I found that people had come to Elephant Fell [in the Special Native Areas] where we are now. I realised that I'd been wasting time in Johannesburg, playing with my money, and not working seriously. My mother was suffering, because she had nothing.

I realised that I had been squandering money in Johannesburg, so when I went back, I wanted to work like a man and not like a woman. I did work like a man, for a time. And I bought cattle, for I had seen, when I came home, that my mother was suffering and I wanted my mother to live well and be happy. I stayed in Johannesburg for five years and returned home.

I lived, and lived with my mother until she left us [roughly in 1952]. When she died, she had a horrible sickness. I had never before seen it in the world. It was the first of its kind in the world. Nobody had ever seen it before. I do not know what kind of disease it was. But when she died, she had maggots in her eyes.

We tried to get doctors, but we failed. We tried to send her to the [European] doctors in Bulawayo. They failed. She died and left us. We remained living as if we were orphans without anyone to care for us, although we still lived in the hamlet of our father, Lupondo. Even today we still live with troubles and troubles. But because we don't have anything from our father, we have things of our own power. We go on still living.

[Baka Chedza told me, but Buka himself did not mention it, that when he returned from labour migration, believing his father did have a reasonable number of cattle, he tried to find out which ones were his father's. Disappointed by how very few they were, he gave up any interest in them, and insisted he wanted only things of his 'own power'.]

### Marriage, Separation, and Remarriage

You ask about the wife I brought home from Johannesburg; well, I met her when I had gone to a kinsman of mine who was living in Sophiatown. That is where I met her, and made love to her; and she accepted me. When I said I was coming home, she said she wanted to come. I brought her home. Later she said she did not want me to have a second wife. And I said to her, 'You have no children, and yet you don't want me to take a second wife, so how are we going to live, just the two of us, without children? Maybe the woman I want to marry will have children, and we will send them.' But she insisted that she did not want me to be a polygynist. She said I should send her home. I took her to the train, and she went back home. [He paused, at length]

Well, it went, and went, and went; and I took a wife, Baka Yenda. I stayed, and stayed, and stayed, then went back to Johannesburg. I worked, and worked, and worked. Then I came home and married another wife, Baka Sala. I stayed, and stayed and had children with them. Before I married Baka Yenda, we were living as close as we are now to [a locality three miles away]. It was just the same as if you'd go to [that locality] to see a girl, and make love to her. It was very easy for me to see her because my sister was married in her hamlet [to her brother]. About Baka Sala, you know I have a kinsman who sometimes comes here, the man who came to give me money, he lives at [a place we had visited together]. I used to go there and that is where I saw Baka Sala. Her father had already been my friend. I was not offered a woman when she was not in love with me [again without saying so openly, he makes an invidious comparison to his brother Dzilo, whose second wife was never his girl-friend before marriage]. No, none of my wives were taken that way, they had all been my girlfriends before marriage. [He laughed, remembering his escapades in courting his girlfriends.]

### Children's Names, Affliction and Sorcery

You ask about the names I gave my children. The first is Sindebele for 'Where shall we hide in order to run away from these troubles?' Those were the troubles I told you about, when I said there were many worries in my mother's household. The second does not mean anything. The third means 'We have got out of your affairs.' ['We have stood aside from your affairs.'] The fourth is a Roman Catholic name. The first of the second wife was given her by a father's sister, and does not mean anything. Her other name, the one I gave her, was Sifelani—meaning 'What are we dying for?' And I gave that name, as I told you, because there were many troubles and sorrows and ill-feeling. I cannot say why or for which thing I gave her that name, but for all those things. This name was rejected by their mother's mother. She said, 'Even if you are dying, you must not call a child by that name.' The second of the second wife, too, has a Roman Catholic name.

I once was a cripple. My feet were painful, and for three months I could not walk.

[He suffered this affliction roughly in 1950, the same year that his brother Mfila, also suffering a severe illness, blamed it on sorcery by Buka in collusion with Buka's mother's brother.]

I had to stay in a hut, and spent the whole night awake, while a big fire was kept going so that there was always warm water for me to put hot rags on my legs whenever I felt pain. But after fifteen minutes, when my feet became cold again, the pain would return. I would wake up, and they would apply hot rags. They would apply and apply. I went to Antelope Mine Hospital and stayed there for a week. They gave me an ointment which looked like grease, and they told me to rub it into my feet. I still did not feel better. Tobela tried and failed. Mtshaeli, who lived near Sibanda, also came and cut my feet. But he failed.

One day an old man, the father of Baka Chedza, who came to visit us, noticed the water that [my first wife] kept always on the fire in my hut, and said, 'What is the reason for always having a fire for this child?' She said, 'It is because his feet are always painful.' [In Sindebele] 'People took some soil where he stepped, and they have done something to it', he said, as if he were joking. He sent Baka Chedza to go and get some herbs, for he said that was why my feet were painful. He treated me for a month; and early one morning, Baka Chedza took me to the fork of two paths and dug a hole there. Then she poured in all the medicines that had been used to treat me, and she told me to step over the hole and to go home without looking back. That was the end of the pain in my foot.

Ah, they had worked sorcery against me, yes [it was] my father's senior wife [Baka Dzilo]. Another thing, ah, I have forgotten the year,—the year Baka Sala was married [roughly 1953], we planted a lot of finger millet. We had heaped it and heaped it at the threshing place. It was a big heap of finger millet. One morning when we came there we found that something like a dog had been lying on top of our heap of finger millet. We did not think it anything dangerous, so we rearranged the heap of finger millet, for we thought it was a dog. The next morning we found the same thing had happened. So I went to the Chief and told him to come and see with me.

The Chief came. Some men here went, some did not [again a veiled remark against his brother Dzilo]. When we got there the Chief said, 'What is this being done, old man?' He was speaking to father. The Chief said, 'Let him go and get Mlilo, that doctor, to come and work [protective magic] on this spot.' Mlilo was brought and he worked on that finger millet in the Chief's presence.

Now, one day when we were coming from [his second wife's home] where we had gone to sell beans at the store, we were told that someone had had a fit, while we were gone. And it was said that this person was bewitched by Mlilo. I said, 'No, Mlilo did not bewitch anyone. He only charmed the finger millet.' Oh, there was a complaint from then till today.

And the man who had the fit is this man who is ill [his dying brother, Mfila]. They went to a doctor and asked the doctor to kill Mlilo and me. The doctor did as he was told, but nothing happened. They then refused to pay the doctor his money. So the doctor sent them lightning. They said they did not want to pay the doctor; they did not see what the doctor had done for them. But the doctor said, 'Did you want me to kill innocent people?' From then, things went badly for them. They said they wanted the doctor to kill Mlilo, too, because Mlilo makes me, his 'sister's child', very strong. But the doctor said, 'I cannot kill innocent people.' But, because they refused to give him his money, he sent them lightning. So too with this money, the 40 pounds that was wanted, it will bring some trouble. The medicine will not work against an innocent person. But if you refuse to pay, because it did not work, it comes to work against you.

We stayed like that, on and on, still being in misery, because troubles did not cease. Even today, we are still in misery. I cannot say where all the misery comes from. But I only say that God knows, and even today God is still with us. So we are still living in misery. I cannot say many things, because there are many things which can be remembered as we live together, as days go by.

### From Poverty to Prosperity with God

I ploughed but did not have very good harvests. Yet as time passed, and passed, and passed, God gave us good fortune, and I had crops. During my childhood, my mother did not get much of crops. But when I was grown and became a man, God gave us good fortune; and we had good crops and were able to live like other people. That is how I lived, till today. I lived in suffering, but God was with me.

Whatever things are said about me, about which I know nothing, I say, 'God knows what it is.' And I only pray to Him to give me good fortune. Many things are said about me, and yet I know nothing about them. I only say that God knows what He is going to do. And I pray to Him to be with me, until the day that He calls me. I do not think there is anything more I can say. What I have said is much, and I am thankful for these words. I can say for the time being I will stop there.

## Baka Sala Recalls

Buka's favourite wife, Baka Sala, was nearly thirty, and pretty, when she told the following life history to me and my assistant, Timon Mongwa. Pregnant at the time with her second son, she was the mother of three children, the first of whom, a son, was born before she knew and then eloped with Buka.

### From Childhood to an Adolescent Love Affair

From the beginning of my childhood, my father stayed with my mother, until he took a junior wife. Then we were chased away by our father. When we were as big as Ndiwa [her oldest child, about six or seven years old] we went to our mother's brother to stay. And we really stayed until we had our own homes, until we had eyes, and saw that we were people. Our mother's brother took us to school then. When he had sent us to school, we learned there. In our school days I was a mad girl, always being punished. It went, and went until I became straight and came to the way. Yes. I went to school and stayed a time.

In the middle I had eyes to see that I had fallen in love. [She laughed.] I stayed and went to school. While I was still there, our mother's brother said, 'I don't see you well, my sister's children.' Our mother's brother would rise very early. And there were two gateways into our hamlet. He would leave by one gate in the morning, looking for footprints, and then he would look at the other gate. We stayed there being trusted children, going to school.

Time passed and passed and, at last, that boy I was in love with . . . well, I was 'spoiled' [became pregnant]. After I'd been 'spoiled', my mother's brother said, 'This child, I don't see her well. What is wrong with this child? This child was a child but now she has turned colour. I don't see her.' Yes. Then our mother's brother said to our mother, 'Find out what has happened to this child. For we shall carry a court case and ourselves be at fault, because these children have their father [who has rights over them, including the right to sue the lover for compensation].' At last they objected, while I was still refusing, and they saw that I was 'sated' and my belly was swollen.

Then my mother went with me to my father to report about me. When she was doing that, my father said, 'Who is your lad?' 'My lad?' I told them his name. My father said, 'I don't want even to hear about the child of so and so. They are not the kind of people who can marry someone. They have no households. Today I'm taking you from that person and giving you to another.' [She laughed, remembering the folly of her early affair and her youthful stubbornness and self-will.]

He sent a person so that I would be given to another. I cried then, because I was pregnant. I felt like hanging myself, because I did not like him. I stayed there. They went to that person [the man of her father's choice] and it failed. When it failed them there, I went with my mother to my mother's brother's where I gave birth. When my father had said, 'The boy who got you pregnant, I don't want to hear of him, nor do I want his [court] damages.'

[A father has a right to receive compensation, an award of damages, from a lover responsible for getting his daughter pregnant, in the case of her first child born out of wedlock. Waiving that right, her father did not want to recognise any connection with her lover.]

I said that since my father does not want the family of the boy I am in love with, it's better that I should refuse to go where they have offered me in marriage. For where I got pregnant I am also not allowed to go. And thus everything will end there. [She laughed once again at her youthful self.]

I stayed and bore a child there. I brought that child up, and when he was as big as Longani [about two], I weaned the child, and intended to go to town. But my mother's brother brought me home again. There I thought of where my father was, when he was at Bembeswani. I went to my father and stayed there a long time. And when I stayed there many men tried, but I said, 'No, I want nothing more of this matter of men. About this, this matter of men I have "joined" [as one does a church, vowing abstinence]. I am only going to work.'

### Falling in Love and Marrying Buka

At last, after I had stayed there, near the store, my brother said, 'It's better that you come to the store and do something.' I went to the store and tried to sew on a machine. And then Buka came and he was well dressed. [She laughed, this time at herself for being attracted by a dapper man.] He said, 'There you are, there you are, girl.' He failed. I said, 'I have failed to get to a household. I have been forced to leave. I have had many troubles.' He tried very hard. He said, 'Anything you'd like, anything you want to do, I'll do it for you at my home. But I want you to be my wife.'

I tried to refuse. Then this brother of mine at the store said, 'It's better to be married. It is not fitting to remain without dignity.' I went along until I was free, and I fell in love with Buka. [She laughed.] And when I fell in love with him, I said, 'How is he?' People said that he has his own wife.

My father wanted to refuse and my mother was not there, she was elsewhere. He complained, 'I have no child who is to become a junior wife. I don't like it at all. I would not want to see the man you are in love with in my hamlet. I don't like it at all.'

I was in trouble. I tried by all my powers, since my mother was not there and I was alone with my father. And I really loved Buka. I would go to the store to buy some corn when my father's corn was plenty, because I loved Buka. I would take some money to buy a fowl which we would eat with this person who was coming from Bango [chiefdom]. I said I'll only go there.

At last Buka said, 'I'd like you to come and see my hamlet.' We left there with my sister whom I come after in birth, and we saw where Buka lives. And she said, 'If you see that it doesn't suit you, say so; and if it suits you, you say it suits me.' And I also saw that it is only a thing of love, once you have loved, you find everything good, because you love that person. We married each other and we stayed, until I was without children. He got me some diviners and doctors until I had these two children, until I had my own household. [She laughed, ending her life history.]

## Dzilo Recalls

### Saying 'One'

I lived as I lived. I lived that life I led, beginning when I was small. I was born. I grew up in my mother's household, and yes, I was herding cattle. So it was, until I came to go to work, leaving behind Mfila [his younger brother] who was herding. I went to work and returned.

Then I began to make love. I first made love to an Ndlovu [Elephant totem] girl, she is the one who said, 'One.' She said, 'One' and I was saying, 'One' with that girl of Ndlovu. Yes, I again was loved by, uh, uh I won't mention their names, they are the wives of men, they will kill me. And then I was loved by a Moyo [Heart] girl. That was the girl who loved me. After that I was loved by Baka Temba [his wife]. Yes, I courted Baka Temba before, and I failed. Then I left for Johannesburg. When I returned, I went to her and courted her. Then it was that she fell in love

with me. Who would I marry of these three? I took her. My soul [air] had
loved her, and I took her.

[They lived in nearby localities, within about three miles, before marriage,
but after moving to the Special Native Area his wife's kin settled in a distant
part of Bango chiefdom.]

We lived for a long time, until I begot Temba and another daughter who is
over there, Nsusu, next Chandi, then I went forever [for a long absence
without coming home each year]. I lived there for four years, in Johannesburg; I really lived there for four years. Then I returned and found Chandi
to be a girl as big as this, maybe she was bigger than this. I returned and
begot Ngoni, and Ndapa followed, and this one here, too.

### Attacked by the Spear of Sorcery

[Dzilo insisted that he would not have left his father's hamlet, had it not been
for the sorcery from which he barely escaped alive. In 1959, lightning struck
and burnt down the hut in which he was sleeping. It was because he was
innocent of any cause for vengeance, he protested, that God protected and
saved him.]

When I was still living as I had been [in 1959], that spear [of sorcery]
entered that lifted me out of the hamlet. It came in at night time. It was
when sleep was just about to come to us. It came then, but I was still
awake. I was not sleeping. I was very awake, yes. And then as I was resting
like this I heard it leaking this way and I pulled [the blankets] this way. I
felt it coming in, and I pulled this way again. I did not pull twice again
here. Ah!

I found myself down there in front of the house. I fought with it and
fought with it. But mother had heard too. She came out and found the fire
burning. The houses were like this. There was one in front. But the one
burning was like this one here. And I was not then holding, I was being
caught like this. [He crossed his arms.]

I came out to sit at Mfila's house, far off there on the stoop. It burnt till
it finished; while I was watching, the women struggled with the blankets
alone. There was nothing that came out, not even a single blanket. She
[his mother] kept on taking things out, alone she took all the things out. I
stayed and then followed the world, going forever. I returned to go to
those people [diviners] who are spoken of as 'Knowers', those who are
said by people. I went to them. They really told me. 'Public' [the English
word here meaning, 'out in the open']—they told me. 'It is so and so.' It is
so? Ah, people are so bad.

[In this tape-recorded account, Dzilo abbreviated what he told me some five
months earlier, which I wrote down in longhand as he spoke. I had asked him
to tell me how he came to leave his father's hamlet and build on his own. He
explained it as having been forced upon him by the jealousy of others:

I had worked well in Johannesburg. There was not even one person around here who had his children dressing like mine. When Pumpo [a storekeeper] was here, he 'gave Christmas' [a Christmas party]; and beer was to be brewed in my compound. Some people didn't like having it brewed here, 'Such a small boy and yet he has it in his homestead!' Some refused to stamp the grain for the beer, and others agreed.

There was not much rain, and a little lightning was seen down at Mambale [a distant part of the chiefdom]. Our first wife had Jela as a young child [born 1957]. Yes, Jela was very young then, when lightning came in more and more, though there was not a cloud in the sky. When I stood up and looked out, I saw rain coming down. I pulled the blankets over, and I tried to pull them over again. Lightning then threw me over, and I was bound like this. [He showed his arms crossed and pinned against his chest.] I said inwardly, 'What is happening? I have no cause [*nlandu* fault] with anyone.' And my wife suspected something, for why should lightning come in like this, and pull the poles down like this? There was one of my huts where no one slept. It was so full of goods it looked like a store. It had everything, beds, clothing. There eight blankets caught on fire, and also that new bed I had never used, ah, many things.

There isn't even one here in Nigoba who had worked as I had, and everything was burnt. In the hut where I slept, lightning struck six poles from the bottom to the top. But God objected, and said, 'This person has no fault.' And the lightning went to burn another hamlet. That is why I left the hamlet.

I went to the diviners, and they told me to move off. Now I am starting to work from the bottom. But my wife and I are hard people. That will raise us up, our cattle and our crops, ah, we are getting many. And if anyone gets into my hut now, he will say, 'These people have never had any suffering.' These are all things we have bought.

That European [Pumpo the storekeeper] had given us a big Christmas; he killed a big bull, bigger than Buka's. Yet when he came, he said 'You should not have to kill someone, when I have given you a Christmas [party].' Yes, I lost much money with the black people, the diviners. Yes, you are killed by your own person, not by someone coming from somewhere else.

[I pressed Dzilo to be less indirect and name his suspects. At last he mentioned Tobela as the one who got the lightning, 'We should never mention it because that man is the friend of Buka' implying but at that moment not saying that Buka was in cahoots with Tobela. 'You must understand what sort of life we lead here', he continued. 'Ah, you can never see him [Buka] coming here. You saw me drinking beer in his enclosure that day, but even if I have some beer here ... Ah ... I thank God for all that power that saved me.']

I returned, and then I went to find a person to make me vomit [a countermeasure against sorcery as poisoning]. He made me vomit, worked and worked over. Then I heard some saying, 'No you should not build here anymore. It is taboo [koyila, avoided] to remain where God has worked. Remove.' I talked to the Land Development Officer [asking for permission to move to a new site]. He refused. [At that time, there was an official halt on movement to new sites.] When he came again, I told him that where Divinity has worked, one must not live. One removes. The Land Development Officer then agreed to me.

I went out to the fallow [close to the hamlet, and not the site he intended to use], knowing that if I showed the people, they were going to peg some things [of sorcery]. I was deceiving them, because they would peg a thing while I was away. I said to the Land Development Officer, 'I'll build here.' Then it was written. My person [the doctor treating the secretly chosen site] came at night in his car and left it there. I already knew. At night I went there. And when he had worked on it, he got up the next morning; and so it is up to this day, we are living here.

Yes, I was lifted up by troubles, that is what lifted me. I would not have left my father. I would still be living with him, and very well. Then, uh, it became heavy for me, a great thing like lightning! You see this house, here it hits the outside supporting poles, so many were hit, six. I was inside. It hit the house I was sleeping in.

[Shortly before Dzilo recalled this, we had heard the Zionist preacher who prayed about the illness of Dzilo's gravely ill brother, Mfila, and rebuked the congregation for introducing sorcery into Lupondo's hamlet, but did not name any specific sorcerer.]

When he heard that man preaching there, didn't we hear him saying, 'This person [Dzilo himself], really I fear him. God fought for him. He had no dispute with a person.' Had I a case, ah I would not be here. No, I would not be here. Then God refused.

God, being like this [a just God], and I say I want to work sorcery against you [who are innocent of wrongdoing], God refuses that very day. The great thing is maybe I'll get poison to set for you, I can then kill you. If I point at you and say, 'Swa' [sicc him] ah, there is nothing that is going to happen. It is never known how it'll work, maybe you will also be alright. It goes back to the owner. [Sorcery sent against an innocent, faultless person is supposed to turn against the sorcerer, leaving the innocent unharmed.] I mean my troubles, as I was troubled like that there. That is when I came to stay here forever, here with my wives. Now there is nothing that troubles me. I'm living very well these days. There's nothing troubling.

People are bad. As I have already told you. Didn't you hear that person [the preacher], that day, what he was doing? He wanted to know. Didn't you hear him talking about our case only. He said, 'Understand each other, being the children of one man.' He was preaching, meaning us. This shows he sees. Didn't you hear him saying that 'If you argue I will tell you that so and so is like this, and so and so is like that.' And it was all quiet. He would have told us if we had argued and said he should say that 'You spoil by doing this and this.' But no, we stop it. It breaks hamlets. We look at it and leave it. People are malevolent. Yes, they are malevolent.

You see, as I live I do not lack anything; I lack nothing. It was starvation as you saw. Even on one day you didn't fail to get beer here. I always held people. They gathered here. I always brought two drums, two drums [barrels of beer]. Food was always eaten. I never went to the place where people line up for bags [in loans from the administration]. I never went there [unlike Buka's family].

No, God gave me power and said, 'Be wise, this way.' Then I met a strong 'house', a strong one, a born woman who is strong. She is really strong. Yah, really strong this woman. Many people here had no grain in their granaries. No, so it is what they are killing me for. They are killing me for power and also my wife. The wife, they really put a thing for her. A thing closes her here some days [he pointed to his chest]. It is at the heart and it comes, but through here. [His wife is suffering from pains in her chest.] I went to the hospital, and I failed there; but still, no. It sometimes says, it sometimes becomes quiet. I have gone to all the doctors. I have gone to them all. I can say, as I see in these past days, in this last month, I lost twenty pounds, yes twenty pounds. Two tens by all the truth. Two tens, in this past month just now.

They are trying us with all things. People give to others saying, 'You go and make that person eat this thing.' [He has in mind, above all, Tobela working with Buka in sorcery.] That is the trouble that troubles me. That alone. They want to make us eat, to poison us. That is the only thing troubling us, that, only one. If it is for living, just living, then I'm not thinking of anything. No. Were it not that they would try to do it again, that injury done to me, I would no longer be thinking of it.

I had so many blankets of mine burnt, new ones, unused, eight unused blankets that were only kept in the house. [Dzilo, like other returning labour migrants, had brought home a store of blankets, representing a part of his savings.] Just as there are blankets kept now in the house for visitors, so those would be given to visitors. They were just like that too. Then I was no longer thinking of it. No, we have again covered them up. They are just like that again. But what troubles is illness. That's what troubles.

### Troubles and Buka's Wind

Do you see well? We have a brother here [Buka]. When he comes, he limps like this. He comes limping along. He does not go, as we do. We go there and sit. But him, you can never see him come and sit here. No. He understands well his friend that side, Tobela. Sometimes he brews beer with a barrel as big as this. They are going to spend a day working at a helping party when we are here, here, here, when we are children of one man.

[Dzilo's first wife later put it even more bluntly, 'This Tobela is the one who is taking out Buka from his father. But it is not that he takes him out because he is of the same "house". They take each other out because of their crookedness.']

People talk that way . . . people talk that way [muttering in an aside, mimicking Buka's unsociable mannerism]. That means the wind [*mhepo*, soul] of a person is not good. He thinks very bad thoughts. If you are children of one man, you should love each other very much. Very much. It may be a small calabash, but you call each other and come to eat together. Not that I should get up myself and leave the people of Nigoba to go and call the people of Bango. That those of Bango should work at my fields, when the people of my home are not there! My wind [soul] is unbecoming. Yes, my wind is bad. Better I should call my own people, my brothers through my father who begot me, we go and take from each other. These, my mothers, we go and work together and eat together. Or there may be one from the other hamlets who finds us. Yes, he can find us then. Here a thing is done [by Buka], and you never see it. But sometimes, one day, he wants to come, because people scold at him, they scold, 'How do you work?'

It happened that one day, that time, beer was brewed there [at Buka's]. And then I thought, 'Shall I go to that man's beer when he has not asked me to come?' I then stayed away. I went, and then passed, and went that way. I went round and came this way. He remained saying, 'But Tata Temba [Dzilo] didn't come to beer! What has happened?' It was then said, 'You say what has happened?' The wife [of Buka] then said, 'He is made to do that by you. You do not go to Tata Temba. Will Tata Temba always be coming to you, when you do not come to him?' The junior one, that one said, 'Tata Temba is acting the way you do. You never go to his home. What makes you do that? Will Tata Temba be eating your things here, when you do not eat at his enclosure?' Now, when there is beer, he sometimes comes and drinks a little, stays for a short time, then goes off.

Here at Tata Temba he didn't step [he didn't manage to step in and succeed in doing harm]. He tried and he failed. He has failed; even fearing, he fears. He says, 'Ah, if I may try here, maybe I'll be injured.'

He tried and he failed. His wind is bad. Very, very bad. His wind is bad. He is my older brother, but we loved him very, very much. Very, very much, too. We didn't say there was that [disposition of Buka's], no. But ah! that one [Buka] has defeated me [I have had to give up on him]. A 'skelem', a scoundrel. Ah, he's no good. He's an unreliable crook, and he's a scandalmonger. Even Europeans know he's a crook. Even that storekeeper.

[Dzilo went on to give an example of Buka's treachery in speaking harmful untruths about other people. At Dzilo's recommendation for a woman of his administrative village, Baka Siya, the local storekeeper had hired her to build the storekeeper's house. Although the house was being made beautifully, Buka tried to convince the storekeeper that it was no good and that he needed a woman Buka would recommend to do it right. But none of Buka's brother's wives would agree to meddle in someone else's affair, and the storekeeper, too, saw through Buka's tactics.]

He [Buka] went to the storekeeper, got to the [brick] house, and said to him, 'This house is no good. They do not know how to build.' [The storekeeper asked,] 'Do they not know how to build?' 'No. I'll get you a person who knows how to build.' He came to [his younger brother's wife] and talked to her. She said, 'I do not go to such things.' He went to the wives of the brothers to go and work. But it was the wife of Siya who was hired to do the work and who built that house. It is a beautiful house. The storekeeper said, 'This man will make me hated by people. He'll make me blamed in the world, by people. This house is beautiful.'

Then, it is not good to be blamed by every person. No it is not good. Ai no. You should have the truth: the truth is a good thing in the world, yes. You will see you will live very well in the world. His kindness is really bad. Ah, his kindness is very bad, very bad. His wind is very bad. Ah, he's not a person. No. Really very bad, very, very bad. He's like that junior wife of his. Only 'rubbish'.

You are living with him there. Do you ever see him going to her [his senior wife's] house? I mean does he ever go to the house of Baka Yenda? Does he ever sleep there? She doesn't know him. That wife of his is a wife for food only. Do you ever see when he is sitting there? But she is the owner, who made him rich, so that he could marry that other one. Yet she is left outside. No, the law of the Kalanga does not go that way. No. One who is in front is in front.

It goes this way. You see these houses of mine here? [He pointed to his wives' huts.] I have turns. You know, even our fathers said so. [Turning to my assistant Timon Mongwa] You are a Kalanga, you know, too. There are turns. I take two weeks here, and then two weeks there. You do it, so that you build well. You should not say a wife should just be a wife, and you do not sleep at her house.

You see Baka Sala did not tell me at first, but then, she had to come straight to tell me. She said, 'Tata Temba I do not see my husband. My husband has got tired of me.' I say she lived for so many days, so many months [nearly three years without having a child]. Is it not long since she gave birth? [He pointed to a young daughter of his own.] Is it not that this one has been long weaned? He never did it again, to go and put there. He stinges her, really. Maybe when you look at her, you think she can no longer bear [children]. But she is able to bear. There is just no one who goes to her.

The law of the Kalanga does not hold it so. It does not go that way, no. To end your work, when you have already done it [made the commitment to doing it]? They may be five [wives], but you must go around the houses. For you know a person is not a bull or a cock that is said to have 'strong' [in English, a ready erection]. You should sleep only. You will one day get one bullet and you shoot. She will thank and say, 'I have an old man, too. We sleep together.' Not that you should just say 'I want wives', and you go and take her to put her in the compound [to exploit her merely for domestic service].

You know that child [Baka Yenda], her co-wife fed her [poisonous medicine] a long time ago so that he doesn't think of her, that she is a woman. And again it does not stand up when he is looking at her. It just keeps still. [He gestured to show that Buka does not have an erection.] She [the junior wife] worked with such charms on that man, so he would become strong on her alone. And you will not see him at that one's house [the senior wife's]. I do not know now, but I do not think so. But then when this one [the junior wife] was not there, he went to rape [to force his senior wife to have sexual intercourse with him]. The [senior] wife refused. Yes, he wanted to grab her. The woman refused. She said, 'Hey, first finish all yours. Today you see that your woman is not here. And you say I should come near you and under you. I! You hold all things, as you see them.' She refused. He thought that, if this one [the junior wife] will not be here he will be scraping'. She refused.

## The Right Way of Seniority among Wives

[Developing his homily on the law and dutiful conduct towards wives, Dzilo elaborated the counterargument to Buka's complaint about his father's mistreatment of his mother and her displacement from seniority. It was that Buka was himself at fault in failing to respect seniority among his wives. Seniority meant recognised authority, a rightful order, and fixed turns among the wives. The husband should give his goods and money to the senior wife who should pass a share on to the junior. The senior wife ought to have charge of opening his granaries and distributing his grain. But Buka respected none of that in his discrimination in favour of his junior wife.]

Such a way, one liked, that is not good. It is very, very bad. The law disapproves of it. It is disapproved. You see, I being as I am, I may get some meat. Do you hear? I will not come and bring it to [the junior wife]. I will bring it to the senior here. It is the senior who must call. 'Ma Ndlovu?' And she replies, 'Ma?' 'Take this thing and cook it.' She has been given by the senior wife, who is the one to say 'Cook this thing.' She will then cook, and it will be eaten. Or if I buy some sugar, I will bring it here [to the senior]. She is the one who will call that other one and say, 'Make some tea.' Or if I brought some bread with me, I will bring it here. It will be cooked, and they will call each other. And they will eat together, gathered that way. Not that I should come and give to that other one. No, you cannot live well. No you cannot. Never, never. No, you can't.

You know, you see this one [his junior wife], she cannot open my granaries. She cannot touch it. No, she never does. She is given. If she has hunger she goes to Baka Temba to tell her, 'I am hungry.' Baka Temba is the one who gets up, calls her, and goes with her. She will say, 'Take some grain from here.' They will put it into a sack or whatever it is and give it to her. She says, 'Take it' and she takes it. Not that she should go too, and dish out, no. She goes to take out grain when Baka Temba is also standing there. The law of Kalanga says so. It was so with our fathers. Yes, it is so, yes if I am to share money. I will call her and count the money. I'll say, 'Here it is, the money. Take it and buy some goods. I'll sit on a stool there and then she'll call her. 'Hey, come this way.' And she will come. She will come and give her money and say, 'Here is money. It was said go and get clothing.' She also takes hers. They divide it themselves, when they are alone. Thus is the law of the Kalanga. You should not go to a store, find beautiful material on sale, and then say, the money is for so and so. She gave it to me to buy this for her.' Yet you know it is underhanded. It is not straight. You do not have the art of building; building is not in you. You cannot build in a straight way. No, there will always be noise. Yes, it is bad. That thing is bad.

So holds the law of the Kalanga, there is nothing I can give this child [the junior wife] unless it is through this one [the senior wife]. There I would be destroying, I would be spoiling. You see, she cooked in the morning, eh? She cooks *chikuf* [food] '*Skuff*'. She then carries the plates and brings them here, here. That one [the junior] does it. They will eat here, lining up here. Didn't you see that day when they were lined up here? In the evening it is Baka Temba who cooks now. They will be called and come here. Tomorrow, it is that one who is cooking, she will carry it and bring it here. Yah, the law says so. You should not have it that she will cook there in a small pot and say, 'I am cooking for a child.' [She should not be allowed to excuse herself, for the sake of cooking a small amount for a child, and thus begin to withdraw from joint arrangements.] It will go on, and go further. If you see her doing that, you must refuse. It should be cooked, but in the big [pot] only, and it should be eaten then [by everyone, husband and wives in turn]. Children will have some food left for them, and during the day they will eat. I speak here of the law, this law, that I be clever about it.

Do you see that 'brother' [cousin] I was with that day, that brother of mine, he is the one who gave me the wisdom that, 'It is lived this way. You will live this way with wives, this way and this way.' He is Gadza, yes, he is the one who gave me wisdom. He has so many wives, three. But they cook in this way, it is the junior wife who cooks; the senior wives like Baka Temba are [seated] making mats. You should not have two pots, these small pots separately. There I object, and the younger wife should not open the granary, when she is alone. It is taboo.

Do you see there? [At Buka's] she [the junior wife] takes all things for herself, as she likes. You cannot hear her saying, she will wait until she is given. She goes and draws out by herself. That one [Buka] acts like a person who steals from this one to give to another that he loves. Or should you get good seed anywhere, you must bring it to the senior wife. You buy it and give it to this one and say 'Here is seed. Sow it.' She will share it out. Otherwise, nothing works well. Can you come and say, 'I'm going to give to my wife' and then you give it to her by a 'corner' [corner in English, i.e. in an underhanded manner]. It is not good. It is a very bad thing. If I have a field, and it is in spring and they are going to collect a thing, they will get a lot. They will cook it, and everyone will eat it. That one cannot go to my fields and get what she wants. No. That is taboo. The law of the Kalanga says it must not be done. You see, we milk here in our compound. Our gourd is one. Right from our grandfather it went on so, we began in that custom. We did not begin with another. No. We began with this one. There are turns, proper turns.

These people you see them doing like this. If she wants secret things, she does these secret things in her hut. If you want to make two, make two with this one and two with that one. Right, you will see how good things will be. The law goes so. I mean the law of the Kalanga is so. You see if she has made some beer, she will take out a small calabash, about this big, and give it to her senior. She will say, 'Here is a small calabash.' Or if I am not there, her kinsman who drinks beer may come and she will give it to him. The law goes that way. I mean the way of life of people. Thus they live. Beginning before I was born, we found it so. There is no other law, no, none. That is the law.

### Cradling Elders

[Lupondo's younger brother, Tata Chedza, and his wife, Baka Chedza, were among Dzilo's staunchest supporters within Lupondo's family. Having heard her version of it, I asked Dzilo how their great mutual understanding had come about.]

[At the old site] four head of cattle were given to Tata Chedza when his wife was going about begging. Don't you see us always visiting this compound? It started right there. While Tata Chedza was at Johannesburg, his wife went to her home. I then completed my four years in Johannesburg. And when I returned, I saw Baka Chedza had come here. Baka Chedza was then working together with [a neighbour] in a nearby hamlet. [The neighbour] would come and help here because she had no cattle, and yet when [the neighbour's] cattle would come to that field, the cattle would all lie down. I could see this, because the fields were all in one place, then.

Yes, I saw that woman was being troubled. And the following year, starvation came, there were no rains. Till then I had not helped them. I was still feeling it in my heart. Then I said, 'I will help you.' I brought five head of cattle for her to plough with.

That year the rains filled up the Semokwe River. We [Dzilo, Buka, and another brother] went bare here [he indicated his chest], in the river together, till it was this high on us. We slept then at my sister's. We got to the cattle posts at night and went then to the Shashi River. The next day, we chose those [oxen] we wanted and slept and rested. On the following day we brought them here. When the Chief passed by here on his way to the post, he and those of Bango found there were seven span of oxen ploughing *hunde* [the service for a senior elder, here for Dzilo's father]. That was the year I began ploughing for Baka Chedza.

Yes, I am the one who carries her on my back. You see Tata Chedza, I am the one who cradles him on my back. I drive the spans of oxen myself. Yes, he had been so poor, and now he is up. Did you see him going to get grain at the store last year? No. Now he passes Buka [in his crops].

[Dzilo had earlier remarked to me disapprovingly that 'Buka is starving really. There is hardship in his compound, and he is careless with grain.' Dzilo took great pride in his ability to work hard and produce enough from his own and his father's brother's fields to more than feed their families.]

Ah, the 'wind' [*mhepo*, soul] I was born with is good. I became good. In this hamlet you can never hear them talking bad of me. They all say [pronouncing the diminutive form of his name very tenderly and affectionately] 'Tata Tembanyana'.

If you see a person angry with me, hating me, you know it is because I have taken people away from him right before his eyes. Baka Chedza was a 'retainer' [*nlanda*, an inferior client]. When I came, I objected and said, 'No, this person must be up.' If I were to come this year and say, 'No, you must plough alone', there would be wailing in that enclosure. Didn't you see [Dzilo's daughter's daughter] living with them [to help them]? It is because we understand each other. Now she [Baka Chedza] says, 'Her grandfather [Dzilo] has done me so much good, how can I throw away this child [Dzilo's granddaughter]?'

If I die it will be because I have been poisoned 'in food' [in English]. That is just because of my kindness. If I were to go to Tata Bokani [the prominent entrepreneur and leader who was the richest of the Chief's close kin] and say, 'Today, I no longer understand you and like you', there can be much wailing in that hamlet this night. Yesterday, when I passed, there was a child waiting for me. Tata Bokani was already asking for me.

In my wind I have no sorcery. I am happy to have you come to me, and when you leave, I feel I have been visited in my own enclosure by men. I am happy because God is making me to live so on earth.

### THE ACCOUNTS OF BUKA, BAKA SALA, AND DZILO IN RETROSPECT

The life histories of Lupondo's sons belong to a genre of heroic narrative. It is that kind of self-account in which the subject as hero actively and consciously finds his way past obstacles despite the efforts of his antagonists to defeat him. The genre of heroic narrative as used by Lupondo's sons conforms to Kalanga ideas of a man as someone who, in his maturity, achieves *masimba* 'force, power, authority' as an outer aspect of the person complementary to the 'wind' as an inner aspect of character. As befits having *masimba*, each of the sons claimed to have achieved 'things of his own', wealth and prosperity as the product of his own efforts. Buka represented himself as having reached consciousness at some turning point in life—after squandering his earnings from labour migration—whereas Dzilo took consciousness for granted, as if he saw no such turning point. But each of these sons gave the self-account of a purposeful and resolute hero who had stood up to the test of his enemies within the family, and would continue to do so. Using this genre of heroic narrative, each justified himself and moralised against an enemy or rival, as befitted his own view of his rightful place within the family. Being a man of public authority as a headman, Dzilo added a homily to his heroic narrative. Rather piously—given the fact that he was himself renowned for his affairs with other men's wives—Dzilo lectured on the law. He dwelt upon the duties of a husband towards his wives, for these were the duties which Buka, Dzilo argued, failed to fulfil. And Buka failed partly because of his being charmed by his favourite wife and partly because his disposition or 'wind' was so bad that he was driven by passion, not ruled by prudence, wisdom and law.

Both of these heroic narratives reflect the fact that what a family member was perceived to be depended on what he was perceived to have felt. Did he give himself over uncontrollably to feelings of resentment, envy, lust, even the lust for one wife without dutiful regard for her co-wife? If so, he could be regarded as someone driven by his feelings to be secretly destructive, to be a sorcerer. Family members fixed identities upon each other through nicknames such as

'Forker' and through caricatures: 'man of the people, 'man of wives', 'man of the town', 'man of work-parties'. Yet character as *mhepo*, wind or soul, remained something inherently inscrutable to family members. Wary of the dangers in that, they argued about who had *that* character, the one that was not as it should be, because of being antisocial. Buka's and Dzilo's accounts of themselves are products of that argument, but as heroic narratives they are also self-assertions carrying that argument forward.

By contrast, the brief life history Buka's junior wife gave me is a much simpler romance, free of moralising or heroic self-assertion against enemies. There is, admittedly, a similarity, despite the contrast, in their shared assumption of responsible maturity. Like Lupondo's sons, Buka's wife looked back on her life as a movement to responsible maturity from a period of irresponsibility; in her case the period of her carefree, girlish affair and in theirs, the time of boyish pranks in herding or free and imprudent spending as a labour migrant. From having been 'a mad girl', wayward with her boyfriend, she had to become 'straight and come to the way'. But what she glossed over was virtually everything that motivated Lupondo's sons in their life histories, such as their concern with past rights and wrongs, with the family debris from earlier quarrels, with self-justification. Unlike them, she commented not at all upon the *mhepo*, the wind, soul, character, of herself or others. She gave no hint of an awareness of herself as the subject of scandalous song—in one she was likened to a crocodile—or of numerous sorcery accusations in gossip. Instead, she gave a flattering self-account in accord with what she valued most, namely her place as her husband's favourite. The very telling of her story was an assertion of that place, since she responded to my request early in January 1961 largely to please her husband. 'And I also saw', she concluded, 'that it is only a thing of love, once you have loved, you find everything good, because you love the person.' In her story, the subject falls in love, the right man gets her, and she comes to her sentimental fulfilment, protected by her husband and, at last, bearing children. The naive romance of it all was almost too good to be true, something she herself had to laugh at, and laugh she did repeatedly, bringing her life history to an ironic end.

Taken together, and understood in the context of the moral argument waged within Lupondo's family, these life histories are revealing. They show how members of the family tried to come to terms with problematic changes in themselves and in their way of living with each other. As inward-looking accounts, they disclose, above all, how the construction of character was a force in the moral dynamics of Lupondo's family during its first two decades in the Sanzukwe Special Native Area. What emerges clearly from the accounts is the inextricable intertwining of the characters of men and women. A man was not judged, evaluated, and known to have a certain character as a man among men solely or even primarily. He was the son of a mother, the husband of a wife, the lover of a girlfriend or someone else's wife, and he was judged accordingly. And so too was a woman's character constructed more according to her involvement with men than with women. Character, and especially antisocial character—which was the paramount concern in the family argument—was held to be dangerously opaque. The shifts in the involvement of men and women with each other were perceived as outward manifestations of such otherwise opaque character. Thus being locked in contention about these shifts, family members were caught in argument about an elusive, ever provisional, inner truth.

# 5

# Remembered Ordeals: Voices of The Unvanquished

## THE VIOLATION OF THE BODY AND THE PERSON

When I returned to Lupondo's family in 1989 and asked the present elders, the generation of Lupondo's sons and their wives, about the years since we had last been together, they spoke passionately about the wartime brutality they had endured. Each side in the war—whether it was in the liberation war, especially in the final years towards the end of the seventies, or in the post-independence counter-insurgency war at its height in 1983 and 1984—terrorized them. Remembering that, they told me of their grief in bereavement, of how they had suffered torture, how they had been violated and not merely physically.

On their side, the Rhodesians made the violation of the person into a deliberately savage form of psychological warfare. Their sadistic tactics were intended to turn the people's own sense of humanity against them in physically loathsome perversions (on the propaganda displaying mutilation see Frederikse, 1984, p. 123, and on the deliberate violation of 'taboo', Frederikse, 1984, p. 131). In many parts of the country, for example, the Rhodesians made displays of the bodies of dead guerrillas, and forced people to look at the degradation. As Bob North of the Rhodesian Intelligence Corps told the reporter Julie Frederikse shortly after the Liberation War:

> Body displays. A nasty but effective operation. See, the locals were told by the *terrs* [guerrillas] that they were immortal, so we'd leave a few bodies lying around of *terrs* that we'd killed in contacts, in the locals' huts and *kraals* [homesteads]. If we had a high hill which could be seen for miles around, we'd stick a body up it. Good deterrent. Or a helicopter would fly over *kraals* carrying a netful of dead bodies for everyone below to see (1984, p. 128; see also Bhebe, 1988, p. 176 on the shock to the people of a body display).

The elders of Lupondo's family had identified with the guerrillas, 'the boys of the country', during the liberation war and for at least some of the time during the later counter-insurgency period. They spoke of them as their 'children', who usually respected elders, but who, nevertheless, for the sake of revenge and in the name of a defence against evil and sorcery, could and did commit atrocities against elders and their families. In place of the controlled, everyday argument in peacetime about moral character and sorcery came something uncontrollably monstrous in wartime: a campaign against sorcery that was brutal and often arbitrary. This anti-sorcery campaign, imposed by youths as strangers, if in the guise of 'children', was out of the control of elders bound by the passions and responsibilities of close kinship.

The guerrillas were themselves fearful of attack no less than betrayal by the very people on whose behalf they fought. In part, this may have been due to the Rhodesians' 'dirty tricks', their posing as guerrillas to sow distrust and dissension among the people and the guerrillas themselves (see Frederikse, 1984, pp. 281–303; Cilliers, 1985, pp. 118–34; Chater, 1985, pp. 128–32; Ranger, 1985, p. 270; Moore-King, 1989). The guerrillas feared the attack from sorcerers as food poisoners and the betrayal by *batengesi* 'sell-outs' as agents or informers of the Rhodesians (see Frederikse, 1984, pp. 215–19, for different eye-witness views of the trials and treatment of 'sell-outs' and sorcerers). The two things were not easily separated: the sorcerer and the sell-out were often equated in practice or were labels different people used for the same victim of suspicion.

In trying to protect themselves and the people also, the guerrillas waged their brutal campaign against sorcery on the basis of suspicions, the guerrillas' own and those which people revealed upon being interrogated in private, one by one. Almost no guerrillas fought in their own home areas; the advantages of local knowledge were held to be more than offset by the dangers of being known and being subject to the pull of prior loyalties. On the basis of suspicion, and sometimes after a trial, the guerrillas punished suspected sorcerers, often by severe beating, or by torture to death. Elsewhere in Zimbabwe, and not to my knowledge in Lupondo's family, young boys and girls as trusted helpers, who carried food, messages and intelligence for the guerrillas, were also blamed by elders for spreading false accusations and making innocent people suffer at the hand of guerrillas (Ranger, 1985, p. 292; Bhebe, 1988, p. 187; Reynolds, 1990, p. 11; Kriger, 1991). Not all of the victims were regarded by everyone or most people as innocent; the victims were sometimes suspects much accused even before the war, and I was told repeatedly that sorcerers who gave up their practice out of fear of being beaten during the war were back to sorcery after it. Even more, I found that people complained that there had been a great outbreak of sorcery since the war. But from the viewpoint of members of Lupondo's family, it is a measure of the monstrousness of the wartime campaign against sorcery that its victims included some of the most esteemed members of the family.

Looking back on the wars, elders such as Buka's brother Gwati saw nothing heroic about them, at least as wars of the armed. Gwati recalled times when the sound of firing would be heard across the country, when each side would shoot in a different direction, each avoiding the other. One would pursue the other's track from the front to the back and not go ahead to engage, because they were all afraid. Their courage was their rifle, and if they would have put it down and fought with their fists, Gwati insisted, he would have beaten them himself.

Gwati told me, speaking in a whisper—it was still something he did not feel free to speak out loudly—that the guerrillas were evil, for if they hated you they would slice you up with a knife. The evil was not on one side, he went on to say, and he recalled how a Rhodesian patrol led by an officer he called a *Bunu*, a Boer, tortured his daughter before his very eyes. The Rhodesian patrol was hunting down Gwati's son Chibindi, a guerrilla suspected of returning home, although actually he was fighting elsewhere. Such hunts were made, the intelligence reports suggest, because the Rhodesians believed that certain guerrillas from Matabeleland came back to their own areas to recruit (Martin and Johnson, 1981, p. 223). Gwati wondered how the solders knew his son's name; he suspected that someone had directed the Rhodesians to his homestead, because 'people do not love us'.

The Rhodesians struck their terror using a barbaric perversion of a sacrifice. It followed what members of the Rhodesian Intelligence Corps called 'psychological operations' or psyops (Cilliers, 1985, p. 137), in which, as one of them put it, 'Shona and Ndebele custom was studied and used against them. Witchcraft, in other words' (Frederikse, 1984, p. 130). First the Rhodesians killed a chicken by hanging it from a noose atop a tree in front of the hamlet and letting its blood run loose. It was a sign of what they meant to do to Gwati's son. Then they came in and ordered Gwati's wife to get a brand from the fire, which she did, innocently, not knowing what it was for. Gwati and his wife were forced to watch helplessly while the Rhodesians burnt their screaming daughter's breast with the brand, demanding in vain to know where Gwati's son was.

### REMEMBERING INNOCENT VICTIMS

The atrocity of the death of my friend Dzilo was a memory that elders of Lupondo's family could not put to rest. They wanted me to realise how senseless his death had been, and I found it painful to listen and become, like them, a grieving witness. Dzilo was killed in the Bango school by ZIPRA guerrillas when the liberation war was reaching a height, roughly in 1977. He was tortured, butchered to death and shot, for hiding his mother-in-law whom the guerrillas blamed for their comrade's death by food poisoning and sorcery. Dzilo's mutilated body was left to hang through the night soaking that Bango schoolroom with his blood. On the same day, the guerrillas also mutilated and killed his wife and daughter. His mother-in-law they wrapped in plastic and burnt alive. Fearing the arrival of Rhodesian troops and the danger of being caught in the crossfire or being tortured to reveal the guerrillas' movements,

Lupondo's family could not give the dead a decent burial (on the guerrillas' policy of denying a decent burial to 'sell-outs' see Frederikse, 1984, p. 218.)

In death, Dzilo became, for his family and the people immediately around his home, what is called *ngozi*, a restless and vengeful presence, innocent yet wronged, aggrieved and dangerous to the living. All of them had failed to mourn him by shedding the tears for their loss in a wake that would have freed them of his presence as a ghost and sent his soul back to rest among *midzimu*, the divinities of the dead. Speaking with grief and anger, Baka Lufu, the widow of his brother Mfila, recalled.

> Dzilo was just seized. He was blameless, he had done nothing wrong. If you die and leave your children without having been ill, without starting on something that you are dying for, and you are killed merely meeting the day—you are pulled along until you hear the rifle shot—what would you be? He grieved in his heart, he grieved greatly. And there was nothing that we could do. We just heard it, sitting over here [in the hut]. We wanted to go out and see what it was. But there was nothing we could do. We couldn't go out there to it. We could only go out in the daytime [because of the curfew]. All we could do was huddle together and worry about the rifle coming nearer. It was heavy, very heavy.

Baka Sala spoke at length about Dzilo's death, when she tried to make me understand how her late husband Buka suffered in surviving the war:

> Those boys of the country [the guerrillas] started at Number Three [a distant locality named after its dip tank] and came around this way, saying, 'There are some people here who practice sorcery.' They meant Dzilo's mother-in-law and later they took a plastic and burnt her alive. First she fled from Number Three and rushed over here to her son-in-law, to Dzilo, who kept her safely. He protected and hid her. And when they came and asked, 'Why have you hidden her so that we have not yet found her? You, it's your own fault that you have hidden her in your homestead. What are you hiding her for?' He said, 'I hid her because she is my mother-in-law, who gave birth to my wife.' While she was still hidden, they looked for her and couldn't find her, so they took Dzilo and killed him at the school. He died first, having protected the old woman. The Holy Spirit makes you mortal.
>
> Father woke up early in the morning, and we had heard the shooting. We said, 'What's happened?' We heard that no one had seen Dzilo. It was already eight in the morning [after the curfew] and they went about searching for him. Father couldn't find, though he went to [Dzilo's wife]. Then he searched and searched until he found him in the school building. He had been shot there. Those boys of the country [the guerrillas] shot him and left him.
>
> We suffered terribly in those days. You can't know it. Those boys [the guerrillas] were staying over there, near the homestead of Lamba [a

grandson of Lupondo's brother and a close neighbour]. They were carrying their guns, and they were 'supported' [in English] by us. We gave them food. The girls, our children, would cook for them. Some food would come from Gwati [Buka's full brother], some from others over there. We took turns. One would cook a pot, and so on in turn. In the morning three would cook, in the evening another three.

They were staying right over here. And when we were keeping these boys, father [her husband Buka] was our senior who had to look after them. So when they went about, they would come to father and say, 'Father, today we are going to cross over to the other side.' Father would answer and say, 'Where are you going to cross over to the other side, my children?' They'd say, 'When we cross over, we're going to Bidi [the next chiefdom to the east]. We'll sleep there, and not come back.' Then we ourselves went to sleep. And so it was that late in the evening when the sun had set, we heard, 'Thump, Thump, Thump', a knock on the door. It was a boy, one of those with a gun, who came where we were staying.

'Ah', father said, 'What's the matter, my children?'

'I don't know, I have come back, father. Some of us are dying', he said [in Sindebele].

Father went out of the hut, and his heart was beating in terror.

'He's dead.'

'What's happened? When did you get back? You told me you were going to cross over [the river] to Bidi. You say someone has died, and how is that? Weren't you going to sleep over there?'

'No, No,' he said, 'we have turned back, father. We returned after we crossed [the river] at Bango and came back this way. When we got there at Bango, we went in [to the Chief's younger brother] and we had tea made for us.'

'Oh, so you had tea made for you, and what happened?'

'Ah, we drank the tea, came back, and said to the girls, "Today we won't eat food here; don't cook for us; tea is ready for us over there."'

Then father said, 'And so what happened then?'

They said, 'We arrived at Dzilo's [after coming from the Chief's younger brother], and tea was made for us. [Dzilo's] wife went to fetch firewood, leaving the children to cook for us. They gave us the tea, and sat us down in the hut. We were to drink it with the sister of Lamba [a grandson of Lupondo's brother], but she refused. When poured tea, she spilled it out behind the table. She refused it, just poured it out.'

'And you?' father asked.

'We just drank, and then we asked her, "Why did you spill it out?" She said she realised that it stunk. And so, father, when we did that one of us died. We realised that we drank something from that tea.

Oh, then all of us, father, Baka Yenda [her senior co-wife] dashed out and raced madly over there. We found that the child was no longer talking. Baka Yenda, who held his head, saw that he was already dead; that he had truly left us.

Then the others said to us [addressing Buka by his clan name], 'You are failing us. We came with a full contingent, and now we are short one. Now that our person is dead, what are we to do? What's more, we are people who are hated. We don't want to be seen by the Boers [the whites]. Today if they find us, what will they do to us?'

Ah, when he said that, we sat and sat, while that one was dead, right over there at Lamba's homestead [where the guerrillas were camped]. Father began to quake in fear. All the people had to meet where they were summoned. A great crowd gathered, many people from Bango. Those boys then came, and Dzilo's wife asked, 'What's happened to them?'

They said, 'You're asking what's happened! You'll eat your own flesh today. One of ours is finished in that hut here. He is dead. When you look after our people, we are getting killed. We don't want you to keep people in this way. And what should we do now that our person has died?'

And they asked for a cart to carry that person to the river. They said, 'We hid, we are trying to avoid being seen again. If we are captured we'll be taken to prison.'

Then they phoned to others [using their radio telephone]. And we found that at the river, they were as thick as the mud, there were so many other boys of the war, who had come with the army.

Ah, then they made us sit down. We were carrying rocks, and we were just quaking in fear. We were quaking and thinking, 'Our children too have gone to the army. They have been protected [in Sindebele, *nciniwa*] by other people. We haven't ourselves borne these, but they have their mothers, too.' Oh, we were trembling in fear!

While others were digging over there, they said to us. 'Carry them [the rocks for covering the grave]'. When it was all done, they said, 'Who is Dzilo's wife?' She said, 'It's me.' Then one of them kicked her with his feet and shoes. He kicked her until he knocked her teeth out, there in the midst of us all, where we were sitting.

We felt the pain, terribly, terribly. Oh, when I tell about it. I begin to tremble again. I tremble.

They said, 'Woman, today you will eat your own flesh.'

Baka Sala was overcome by her memory. The horror of it left her speechless for a moment, and when she recovered her voice, she spoke in a whisper at first,

When they finished digging, they asked the people, 'Hey, those people that you lived with and went with were they practising sorcery or what were they doing?' People said, 'We really don't know what happened.'

After they finished covering over the dead, they divided us into bunches. 'Those who have children who have gone to the army should raise their hands.' In those days there were still not many people whose children had gone to the army. So I raised my hand and Baka Lufu [the widow of Dzilo's brother, Mfila] did too. We were only two.

'Ah, this is why you gang up, and kill the children of other people. It's because you all have your own children still. None have gone to the army.' When they were casting away the dead, they called father and rushed him into speaking in his own defence. Then they summoned the grandmother of Lamba [the neighbour closest to the guerrilla's camp]. She feared they were going to batter her and finish her off. But they left her. When we returned to our homestead, just when we got to the gate, we heard that another one of their people had died. [Baka Sala pointed to the sun, to show that it was about one o'clock in the afternoon.] He died over there at [a nearby place] and was buried by [a neighbour] just behind the homestead.

When those lads went away, they called together all those people over there at Bango. We were not yet summoned, but they went to the homestead of [the Chief's younger brother] to order everyone, 'Go, you are going to see the killing of a dog.' What did they mean? They meant the wife of Dzilo, and her daughter.

At that time, we forgot that we were at home in our own homesteads. We were suffering so in that time of the war. It was all going on in front of that homestead we were building when you left us. We kept on hearing the sound of, *kwakwa, kwakwa, kwakwa* [automatic rifles firing]. We heard it after their people died, and father said, 'What's happened?' So we rushed out of our hut with no blankets around us, and when we were in the thick of the mopane trees, father said, 'There is nothing we can do about it, even if we hurry. But the place belongs to me, and I am the one who is the senior over here. If I run away, what can I do? Where there is death, I too die. They will come back and ask, 'Where has Buka, the place's master, gone?'

So we returned and went into [her co-wife] Baka Yenda's hut, all of us: including Lamba [an adult grandson of Lupondo's brother]. We slept crowded together like that [she showed one fist clenched within the other hand]. We said that when it's finished, we'll hear about it. We can't go to hear about it without being summoned. Eventually, we'll hear about it. [Then she folded her hand by her head, showing them all sleeping.]

Ah, we slept, and woke in the morning about 8 o'clock. Children arrived coming to father, children of Dzilo, saying that granny was killed last night. Ah, then the child of Lupondo [Buka] went out, terrified, and when he got to where she had been killed, he found the old woman fallen down here and her child outside over there. Her guts were spread on the ground. Father looked, and he thought, 'How can such a thing be done? She has not been left alive as a person. [She died mutilated in a way that denied her humanity as a person.]'

Father and Gwati [Buka's younger brother] were suffering by themselves. They pulled and lifted the corpse laying it down in the hut. Others were afraid to come near them.

'What can we do? Can we dig once more? [They had dug once to bury Dzilo.] If we are found digging a grave once more, we will be taken prisoner.'

'So we'll be taken. What else can we do? If we are taken, we are taken. What comes will come.'

Then they took a pick, over there at the river, found a little ant heap, and hurriedly dug very lightly into it, for they were afraid that if found doing it, some more of us would be killed. This time the Boers [the whites of the Rhodesian army] would say, 'What are you doing over here?' Baka Gumbo [Gwati's wife] and I pulled the cart with the people in it, and Baka Yenda [her co-wife] and Chigegwe [a crippled son of Lupondo's brother] pushed it from behind. Having merely scratched the surface, we took those two people and just stuffed them in the hollow. We were, father, Gwati, and [a kinsman], Baka Yenda [her co-wife], Baka Gumbo [Gwati's wife] and Chigegwe [a crippled son of Lupondo's brother]. All the rest had fled, just fled. After we had barely covered them, we turned around and went back home. There was no wake, no wailing, no lamenting the dead.

Oh, [Baka Sala groaned] to just be covered over and hidden in your own home place! They [the guerrillas] said, 'They had practised sorcery, and they are the ones who killed those people over there.' When father had just cast away the bodies, they came back to him and said: 'Elder, today we load the burden on you, because you are the father. You are the first among these people. Do you see the infant that has remained, the little red one? You are the one who knows what must be done. Soon something will happen to these hamlets, and the people will flee carrying their children on their backs. And you will see to this one.'

Ah, that little red one came to me, and he cried through the night.

And it did happen that we had to flee and sleep without eating. Yet in our homestead there was enough food to feed us all. Smith's soldiers [of the Rhodesian Army] came and camped by our goat pen. They ate our chickens, they slaughtered our goats, and they made our pen feed their camp. They would spend the whole day there, sometimes going about shooting. We were terrified, and while they were there, we had no homestead of our own. How we grieved and suffered in that time of the war! Father and Gwati suffered very, very greatly.

## THE ORDEALS OF THE SURVIVORS

Baka Sala spoke with a painful realism that reminded me of the way that, in the earlier generation of elders, Baka Chedza gave witness in peacetime. Not only had Baka Sala reached the same phase of elderhood, but the wartime ordeals of her life no longer allowed her to look back, as she once had, telling a naive romance. Placing Buka as father at the centre of her account of their wartime lives, Baka Sala, like Baka Chedza, talked to me as a mother does to her child. By contrast to Baka Chedza, however, and being a more active Christian, she took much more comfort in the power of God, in seeing the presence of God in the good that survived the terror.

Baka Sala's realism revealed her strong ambivalence towards the guerrillas. On the one hand, she told very painfully of the terror they struck in committing the atrocity of Dzilo's death. On the other, she recalled their respect for Buka as father, their concern that he take responsibility for the others as his children, their care for the helpless orphan of the man they murdered, and their warning about the imminent danger from the arrival of the Rhodesian Army. Later, when she told me about the guerrillas during the recent counter-insurgency war, she also recalled the guerrillas' careful warning of the danger from looting by soldiers.

There was no such ambivalence in what Baka Sala, or for that matter anyone else in the family, remembered about the soldiers in the liberation war or in the post-independence counter-insurgency war, especially the soldiers of the notorious Fifth Brigade. Each of these forces was an unmitigated evil, although the Fifth Brigade was felt to be an evil even greater than the Rhodesian Army.

In the light of their earlier inward-looking concerns, I found a great change in the accounts family members gave me of their lives and in the personal stories they told among themselves at feasts and beer drinks or, more privately, at night around a hearth in the compound. They made ordeals the focus of many of their current stories. If, in the past before the wars, they had woven a world of family understandings around quarrel stories, they were recreating another world in its place, after the wars, by telling of how they survived in the face of the suffering which war and its aftermath brought them. In this change, some older women told of how, unarmed yet driven to resistance in defence of their homes, they had acted with that heroic quality, usually attributed distinctively to men, of *chibindi*, 'fierceness, reckless courage'. But most of their ordeal stories were about heroes or heroines as victims of terror and superior force. They were terrorised by the armed forces or, in the case of labour migrants, as ex-combatants accused of going to South Africa to train to be 'dissidents', by the police. Even more revealing is the fact that certain ordeals remained largely outside the personal discourse in which family members recreated their experience as shared memory. The unspoken and, perhaps after the atrocities of the post-independence war, the unspeakable, were the

ordeals of the family members as guerrillas. 'Freedom fighters' remarked the
teenage younger brother of one, 'don't like to talk about the war and their
fighting. They sometimes sit alone or with others not talking, and they don't
want to tell others about their experiences, which grieve them and trouble their
thoughts so much they just want to forget.'

The end of the liberation war and independence for Zimbabwe in 1980
brought a brief interlude, more a fleeting ceasefire than a peace in the province
of Matabeleland South where Lupondo's family lived. The ex-guerrillas left
the army, and many returned home in that year and the next. The war had been
so catastrophic that it was hard for some mothers of guerrillas in Lupondo's
family even to hope for their sons' return. Mfila's widow Baka Lufu remembered having to be stoical:

> I tried to disregard them [the sons who went to war], not thinking I would
> ever see them again. Then I heard he [her second son] had crossed over,
> but I just disregarded it, expecting his death at the war. [A neighbour]
> then found he was at Plumtree [the district headquarters], injured. I
> refused to believe it and said, 'You are lying, when you say you saw him at
> Plumtree. Oh, how can he return, when he has gone in that way.' She
> said, 'I really saw him.' I still refused, 'Don't try me on. I'll rejoice when I
> see him actually coming into the homestead.' And when I did see him, I
> was astonished. I just looked at him at first, looking and looking and then
> after some time I greeted him. 'Is it really you?' 'Yes, it's me.' 'Oh, yes?'
> 'Yes.' He came when the soldiers weren't here. I said, 'They'll return and
> shoot him', not wanting him to be here. Others came and just squatted
> here, too, looking and being astonished. He came with some others he had
> been 'working' with, and then they went off. They were a dangerous
> gang. If they had come without their guns, we wouldn't have feared so
> much. A gun is very frightening, and when we see it, we are terrified that
> we might get killed. People with guns are made mad by them.

### THE CATASTROPHE OF QUASI-NATIONALISM

The period immediately after independence became a time of sporadic violence between opposed forces of ex-combatants. It was also a time of attacks by
bands of ex-combatants against civilian targets, including white farmers, still
in control of vast areas of Matabeleland despite the liberation war. The
hostilities advanced struggles for power which had been waged during the
liberation war, but not resolved.

Two separate guerrilla armies, the Zimbabwe People's Revolutionary
Army (ZIPRA) led by Joshua Nkomo and the Zimbabwe National Liberation
Army (ZANLA) under Robert Mugabe, fought the liberation war. They
made an uneasy alliance towards the end of it but, as Martin and Johnson
reported:

> There had been difficulties between ZANLA and ZIPRA from the outset,

and at two joint training camps . . . there had been clashes and a considerable number of ZIPRA guerrillas had been killed. There had been
differences over political education, strategy and methods of mobilization
(1981, p. 243).

The two forces were unlike in so many ways, and perhaps most importantly
in ZIPRA's greater emphasis on the build-up of a regular or more conventional
army outside the country. In accord with their differences, they had rival
sources of support: among others, the Russians heavily backed ZIPRA and the
Chinese, ZANLA.

All the guerrillas in Lupondo's family joined ZIPRA. They joined it as most
others did in the region immediately around Matabeleland and centred on its
major city, Bulawayo. ZIPRA had its main base in Zambia along Zimbabwe's
north-western border from which it recruited guerrillas primarily, though not
exclusively, from western Zimbabwe. Apart from English, and for some their
first language was Kalanga or Venda or even Tswana, the *lingua franca* of these
guerrillas was Sindebele. The rest of the country, dominated by speakers of
distinct Shona dialects from numerous colonial tribes, provided most of the
guerrillas for ZANLA, which was by far the larger of the two armies. Neither
of the armies was homogeneous, ethnically or racially, and each of the armies
espoused the causes of unity against colonial domination and of freedom for all,
irrespective of race, tribe or gender. But the recruiting of the armies on a
regional basis was itself a process that polarised people who came to be
identified by language as Shona or Ndebele. The nationalist struggle thus fed
and in turn was fed by its antithesis, the polarisation of two quasi-nations or
super-tribes, the Shona against the Ndebele.

The powerful reality of that polarisation was and is a creation of present
politics, not a mere survival of pre-colonial chiefdoms. Nor is it to be explained
away as simply a consequence of a colonial policy of divide and rule according
to which white settlers invented two hostile tribes, for their own purposes.
Such invention, elaborated in settler mythology and settler state propaganda,
was perhaps a necessary but certainly not a sufficient basis for the polarisation
(on the invention of ethnicity in Zimbabwe, see Ranger, 1989b). Quasi-
nationalism, like the nationalism with which it breeds, is a movement of ideas
and practices that wins its often cruelly violent moments within the formation
of the nation-state in the twentieth century. If energised by a myth of being
prior to the nation state, of revenging old scores left as unsettled from ancient
hostilities, quasi-nationalism is none the less made in and by the struggle for
power and moral authority in the nation state. Nor should quasi-nationalism
be confused with ethnicity, which operates differently in different situations,
irrespective of any dominant cleavage dividing the nation.

The catastrophe of quasi-nationalism is that it can capture the might of the
nation state and bring authorised violence down ruthlessly against the people
who seem to stand in the way of the nation being united and pure as one body.

In such times, agents of the state, acting with its full authority, carry out the violation of the person. It is as if quasi-nationalism's victims, by being of an opposed quasi-nation, put themselves outside the nation, indeed beyond the pale of humanity. They are dealt with ferociously not merely for the sake of political dominance by one part of the nation over another, but importantly also for the sake of the moral renewal of the nation as a whole. The attack by the state on the victims' own bodies, in the present instance, by starvation and torture, even to death, seems to fulfil the objective of purifying and cleansing the body of the nation.

It took some years after independence for quasi-nationalism to command the full force of the state against the people of Matabeleland. The independence elections followed the regional division fostered in the course of the liberation war (see Cliffe *et al.*, 1980). Mugabe's party, the Zimbabwe African National Union (Patriotic Front) (ZANU, PF), which won most of the country apart from Matabeleland and areas nearby it, gained almost three times as many seats in Parliament as Nkomo's Zimbabwe African People's Union (ZAPU). Reconciliation was Mugabe's announced policy, and to overcome the division between people in different parts of the country, Mugabe as Prime Minister formed a coalition government that included Nkomo and several other ZAPU members in the cabinet.

The coalition did not last, however. Mugabe ended it and fired Nkomo from the cabinet early in 1982 in the face of the increasing violence in Matabeleland, including a major battle between ex-ZIPRA and ex-ZANLA forces in a township of Bulawayo, and in the face of government suspicion, rejected by a treason trial judge, that arms cached on farms owned by Nkomo and his party were meant to be used in a coup d'état (Lawyers Committee for Human Rights, 1986, p. 21). It was feared also that there was an alliance between the enemy within and the enemy without; that 'dissidents' had the support of South Africa as part of its destabilisation policy intended to undermine the neighbouring states in the region (see Nkomo, 1984, pp. 222–8).

Holding Nkomo's party, ZAPU, ultimately responsible, Mugabe decided to quash 'dissident activities', 'banditry', 'lawlessness' in Matabeleland. The Lawyers Committee for Human Rights reported:

> in a speech to a rural Ndebele audience near Nkayi, a particularly volatile region, in April 1983 Mugabe publicly alleged Ndebele support for the rebels and articulated the strategy behind the government's response: 'Where men and women provide food for the dissidents, when we get there we eradicate them. We don't differentiate when we fight, because we can't tell who is a dissident and who is not' (1986, p. 38, citing from *The Times* of 27 April 1983).

One of the extreme measures of the late Rhodesian state, from 1973 onwards, was 'collective punishment', imposed under the emergency powers, directed against whole communities as supporters of guerrillas, and including the use of curfews and in some cases the closure of schools and stores (Cilliers, 1985, pp. 16–17). Under Mugabe's government, using the same emergency powers, the new nation state brought back 'collective punishment'.

Early in 1983, Mugabe's government unleashed an army of mostly Shona-speaking soldiers, ex-ZANLA guerrillas who came from outside Matabeleland. Among them was the elite force known as the Fifth Brigade, trained by North Koreans and directly responsible to Mugabe, thus by-passing the usual chain of command in the rest of the army. The army, if a national army in name, was quasi-national in intent and practice. It was a punitive army which, along with the police, behaved like an occupying force come down upon an alien people to strangle them into submission, and if need be by starving everyone, women, children and the old indiscriminately.

There is already a considerable body of evidence documenting the looting and atrocities committed against civilians by that army and by the notorious Fifth Brigade. The Lawyers Committee for Human Rights gave this résumé of the evidence:

> The pattern of abuse [of human rights] can be broken down roughly by year. It began in early 1983 with the deployment of the army's Fifth Brigade, which was accused of massive abuses against civilians in Matabeleland; it advanced into 1984 with the imposition of a 24-hour curfew on Matabeleland South and the use, for the first time on a large scale, of food as a tool of coercion; it continued throughout 1985, beginning with the abductions of Zapu officials and ex-Zipra combatants in the first four months of the year, and concluding with the detention without charge of more than two hundred Zapu leaders and supporters after the Parliamentary elections in July (1986, p. 300).

The terror brought back the most brutal methods of the Rhodesians but imposed them even more ruthlessly and far more devastatingly throughout southern Matabeleland.

At Bango, although the Fifth Brigade as a whole was considered to be merciless, some people told me that certain attacks on them were by soldiers taking the law in their own hands. But many people dismissed the idea that the attacks were simply a matter of soldiers running wild. The attacks were seen to be well planned and deliberate, aimed against some of the most prominent men. As I reported in Chapter 1, the Chief himself was murdered at his own homestead by soldiers of the national army in May 1984, although he was officially reported slain by 'dissidents'.

A popular name for this period of counter-insurgency, *Gukurahundi*, is revealing. According to a school textbook, written from a ZANU point of view to teach the nationalist lesson of history to the children of Zimbabwe, 'ZANU President Mugabe named 1978 the "Year of the People" and 1979 *Gore reGukurahundi*, the "Year of the People's Storm"' (Seidman, Martin and Johnson, 1982, p. 129). 'Rain after threshing, early spring rains' is the pre-war translation in the *Standard Shona Dictionary* (Hannan, 1959, p. 228). *Gukurahundi*, as Mugabe named it, was the culmination of the people's war, the year when the storm of the nationalist struggle brought the victory of majority rule; the Lancaster House agreement, ending the war, was signed in December 1979. That was the *Gukurahundi* of nationalism, with its promise of moral renewal in the image of spring rains.

The name took on a different force, however, transferred in place and time to the region around Matabeleland and the war from 1983 onwards. For people of Bango, it was a *Shona* name that meant, 'the sweeping away of rubbish', and they explained to me that the 'rubbish' the Shona soldiers intended to sweep away were the people of Matabeleland themselves. 'Rubbish', *malala*, is used among Kalanga for the pollution of death. 'Those MaShona wanted to finish off all the people in Matabeleland' was the expressed opinion of many at Bango. It is significant that the intent of the attack was perceived, not simply in terms of old scores—and I was told by members of Lupondo's family that the Shona soldiers took loot from them, Kalanga, calling it 'the cattle stolen from our forefathers by you Ndebele'—but also in terms of a moral renewal, the purification of the country from rubbish. The Fifth Brigade, known too by the people of Bango as *Gukurahundi*, was perceived to be, as Lupondo's son Tengi said, 'evil without humanity'. The *Gukurahundi* of nationalism gave way to its monstrous twin in the *Gukurahundi* of quasi-nationalism.

> That was not an army, [Buka's brother Gwati told me in great anger], an army does not beat up women and old men like that and burn people alive in their huts. All of it was against the law. And why did they fight in the country and not in the city? When we were starving in the country, people were eating well in the city. People who fled there were safe. Next time, we won't stay. We'll just leave everything, and not listen to them when they tell us you must not leave your homestead empty. No, if it comes again, we will just die, we can't survive another one'.

Virtually all of the former guerrillas from Lupondo's family who came home after the Liberation War ended in 1980, had to flee from the countryside during the ensuing counter-insurgency war. Like other ex-freedom fighters, who had fought under Nkomo in ZIPRA, the former guerrillas from Lupondo's family became prime targets, among others, for torture and beatings. To be an able-bodied young man was, by that very fact, to be guilty. It was simply too dangerous for the former guerrillas to stay home. Their lives were at risk in the countryside. Towns in Zimbabwe, Botswana, and South Africa became their refuge. After the counter-insurgency war, despite the government's withdrawal of troops, the declaration of an amnesty in 1988, and the end to any immediate threat to their lives, some of them remained uneasy about coming home. Almost none of them were home during my return visit in 1989; most were in South Africa working as labour migrants. Their absence was due in good measure also to the impoverished state of the countryside, following the looting of crops, cattle and personal goods and, most recently, the run of bad years and severe drought.

The only former guerrilla among Lupondo's grandsons who was present during my return visit was Mbulawa, a young man home for ritual treatment while convalescing from a nervous breakdown. Mbulawa had joined the national army after the liberation war, then left it during the counter-insurgency hostilities, and remained in town until the worst of the danger was past. This is what he told me about his war and post-war experiences and the lessons they taught him:

I went to war in 1977, going through Botswana, where I stayed for about two or three months before moving on to Zambia. I was with Mphundu then Mayeba while in Zambia and then I went to Libya to be with the Arabs and Gadhafi, Mohammed Gadhafi, the leader of Libya. It was a pleasant country. They were training us for battle. They spoke about their revolution, and taught us that we too must rule ourselves. During the war we fought in the operations at Nkayi and Gokwe, where we would get into the open country and have engagements, many of us going during the day time. People were all mixed together. Europeans and blacks. We often sat down to hear that we must join together all of us, and not divide as Europeans and blacks; that we must be one people. Together we were fighting to free the country so that we could live well. I don't think we can ever agree if someone comes along and says we must fight again. We fought and it is finished. Now we must make 'Unity' and have mutual understanding. [Mbulawa spoke at a time when Mugabe had received Nkomo back into the cabinet and ZANU and ZAPU were negotiating their unity in one party.] That will be just. We don't want 'tribalism'—you are a European, you are Ndebele, you are Shona—no, we don't want that; we want all of us to be one people.

After the war, I spent some time in the national army and came out of it to stay in town. I wanted to work at home, not just anywhere or abroad. I had fought for the country and I wanted to live in it, to live and work at home. I had gone away suffering, and had enough of that thing of going here and there. I wanted to be home and to work in the country of our home. So I went to work for myself, with a licence, peddling tomatoes and vegetables.

I met my wife when I was peddling. We had two children and lived in town until I brought her here to live. That's when we started not to get along with each other. She didn't want to build here, she wanted to live in town, but I wanted very much to build at home.

Peddling wasn't much money, barely enough to live on. Some days you'd sell little and it would rot, sometimes you'd get as much as $30 a day. You couldn't tell from day to day. It would have been better if it had been a small shop, where I could have sold soap and other things. But I

found that I was getting more and more ill, and decided I would be better
off going home to stay here. Now what I want is to find some work, feed
my children, and have enough to eat and live on. If we have enough to eat,
things are right; if we go in hunger, they are wrong.

Having suffered frequent bouts of weakness and depression living in town,
Mbulawa suddenly lost control of himself, ran amok, and was brought home
by friends at Christmas in 1988. His ritual treatment, initiation into the
possession cult known as Sangoma in Sindebele or Changoma in Kalanga, was
meant to bring him into better communication with the dead. I say more in the
next chapter about the participation of Lupondo's family in the revival of this
cult. Safe in town during the eighties, Mbulawa had no personal experience of
the Fifth Brigade and its immediate impact on the countryside, and compared
to those who had known that directly, he spoke with much greater hope in the
promise of a coming 'unity' of 'one people'.

But how did comrades of family members remember the liberation war?
What were their memories of how they fought and what they were fighting for?
My attempt to discover the answers was largely, if not totally, unsuccessful.
The failure arose from the very predicament I sought to understand: the
heroism of the guerrillas, their glories, and their wartime suffering had been
marginalised, blocked from the personal discourse shared with people at
home. Nevertheless, I did put my questions about the war to neighbours and
comrades of the former guerrillas from Lupondo's family. What they told me
expressed their anger and frustration at being impoverished and brutalised in
their own country after having fought and won a war 'to free the country so that
we could live well and rule ourselves'.

One such comrade was Keti, who had gone to join ZIPRA with Gwati's son
Chibindi, having let it be known first, as a cover, that they were going back to
work in South Africa. Keti recalled.

We went together on foot, and our journey was not much to talk about,
although we suffered along the way crossing over to Botswana. The
soldiers were around us, and we had to hide and cross over in the evening.
Later we went to Zambia and then Angola for intensive training so that
when we went forward we wouldn't be in trouble. We had to eat rats.
Sometimes we would be woken up from sleep and rushed into water. It
was cold, colder than these past three days of winter, and you'd get into
the cold water with everything even your blankets. We suffered hardship
there and when we fought, but I wasn't surprised by that, because that's
what we went for, what we were prepared for. The thing that shocked us is
what happened here. We thought we had won the country and then found
we were being killed [in the counter-insurgency war]. Why was the
government killing us for what we won? We are the ones who won
Zimbabwe and made independence. Yet we were being killed again. We
couldn't understand that. We struggled and we made Zimbabwe great.

When we went off to fight, we thought that afterwards we would find work in our own country. But now we can't get any work. We are just sitting, doing nothing. We see nothing that is really helping us. We thought that if we ruled ourselves, we would find work. But it's still as it was. Ah no [expressing disgust and dismay], it's just the same.

A son-in-law of Buka's, a comrade who joined Gwati's son in Zambia, said: When we started to fight for the country, we went to Botswana and from there to Zambia, where we stayed as refugees. Everything was in short supply. Airplanes came and bombed us. Then we went for training in Angola, where we stayed a long time, about six months, until we finished our training and came back. We fought in Sipolilo and in Kariba living in the open country. We'd go great distances on foot, more than from here to Plumtree [over 70 miles], day and night. When you're in the war, you can't live well. You have to bear hardship. That's when you fight with all your strength, and the war was fought fiercely. Many died at the war. Now we see that things are still not right. People are starving. Rain doesn't fall. Nothing is all right. Things are just the same, the way they were a long time ago, before we fought, only now they are worse. You can't find a job. Instead of 'developing' everything is going down, down. They don't consider us now the way they did when we were fighting.

I found that unemployed former guerrillas expressed much resentment at not getting work in Zimbabwe, because they had taken it for granted that one aim of fighting the war to win control of the country was to secure jobs in Zimbabwe for the people, above all the freedom fighters. It was not solely a matter of being able to earn a decent wage but, as Lupondo's grandson Mbulawa and others explained it to me, of truly coming home after having suffered abroad.

And how did the people who remained at home see their predicament? Peace had come at last to their chiefdom of Bango in 1988, the year before my return. But the elders of Lupondo's family said they were not yet truly at ease, that they still felt anxious, tense in their very guts. 'We worry that the war will come back', said the widow of Dzilo's brother Mfila.

We really think it hasn't finished. We say that someday we'll hear the rifles shooting again. So here it is not truly well and all right. We have rejoiced, but we still remember.

Feeling outraged, they had been virtually helpless to defend themselves and yet, they insisted, they remained unvanquished. 'We have been burnt, but we have come through the fire alive', one of Buka's widows, Baka Yenda said. She and other elders told me that they were deeply glad that I had returned, but they thanked God that I had gone, for had I remained they were sure I would have been killed.

'At that time [during the recent war] people fled their homesteads',

Lupondo's son Tengi said, explaining that he himself had lived at a distant
village or 'rural business centre' as a storekeeper, fearful of coming home. He
continued:

> Now people have come back to begin to rebuild their homesteads. It was
> heavy in those times, and the people who remained behind, oh [he
> groaned painfully]. Over here, people were troubled and beaten, some so
> badly they had to be taken to a hospital. But over there [at the village] that
> was not done by the soldiers. They camped at their base by the store.
> When they went outside to the countryside, then they troubled the people
> there. Here at the store they would leave us alone; they would simply
> come and buy at the store. We would open for them and then they would
> go, after paying. They didn't take it free but paid their money. Some were
> bad, some were right. You couldn't tell in advance. Some would come and
> be rough and wrong. Some would be all right, but the Fifth Brigade were
> only evil. If you made them puzzled [suspicious] about you, they just
> killed you.

'Life really goes on', Baka Sala, the second of Buka's widows, said, beginning her recollection once again, but this time speaking with almost none of the
laughter she had so enjoyed when telling her romantic life history as Buka's
young and favourite wife. This time we spoke virtually alone at her compound,
apart from the brief presence of a young neighbour. Very recently widowed—
her husband Buka died in old age after she nursed him through his last years of
a lingering illness—Baka Sala wore a black kerchief which heightened the
tormented look that came over her face fleetingly as she went on:

> And we are surviving. We are truly alive because we are able to see you
> once again. But we were not very much alive before when we had no way
> of knowing whether we would ever see anyone like you again. The [most
> recent] war was so overwhelming. We lay down, but not to sleep. We had
> nothing to eat. We fled our homes. We were beaten [with poles]. What
> could we do? They [soldiers of Zimbabwe's national army] drove lorries
> into the field over there, took all our maize, filling their lorries, and ate it
> up by themselves. We ourselves had to climb trees to escape. We thought
> our people were going to be killed in our homes. And we who had climbed
> the trees begged them to let us alone. We went along like this, shivering
> and trembling. Yet God is here, and we lived. But others among us did not
> survive. We who survived are now really alive, seeing again our child with
> whom we lived so well.

I asked Baka Sala to tell me more about what had happened in the later war
of *Gukurahundi*, and she responded.

> Smith's army brought us grief, but later we saw that Smith's war was
> better than the war of *Gukurahundi*. That war which came later, the
> *Gukurahundi*, we saw that it went much, much further, because our
> children who had gone away to fight came home and found war again at

home. It finished people off. Oh, those Mashona who came to be too many here, oh [she groaned in pain].

Yes, Smith's war was better, we found later. That war did not leave so many corpses of our people around here. Compared to this one just now, no [she shook her head to convey how much worse the recent war was]. In this one people have been taken and stuffed into mines. At Balagwe [in another part of Matabeleland] a very large mine has been dug for all the corpses. People have just been finished off. They [the soldiers] were simply killing and stuffing them in until it made the missionaries object; and they wrote to other countries, saying that what's being done here is wrong, people are being killed off. It was devastating. That other war was better.

During the curfew [in 1984], we lived on marula fruit juice and water. The stores were shut, and you could die with your money because you couldn't buy anything. It went on for two whole months. Whoever died, died; and if you had God with you, you lived. Some became cripples. We were beaten then by poles the way today we are beaten by the wind. They would beat you severely, and force you to lie down, shouting 'You are a liar', until you'd say, 'Yes, I saw them [the guerrillas]'. In that time of the curfew, we spent the day clapping hands and singing. We had to draw water for them, and we had to go on singing [for them] until the sunset. We really suffered. But God came and freed us. So now though it is not forgotten, we act as if we have forgotten. But when you do think of it, you remember others of yours who are gone. Yet God has come to us, and he gave them that gift that made them die as they did.

In those days, church meetings were not allowed, and schools were closed. It was very bad. Girls were taken by force and made to draw water. You couldn't ask a girl who had gone off where she'd gone and what she had been doing. And if they thought you were bad, they just beat you. They had their own law. It had nothing to do with what you wanted, what you wanted to build up. You couldn't rule your own child. They would just say, 'Girl, come right away' and the child would have to get up and go. They would take her, do what they wanted and let her go.

Sala [her first-born, an ex-guerrilla] had a wife he came home with after he had been a soldier over there. Then the war began again and everything was so much worse. The soldiers came, they entered into our daughter-in-law and raped her. The lad [Sala] said, 'Uh, uh, my parents I see that you cannot live in this way. You may try sometime to ask about what they were doing.' The woman, too, said to us, 'My parents, if you try to find out, you will fight, and you will die.' So my son said, 'Better she should just go back to her home.' That is when the lad freed his wife and let her go home. He went then to South Africa, to Johannesburg. He said also, 'I am still thinking about you. Don't feel that I have abandoned you. God will want to give me what belongs to me, so that another one will live with you at home.'

Once when the shooting broke out, I was by the bus stop over there, driving our cattle. I panicked to get to the river beyond that, and I stopped near a Ntshentsheni tree. I said to myself that the Bible says, 'There will come a time, when it is the time of Armageddon.' It is a time when you go here and there and can find nothing to hold on to. Everyone grabs for someone to hold on to, and everyone tells the other, 'Let go of me.' That way was mine on that day. I let the cattle go. Even though the river was full, I crossed to sleep at a son-in-law's. I was doing something that was unbecoming, a mother-in-law going to sleep at the son-in-law's. I said, 'Am I to climb the Ntshentsheni [tree]? I'll fall down.' So I slept there at the son-in-law's. Oh, in that time of war, we suffered, we really suffered, my child. But when you think of those events, you realise that God is here. He really is here in this time. He works.

Father [her husband], yes, he suffered, that person of [calling him by his clan name]. We had to take the clothes and goods of Ludo [her son] and hide them under the grass in that field. We stashed away our money, our blankets, anything and everything. Then the soldiers came, found it all, and took it away with them. Some of it they just scattered on the road, but they searched and searched for everything. They came with their lorries and packed them with our maize from our field.

Then the 'boys' [the guerrillas] came and said, 'Father speaking to Buka], you must take the rest, all that remains, and hide it, or they'll come and finish it all.' So we took away all the corn and stashed it in the threshing ground way over there.

Father was the one organising all the children [everyone else in Lupondo's family, especially the ex-combatants] and telling them you must support each other in this way and that way. Even in matters of hiding their clothes and things, they came to him seeking his help.

That's when we left that place and moved from our old site at the Mopane trees over there. They [the soldiers] had been saying, 'Why are you staying in the thick of the Mopane trees? You are the ones who are cooking for the "boys" in the woods.' So we removed from there to this place, and here is the place where father [her husband Buka] left us. And now we say, 'Thank God who has taken him from us here in the midst of people, and not over there at the Mopane trees.' We are thankful for that, that He kept him in the midst of people. God sees that you will die and follow others.

Baka Sala did not isolate her own family's suffering at the hands of the Fifth Brigade. Like other family members and neighbours, she saw their suffering in the light also of widely known stories of mass murder and other atrocities by the Fifth Brigade in different parts of Matabeleland. What she and others conveyed to me was their sense that the horror was beyond anything they had thought possible, that they could have imagined before.

Some of the nightmarish quality of their experience came from a virtually surrealist re-enactment of certain parts created in the liberation war. The Fifth Brigade soldiers were the merciless enforcers of collective punishment by the state, re-enacting the part of the Rhodesian forces, yet they represented themselves also as having the moral authority of freedom fighters, and they demanded displays of support of the kind they had known as freedom fighters. Such displays had been made during the liberation war in the night-long rally, known as *pungwe* in Shona and much used by ZANLA, and rarely if at all by ZIPRA (see Frederikse, 1984, pp. 60–3, 232; Nkomo, 1984, p. 162). In the *pungwe* the guerrillas led the people in discussions and in singing songs of liberation, to which the people clapped hands and responded with supporting choruses. The *pungwe* was a means of political education meant to mobilise the people and raise their consciousness in the national struggle. In their revival of the *pungwe*, or rather their introduction of it to people who had not known it before, soldiers of the Fifth Brigade acted as if they were the true makers of Zimbabwe as a nation. They were the heroes about whom and for whom were sung the popular Shona songs of *Chimurenga*, as the liberation war is known in Shona. In accord with that, the people they came to discipline were compelled to re-enact the parts of choruses supporting the freedom fighters—they had to learn the Shona songs, although few spoke Shona, and they had to clap while singing them in rallies that lasted the whole day. For the sake of making the people submit to their discipline, which also entertained the soldiers as something of a sport to watch, they pitted women from the chorus against each other as if they were gladiators. The women had to beat each other down, using poles. If the *pungwe* had taught some people the lessons of nationalism, the revival of the *pungwe* was political education of another kind entirely; it was a parody further alienating the people from their own state and raising their consciousness of quasi-nationalism and their awareness of the role of their own state in the polarisation of Shona and Ndebele.

Mfila's widow Baka Lufu testified to these lessons of alienation and distrust in her account of *Gukurahundi*:

> While they were here, I was beaten with a fence pole, and they had us beating each other until, when they thought we weren't beating each other well, they took the poles and beat us themselves. At the school, we the mothers were forced to fight each other. A woman thrashed you and you had to beat her too. They wanted to find out who would win against the others. When the soldiers forced us to do it, we were afraid and tried to beat carefully. But they urged us on, 'Beat hard'. And we did. 'You are idiots, cripples. Lift up the stick', they said. What could we do? So each of us went on [she snapped her fingers and made the sound of slapping], and in turns, until one ran away. Then they laughed and said, 'Ah, you have been defeated.'

We had to sing for them and clap. They ordered us, 'Sing'. I can't remember the songs any more. I have become like a bird on the wind now. Let the child sing them for you. There's no one who doesn't know them. We were co-operating so that maybe they'd open the stores.

Do you think that was living? That wasn't the life we had under Smith. No, no, Mugabe, oh . . . [she groaned in horror]. Mugabe made us live a life without any joy. That [curfew] of Smith's was 'right' [in English]. We were never set off fighting against each other. There was no killing of everyone including children. Children were never shot. The curfew that he [Smith] gave us was a proper curfew. If you didn't have a watch, you could look at the shadow of the hut, and see that the time had come for you to be able to go out. Then we could go without fearing anything. That curfew of Smith's was 'right'. You could go out when it was sunrise. But Mugabe's curfew didn't allow us to do that. Mugabe's curfew was heavy. You weren't allowed to go out of your hut at night [even to relieve yourself].

How could you help anyone else then? You couldn't. If you were going to help someone else with food, where would you yourself get it? And if you did give it to someone else, you'd get beaten, 'Where did you get it from?' Only the teachers were allowed to buy from town, and only in small packets, not a whole sack [of flour]. They weren't even allowed to buy two packets at a time. One, one only. How could that last when there were children in the homestead? Could it last even a week? Even the teachers could hardly make a little porridge for the children. Even water was short and enough couldn't be drawn for all.

How could we help each other? We would be sitting here when they would come and say, 'Where are they [the dissidents], Ma?' And you'd answer, 'No, I haven't seen them.' The soldiers would then ask, 'You haven't cooked for them here?'

How could you go on talking in that way, saying you haven't seen them, when the soldiers were after you in their way? They would say, 'You tell us the truth, you know you cooked for them.' Then they would beat you and beat you, 'Tell the truth. Tell the truth.' So then I just lied, because I felt such pain, 'I saw them over there where that woman was cooking for them', and that woman would get beaten. I just protected my own flesh, because I had already suffered so badly. I told about her, and she was beaten. And what was that? Was that life?

No, no. We slept in the countryside, in the woods. We couldn't sleep here in our homesteads. You got there and found a bit of grass to get under and just slept. You fled and hoped the army went past. You feared that over here they could find you in the homestead, and even if you told the truth, they would beat you. Oh, those people made us live weighed down by heaviness. Those people of Mugabe, oh [she groaned in horror], no, no. He was supposed to be governing the country, but they were making us live weighed down by heaviness, beyond anything we had ever known.

Smith was [in English] 'right' [by comparison].' Those [soldiers] of Smith's never did to us what *they* did to us. Smith never shut us out of the stores, but those people did. They wanted us to die of starvation. We spent the days crushing and eating marula fruit. We would put aside water for drinking, and simply lived from that tree. We took from it what we needed. When we went out at night [to relieve themselves], they didn't want to see you, and if they did, they would shoot you. We went about bent over, hiding ourselves. We had to get the goats into the pen well before sunset. We were merely squatting in our homesteads. It wasn't allowed for even a child to go out. If she did she would be killed.

'Where are you going? Aren't you going to give something to "those of the country" [guerrillas]. Why are you going out, if not to give to those *magandanga* [the Shona word for a thug or a criminal used by the Rhodesians for a "terrorist" and then by the National Army for a "dissident"] outside?' Then you'd get shot. They'd say you are lying. At night if you wanted to go out to urinate, they ordered you to go with a light, 'If you have no light, we'll shoot you. If you have no light, get yourselves tins. Stay in your huts, and don't go out at night, stay sleeping.'

Oh, the grandchild of this old woman here [she pointed to Lupondo's brother's widow Baka Tandiwe who sat with us along with other neighbours], she was nearly shot when she was bringing soil to smear the floor. She was trying to sneak out to get the soil. They came very quickly and surrounded our homestead, overwhelming it, they were so many. Lufu [her son] had gone out saying that he was going to see an ill child at the place of his father's younger brother. No sooner was he out than the whole homestead was full of them, bang full [she made the sound of 'pam', bang]. I was with my daughter-in-law [Lufu's wife].

'Who have you got with you'? they asked.

'We are alone.'

'You are just alone?'

'Yes, we only have the owner of the homestead [living with us], and he went to sleep where he was called to visit a sick child of his father.'

'Where?'

'Over in that homestead.'

'Did he go yesterday?'

He had gone earlier in the morning [breaking the curfew], but I said, 'Yes, yesterday.' The wife of Lufu was being pushed around to get her to tell the truth. But she said, 'He went yesterday at the right time. The time passed and he must have been afraid to come home.'

'Is that so?'

'Yes.'

One of them was then at the pen, and perhaps he saw something odd, seeing the child who was taking the soil. Suddenly, the one who came to the homestead opened the hut and said, 'Shoot, Shoot, man, shoot.' I was watching from inside, and cried out [the child's name], 'People, it's just [calling her name] a child.' That one was just going to open his rifle and shoot, when he was told not to kill, and it was finished. Otherwise, he would certainly have killed her. I was looking on, watching it all, early in the morning.

One of them was a Coloured, and when Lufu's hut was opened, he was tired and stretched out there, carrying his machine gun. He said, 'These are church people. There's nothing that's happened here. Others are telling lies about them. And the others are the ones who are protecting "the people of the country [guerrillas]."'' But another one went behind the granary, stole the knickers of our daughters, and threw clothes away outside. When we looked for Lufu's clothes, we found that the soldiers had stolen them. Ah, such people, they came as crooks, and they lied and stole clothes from us. Ah, those people, we will never forget them. And if we meet them in town, we will recognise their faces, and know they are the ones who troubled us so much.

We had to fill their canteens and bring them water. Once I said, 'There's no water, it's finished in the hut.' Ah, what had I said? What had I done? How they beat me! And they cursed me. They didn't want to go and get it elsewhere. [She gave a bitter, sardonic laugh at the memory.]

We may die but we can never forget. When we sleep, we wake up remembering it. However many years we live, we can never forget. We remember the suffering we endured. God was refusing to let us die. If He had wanted us to die, no one would now be left alive in this country. He said, 'The children should not die for a fault about which they know nothing [being innocent].' Some people did die, others remained, but most have died. Many homesteads have been closed, and no longer exist. Only children remain.

Did we really live? We can never forget that life that captured us. No, we can never forget. How can we ever forget?

The questions Baka Lufu put, reflecting upon the experience of surviving *Gukurahundi*, were rhetorical, to some extent. How could one manage to share food? How could one join in burying others? How could one avoid betraying others to the enemy, when the betrayal meant protecting oneself and one's own immediate kin? The answers were implied, up to a point. Baka Lufu was speaking to me at home, surrounded by some of her favourite kin, children, grandchildren, and immediate neighbours. She addressed herself to them as well as to me, asking, even urging, their agreement as witnesses who knew and understood from their own experience the self-evident truth. But Baka Lufu's questions were more than merely rhetorical in the sense of being simply for stylistic effect and thus not demanding a reply, spoken or tacit.

My companion and guide to her homestead, a youth about to marry into Lupondo's full brother's family, having fathered his girlfriend's child, was the son of a woman Baka Lufu had beaten, under duress from the soldiers, to the ground. It was a matter of some embarrassment to her. She admitted it freely, but with a rather uncomfortable, nervous laugh; and in talking about it, she seemed to be asking my guide, too, to agree that any other woman would have done the same, under the circumstances. If she wanted the truth she told to be taken as self-evident, she could not help but know that it was actually a contested truth. Her questioning, like the rest of her telling of the ordeals of *Gukurahundi*, had a force of self-justification in the continuing rehearsal, among intimates, of how the survivors had conducted themselves during the wars. Such questioning, understood within ordeal stories, were significant after the catastrophe of war for the reconstruction of character and the redefinition of the person as a moral being, no less significant than was the telling of quarrel stories after personal misfortune and moral disturbance in peacetime.

The significance of questioning such as Baka Lufu's went beyond even that, however. Being an active member of an Apostolic church, Baka Lufu represented the fact that she and others had survived as if it were a proof that God had protected them for the sake of their innocence. But her questioning seemed to me to be addressed to herself, at least as much as to others; it revealed an inner disquiet, an irresolvable doubt, and it conveyed the anxiety, perhaps the guilt, of a predicament she shared with other survivors of the catastrophe of *Gukurahundi*. It was the predicament of having to go on living as usual, taking things for granted once again, despite their experience of having had certain taken-for-granted truths of human existence called into question. The very fact that *they* had survived and at such cost, when so many others had died threatened their efforts to recreate that taken-for-granted world by renewing its truths in everyday practice.

Having survived one guerrilla war after another, members of Lupondo's family bore the lasting marks of collective punishment and terror on their bodies and in their memories. After the amnesty, although some did say they felt free once again, free 'as a bird on the wind', in Baka Lufu's words, they remained wary. They could neither forget nor forgive the atrocities of the wars. Nor could they make sense of their suffering in the liberation war by its part in making their country free of alien domination. The later war against *them* by their own state had cast the significance of their suffering in doubt. They had known the danger that the state becomes when it empowers quasi-nationalism, when it fixes collective guilt upon people as a quasi-nation within the nation and terrorises them as the dehumanised enemy within. Whether it would ever become possible for them to look forward to the future without a sharp regard for that danger remained an open question.

# 6

## Away From Home: Granddaughters, Mutual Security, and the Revival of the Past

Lupondo's granddaughter, Baka Ngoni, laughed in amazement, seeing me once again, after nearly thirty years' absence. We met in Bulawayo, outside the crowded house she rented from the municipality, and she was the first member of the family I found on my return. It took her a moment to realise, as she repeated to a great stream of curious neighbours, that the grey-bearded white man greeting her in Kalanga, was the same Mabuyani—my main Kalanga nickname, which is itself the greeting 'How have you returned?'—who had lived in the hut of her father Buka and who had been 'reared' in her mother's compound. My own amazement and laughter matched hers, she remarked, also, with some good humoured banter. An unmarried mother, nursing her first child, when I last saw her, she was hardly more than a child herself then, nearly sixteen, well developed but slim. If girlishly playful—and she enjoyed teasing me about my lack of appetite for the Kalanga delicacy of roasted caterpillars—she was very much the eldest daughter, aware of herself as the first born, the responsible senior; and she was given to being caring yet bossy towards her juniors. In her forties, now a buxom matron, the mother of twelve surviving children and grandmother of nine, she had grown huge. Yet for all my astonishment, I easily recognised her, and I felt that our shared laughter was itself a mutual recognition: we were aware of each other reflecting upon our old selves in the presence of our new appearances.

Baka Ngoni brought me to her front room, where she explained that her husband, a Mozambiquean immigrant, had not been long in the city when she met and married him. At the time she herself was also a newcomer, having left the countryside as soon as her first born was old enough to be weaned and given over to the care of her mother. Her father Buka who, she reminded me, 'loved the city' came to visit her regularly, often stayed about a week at a time, and would take back home clothes she sewed on her electric sewing machine for sale in the countryside. Seeing her settled permanently in town fulfilled her father's own ambitions for a life more like the one he had known during his many years in Johannesburg.

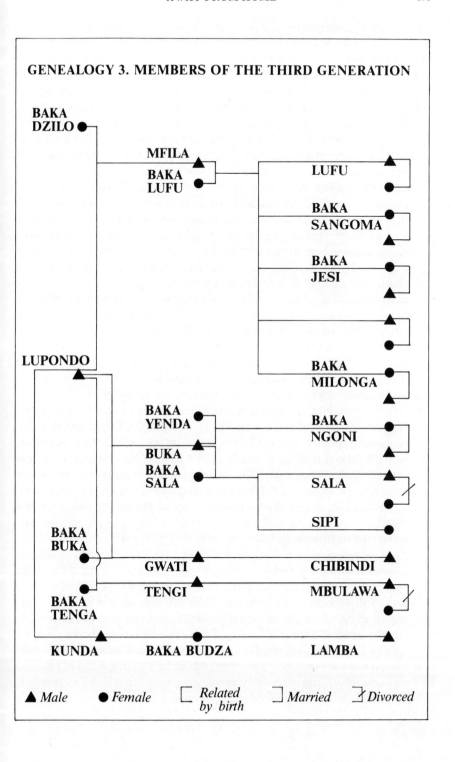

GENEALOGY 3. MEMBERS OF THE THIRD GENERATION

Baka Ngoni remembered the way her father had discriminated against her mother and favoured his junior wife Baka Sala. But that, Baka Ngoni told me, had not estranged *her* from her father, his junior wife Baka Sala or Baka Sala's children:

The way we were living at home, having two mothers [her own mother and Baka Sala], was heavy. Our father loved us, even though he didn't love our mother. Baka Sala was the one who was beautiful, and once our father lived with her, he couldn't be separated from her. But our father loved us more than Baka Sala's children, and he had no trouble with us. If our mother suffered, we ourselves didn't feel that, because our father cared for us. You could even see that for yourself. He didn't reject us no matter what we did. He still loved us. Even though he's dead now, we are in sympathy still. So too there's nothing wrong with Baka Sala. We have mutual understanding, and there's nothing else between us. Baka Sala's children come here to stay with us, for a month or a week, whatever they want, and we get along very well. You couldn't tell that we are the children of a polygynous marriage. Our mothers hated each other, but we have none of that. No, we children don't hate each other. And Baka Sala has no ill will towards us. I am not lying, she really loves us, and however late at night we come, she always rejoices to see us.

At her own homestead in Bango Chiefdom, Baka Sala reconstructed, in *her* memory, more of a basis of good will and mutual understanding between herself, her co-wife Baka Yenda and her husband Buka, when I broached the issue of the difficulties so many others had living as co-wives:

Yes, we ourselves did fight in the past, but you would not have seen that we did fight. When I came to marriage, I found Baka Yenda already at her compound. Father, Buka, arranged it that we ate together from one plate. When food was cooked, he would call us, saying 'My children, come and eat and drink all together.' We ate our plate of porridge together in that way. Our plate was one. Whoever cooked would say to the other one, 'Come and let's eat.' And when it came to ploughing, we were two together, one driving the oxen, the other holding the plough. So too, when it came to drawing water, we were two. There was never a third who came between us. [In Chapter 4 I record the contrary, the subject of some fierce quarrels between Buka, on one side, and, on the other, Baka Sala and her senior co-wife Baka Yenda, during the period of my first visit. Still something of a romantic, Baka Sala now ignores what she could regard as an exception of no consequence, and not part of the family's current image of their relationship. Such a third was actually the youngest wife of Lupondo's cousin Tobela, on whose behalf Buka tried to make special work arrangements and with whom he was suspected of committing adultery.] And even today people are amazed that Buka's wives hold on to each other and understand each other.

The ordeals the wives and the children suffered during the war had, if anything, brought them even closer to each other, according to Baka Sala:

Whatever little our children had, they would share with each other. Even during the curfew, when we were starving, if one of them picked something up, even something little, it was for all of them, and they would call each other together. They were all children of one person.

When I asked Baka Ngoni about the war years, she recalled:

In Smith's war, things were all right here. The suffering came later, in the time [1981, shortly after independence] of the shooting here [between ex-combatants from ZIPRA and ZANLA]. We almost died in our own house. The shoot-out began when I had a two day old child; yes, it was on the third day, when we were just home from the hospital. It started at Entumbane [at the nearby holding camp for ex-combatants]. Sipi [her half sister, Baka Sala's daughter] and I fled, trying to cross over to the other side. We tried to cross in this direction but we failed and then tried the other way. Running, we fell down right by that tar road [a main road not far from the house]. Sipi who was running with her child had to pick up the things she had been carrying. A bullet came and hit her child. She lost blood and died right there in that battle. Oh, we were being shot at and dying, when they were shelling each other at Camp Three [the holding camp for ex-combatants]. We fled until we got to Magwegwe 'location', to a child of my mother's brother, where we hid. How it started we simply do not know.

I didn't see anything of the *Gukurahundi* [the Fifth Brigade], because I was in town [during the counter-insurgency period after independence]. They didn't trouble us here. The trouble we had was during the battle in Entumbane. But at home, it was very, very hard during the curfew. No one could go about. They stopped the buses. I didn't go home during that time.

During our conversations, Baka Ngoni continued to speak of the countryside, and Bango Chiefdom, as home. She told me that she now thought that it was better to live at home:

There you plough and you can get all that you want, and if you don't you can still manage to buy it. But here, oh, the house costs money, food costs money, water costs money, electricity costs money. How can you find enough for all these things? At home you can get firewood for yourself. And at home this year, the people of our home do have crops. When you left us, it was very very pleasant still, because we were all still at home and not yet suffering. Now here in the city we really do suffer to support ourselves. It used to be so good at home, when you could build for yourself and buy what you wanted. Even if you went about at night, you had nothing to worry about. When I think of home, I think it is truly right there, because here in town you are troubled all the time by money. And recently, in these days, it has got much worse [in the recession and severe inflation following the boom immediately after independence, see Herbst, 1990, Chapter 9].

If the city was not truly home for Baka Ngoni herself, and if compared to the countryside, it looked worse in the face of the soaring cost of living, the city was, nevertheless, the place in which she had created a stable home for her children and her husband. Proudly displayed at the centre of her front room was her husband's framed certificate from the municipality. It honoured him for twenty-five years service as a municipal worker, most recently as a petrol pump attendant.

But did Baka Ngoni intend to give up the city and go back home to live there permanently? Not if it meant abandoning her husband; and he was much against living in the countryside. Although he once did accompany her there, since then whenever she went home, she did so by herself or, rarely, with some children. Her children, too, had little direct involvement in her home. Most of them could not speak Kalanga, and hardly understood it; they spoke Sindebele or English, and all had English names. When I asked my question in the presence of some of her cousins, including Baka Milonga, it was treated as a great joke, evoking peals of laughter. To expressions of agreement from Baka Ngoni and the others, Baka Milonga said,

> Could we really go back home? What could we do there? We still do know how to stamp grain, but it is heavy. We have got used to living in town, and we can't endure that now. Here we work, and then we rest. We work nicely and easily. We have days when we wash, and other days when we can stay without having to do hard work. The great thing is washing and ironing. We cook, but we don't have to stamp grain and carry water and fetch firewood. We just cook on the stove with electricity.

Baka Milonga went on to say how much worse life in town had become, compared to 1971, when she and her husband first rented a house:

> We yearn for Smith now. Where is 'our country' ['our country' being the country hoped for and promised before independence]? Where can we see it, when we are suffering so much? My husband is a machinist who sews, and I peddle paraffin. In Zimbabwe you can't live without doing many things. If you don't, you will lie down to sleep with nothing on the fire. The country has changed, and in Zimbabwe, there is no one who does not suffer. Can you manage in Zimbabwe without selling something? Those who sell, who go 'out' [around the city and to the countryside], are the ones who are all right. If you just stay sitting, not doing anything, there is no life in that. Both the husband and the wife have to do something to earn. You can't live well otherwise.

Listening to Baka Ngoni talk somewhat nostalgically of home and then visiting other granddaughters of Lupondo with her, I realised that even while leaving home, Baka Ngoni had managed, in at least one important respect, to recreate home around her. With much effort and great care, she helped to form a circle of sisters and cousins in town. The accomplishment of a home circle represents a remarkable change that distinguishes the third generation of Lupondo's family from the second. At present, half of Lupondo's grand-daughters, eighteen out of thirty-six, have settled more or less permanently in towns, mainly in the city of Bulawayo. Yet none of Lupondo's daughters had been able to do that, although at least one had gone to work in the city and returned home pregnant, to die in childbirth. It was the third generation of women in Lupondo's family who colonised the city, the second having failed to do so. Some of the granddaughters went as young girls; others as the mothers of several children whom they left behind in the countryside after divorcing or separating from their husbands.

Baka Ngoni was the pioneering settler among the women of her generation in the family. As the first of four full sisters, and already their leader in the countryside, she was well placed to become their pioneer. Even the fact that her father, being something of a misfit in the countryside, preferred town came to be an advantage for her. In the early 1960s, she set an example and then helped a number of Lupondo's granddaughters to follow her example in increasing numbers during the sixties and seventies. Baka Ngoni told me that when she herself went to the city to find work, she stayed, at first, with her mother's sister. Once married and in her own house, Baka Ngoni in turn brought sisters and cousins to stay with her, until they established themselves in the same or nearby parts of the city. In this way, and with the support of her husband and his friends, she made herself into a mainstay for a circle of kinswomen, including a core of eight granddaughters of Lupondo, her sisters and cousins.

Lupondo's granddaughters who chose to leave the countryside did so at a time when husbands were becoming scarcer, because women had lost the option of becoming junior wives. Instead, monogamy now prevailed through-out Bango Chiefdom (for a discussion of a major shift towards monogamy in much of southern Africa, see Solway, 1990). The change began even before my first visit, although I did not appreciate it at the time. In fact, Lupondo's leading sons, Dzilo and Buka, were the last family members to marry more than one wife, and they did so by the mid-1950s. At the time of my first visit, I was aware that their younger brothers were all monogamous. Yet the long-term, historical significance of that fact escaped me. It seemed simply to fit an early stage in their lives, similar to the stage polygynists had gone through in the past. Polygynists complained, I knew, that it had become harder and harder to support several wives and all their children. But I mistakenly took these and other complaints, which I report in earlier chapters, to be symptoms of endemic friction, and not a force for change or a reflection of fundamental rethinking about marriage and big families. In reality, that past was being rejected as a guide for the future.

By the time I returned to Lupondo's family, family members and their neighbours attributed the change quite simply to economic necessity. It had become the conventional wisdom, repeated to me by young and old, that it was bad to marry more than one wife because these days no one could support the children of more than one wife. The burden mentioned most often was the cost of the school fees, which had become all the more important now that children had to go to school for so many more years.

The exodus by so many of Lupondo's granddaughters and the end of polygyny in Bango Chiefdom, if not in itself a major cause for the exodus, were both aspects of the same broader transformation. The home economy was simply not growing at the same pace as the population or its spiralling needs for cash. The overall dependence on outside resources and outside income, especially as remittances, was increasing disproportionately. To reproduce Lupondo's family from one generation to the next, while keeping some members of the family at home permanently, more and more family members had to support themselves for long periods, or even permanently, away from home.

The specific kind of husbands many of the granddaughters chose in town has had important implications for the reproduction of Lupondo's family. Here, too, Baka Ngoni was a pioneer, initiating and then fostering a trend. She, and many of the other granddaughters after her, married ethnic strangers, in her husband's case a foreigner; and they remained married to them in relatively stable unions. In part, this pattern came about through Baka Ngoni's active intervention. She served as a key link in the marriage chain. A number of the other granddaughters met and married friends of her husband who were also foreigners or strangers, mainly Shona. Most were semi-skilled or unskilled workers like the majority of Lupondo's grandsons, but unlike them they did not concentrate mainly in domestic, hotel or catering and retail services. In at least one respect, marrying such strangers helped the growth of a home circle around the core of Baka Ngoni's sisters and female cousins. Although some of their husbands kept in co-operative contact with their home people by being active in burial societies, the husbands largely lacked other kin of their own nearby. Instead, the granddaughters of Lupondo were the kin who provided long-term, mutual security: they visited each other constantly, kept track of each other's affairs, turned to each other in crises, gave comfort in illness, and looked to each other as the best sources of the help expected from home people. They learned that, in practice, they could rely on each other for moral and financial support.

Although the brothers of these women were, on the whole, less important on a day-to-day basis—most of the brothers worked in South Africa—some of them nevertheless took an active part in sustaining their home circle for mutual security in Bulawayo. It was a part that became all the more important during the present economic recession and following the erection by Zimbabwe of trade barriers against South Africa. These barriers were intended to block the flow from South Africa of cheap and abundant consumer goods. In response, a division of labour developed within the family. Brothers tried to keep their own wives at home, producing crops and tending the surviving cattle in the countryside. At the same time, brothers relied upon sisters in town to sell the consumer goods which they brought back on their return from South Africa. It is worth noting that although some of the brothers also brought home wives they married at their work places, none of these foreign or stranger wives remained for long in the countryside. Each of their marriages, with one exception so far, ended in divorce or separation.

Baka Ngoni had no full brothers who could facilitate her petty trading by their imports. The half-brothers she had were the sons of her father's favourite wife Baka Sala, the one he pampered at the expense of her mother. Two of Baka Ngoni's sons were working in South Africa. But they were still young, too young to be relied upon; and although they wrote, and even phoned, they did not send her money to help support her other children. Among her married daughters, one, her first-born, remained at home in the countryside, and the other lived very nearby, so close that she and Baka Ngoni easily helped each other in their day-to-day tasks. In Baka Ngoni's place, another person, less forgiving, less generous and perhaps less astute, might have been unable to co-operate with her half-brothers. Instead, she had overcome her girlish resentment of the unfair treatment of her mother by her father Buka. Even more, she had actually become convinced that Baka Sala had very good will towards her and that Baka Sala's character was in reality good, 'Baka Sala does not have a bad *mhepo*, soul (wind)'.

On her side, Baka Sala had nothing but praise for her co-wife's daughter, Baka Ngoni, and gave me this description of Baka Ngoni's leading part in the co-operation between her own and her co-wife's children:

Our children get on very well. Yedu and Zana [two of her daughters] were reared in Baka Ngoni's hands. For she collected them and went with them to show them the city. Now you would not be able to tell that some of these children are from the senior compound and the others from the junior. They hold on to each other like this [showing a tight fist]. They live together there making each other happy. Gwaha [her second son] too went to the city and stayed for a time at her house. And now when Sala [her first son] comes on holiday from South Africa, he goes to Baka Ngoni's house, first. After about a week, he gets on a bus and comes over here. Their way of getting on with each other makes us rejoice very greatly, for our children love each other following along in a straight path, not straying from each other. There is no outsider who can come between them. So great is their mutual understanding that such a person would be afraid to come between them. When Sala [her first son] is away in South Africa, he

writes to his older sister Baka Ngoni and to her mother. And he buys her
blankets and other goods for selling, and she tries to sell them for him.

The home circle in which Baka Ngoni played so important a part came
to have a fairly stable core of long-term residents in the city. Yet some
members were more temporary than others. A few came to the city, moved
to another part of the countryside, and continued to circulate back and
forth between town and country. One of these kinswomen was Baka Ngoni's
cousin Baka Jesi. Baka Jesi reminded me that I had myself brought 'the bright
lights' of the city to their home. On otherwise dark nights, she had been among
the small girls who jived tirelessly at our hamlet by the light of my car's
headlamps. I brought her home on a visit to her mother Baka Lufu, and she
gave me this account of her past, speaking at her mother's homestead in Bango
Chiefdom:

> I met my husband Dan in the city, where you found me at Ntumbane, at
> Baka Ngoma's [her older sister's], and I have never had any other hus-
> band. He met me while I was at my older sister's in [house number]
> 10998, and he was at 10999. He really courted me, and I had my first child
> in the city, when I was seventeen. He promised to give bridewealth
> (*malobola*) for me, and actually did make marriage payments 'to enter the
> homestead'.
>
> Dan took me to live at his home at Shabane [in the Midlands, to the east
> of Bulawayo] where I now have a homestead that I left behind. Yes, his
> home was far, but I wasn't afraid of his home being far, because it is
> actually near by bus, and I can manage to get from there to here [at Bango]
> in one day.
>
> His parents and I lived together in mutual understanding. We would
> speak Shona to each other, and I've learned to speak it so well that you
> can't tell that I'm a Kalanga from the way I speak.
>
> Our customs and theirs differ. Here we have the *wosana* [adepts of the
> Mwali cult (see Werbner, 1989, pp. 245–98)], at their home there are
> none. Here we have *midzimu ye ngumba*, divinities of the hut [the demons
> of the domestic cult of affliction, (see Werbner, 1989, pp. 61–108)], but
> there are none there, and over there they have *midzimu ye sangoma*,
> divinities of *sangoma*. Over there, their fathers who died long ago awaken
> and come to possess a person, but at our home we don't have that—once
> cast aside and buried, the dead don't come back that way. They set aside a
> head of cattle and dedicate it to be Father, and they make offerings of beer
> to it. Again, we don't have that at our home. I first found it over there.
> Here a married woman should not sit the way I'm sitting, bareheaded.
> Over there, they don't care. Over there, too, I could even eat from the
> same plate as my father-in-law, and they wouldn't be concerned. And all
> our respect and avoidance by the son-in-law fleeing from his mother-in-
> law, that too they don't have. A son-in-law may eat porridge with his

mother-in-law. But my husband would respect and avoid my brother's wife; that's the custom over there.

Their custom is right, and it's not 'dry' and inflexible, the way it is here among Kalanga. Their custom seems to be light, not heavy, as it is at our home. They don't really have so many customs and rules, not as many as we do. You don't have to be so respectful, so careful about avoidance. Here you have to stay in the homestead after the harvest. Over there, you are free to relax, go to town for a holiday, and be with your husband. I would enjoy town, stay there till November and ploughing time then return again in April. In town I would sell ground nuts, and things I had made like jerseys from wool, and we would also sell sunflowers and cotton. Growing the cotton was a lot of hard work. You had to cultivate, and then spray when it was a few feet high, and then spray again against boll weevils. But over there it was all right, and there was no hunger like there is here. The cattle over there are bigger, but they are few and don't die in large numbers during drought. Here the cattle have been many, but for lack of food they have died of hunger. There they'll have about five head of cattle and no goats. They simply don't drink goat milk, and they laugh at you for drinking it.

Among the Shona, they didn't have as bad a war and didn't die in such numbers as here, where there was Smith's war then again Mugabe's war. [During the liberation war, in Mashonaland] I cooked for the boys of the country [the guerrillas]. Sometimes, while you were still cooking, they would run for it, and the soldiers would come and beat you. You wouldn't know where the boys had gone to, but after they had gone you would have to stay alone, facing the soldiers.

We feared Smith's soldiers and we feared the boys. Smith's soldiers would come and say, 'Do this'. The boys would come and beat you, saying, 'What are you doing that for?' [Baka Jesi laughed at the absurdity of the contradiction.] Ah, it was just heavy. If you went without a *situpa* [registration certificate or pass] you were beaten, while they asked where you came from without a pass. Smith's people demanded the pass, and you were also beaten by the others if you didn't have the card of ZAPU and ZANU. Smith's people and the others [the nationalist parties] were alike, each had a card, and they still have a card.

In those days [during the liberation war], if they [the guerrillas] hated you, they would just say that you were a sell-out or a witch and come and beat you without asking a lot of questions. If your *midzimu*, divinities of the dead, were looking after you, they would beat you without killing you, but if they weren't you would be beaten to death, and they might burn you too, and set your hut afire, while you were in it.

Those who fought in the country [the guerrillas] did that to one man while we were present. He had fled from them to join Smith and wanted to change over. They came by again and caught him. It is a sin to burn a person. It would have been better if they had beaten him and just left him after that.

Ah, they had malice. They won't go up to Heaven. Those people went about with knives and guns, long, huge knives. But they didn't discriminate against you because you spoke Kalanga. That didn't matter. If someone were to say, that person is not of our tribe, they would ask her, 'What does it matter? Why are you despising her? Zimbabwe means that you are all one people, even if you speak different languages.' And that person would shut up. But when the present soldiers come [after independence in the Fifth Brigade] and saw a man from here going to Mashonaland they would beat him, saying 'You are a dissident. How did you get here?'

Over there, at Shabane and Belingwe, people were mixed together, Ndebele and Shona, and nobody spoke against you because you were Ndebele. It's a place that has no tribalism, no discrimination.

In December we [Baka Jesi and her husband Dan] divorced, because he takes too many women. He would find another woman, live with her and ignore me and my children. A year later he would remember me and say, 'Come back, my wife, and live with me.' Is that right? No, it is not right. And if I would write to him, he wouldn't answer. He just went about and ate up his money without a thought for me or for his child. He has a child in Form 1 [in secondary school] and doesn't care about her. I want her to study through Form 6 and I am the only one who supports her. If I would ask him, he would say, 'I'll do it, eventually'. And he would go off to another woman. He wouldn't curse, or fight. He would just keep quiet, go his own way, and leave you in the lurch. I am the one who supports the children by knitting and peddling. In a week I can knit a jersey. I suffer when I have no wool, but not when I have it.

Here in the city, the women help each other more than the men, they are better than the men. You see Baka Magwadza [one sister] is in Lobengula [a nearby part of the city], Baka Ngoma [the oldest sister, with whom Baka Jesi lives in the city] is in Entumbane, Baka Ngoni [her cousin] is in Entumbane, and Baka Siamwa and Baka Bayani [two other cousins] are in Mpopoma [another nearby township]. If someone gets into trouble, the others manage to help, sometimes with money. We rush to get together when we hear that there is trouble. But if you tell a man something, you will just spend the days waiting, without him helping. He promises he will help, when he gets round to it. His mouth talks, but he fails to do anything at all. Lufu [her oldest brother] is better, and so is Bonani [her youngest brother] who helps his mother and remembers his sisters. They are thoughtful. You see, in Johannesburg where they are working, things are very cheap. They buy things and send them here for sale. And it is a help. But Kangangwani [an older brother] doesn't think of anyone at all; he goes to Johannesburg and has no concern for others.

When I asked Baka Jesi whether she thought that the country had gone forward since independence, she insisted that it had not:

The country has fallen down, not risen up. Under Smith things weren't made so costly for us. Schools, flour, clothes were all not so costly. Smith was better.

I had heard this refrain, 'Smith was better', all too often. At first, I simply listened to it in horrified silence, for it ran sharply against my own convictions and yet I was dismayed by the unmistakably bitter disillusionment it expressed. Still appalled, I felt that I had to argue the point with Baka Ngoni, and we began to discuss it after I objected, 'But didn't Smith steal the chiefship from the people?' Baka Jesi admitted that and yet, troubled by inflation, she still argued that the past was better than the present:

I don't deny that he stole it. But the price of his goods was low and so his rule was right. We used to be able to buy flour for three dollars. Now how much is a half sack? Six dollars. So which one is better?

R.P.W.: But in the past you used to be given very little money for working.

Baka Jesi: It didn't matter that it was very little money. Now they give you a lot of money, but it doesn't help. Things are too costly. For secondary schools we're paying more than sixty dollars 'per term' [in English], so that in a year we're paying more than three hundred dollars.

R.P.W.: But in the past whites owned the farms, went to the advanced schools, and owned the great houses in the city. But now blacks are owners, too.

Baka Jesi: But all the things are going up in price all the time, so that everything becomes more and more costly. The European was better; even if he swindled the country which was not his, he was still better. What you buy now with a dollar twenty you used to buy then for six pence.

R.P.W.: But in the past, very few of your relatives completed Standard Six [in primary school], yet now some complete Form Six [in secondary school].

Baka Jesi: The old people were not awake. They were fools, and that's why the children didn't go further.

R.P.W.: So don't you see that the government is lifting people up and awakening the country?

Baka Jesi: No, they are not awakening the country. Many children are simply school-leavers for lack of money. Don't you see that now the price of flour for workers is being raised? You can't get work that earns you enough money. Maybe they are lifting the country, but their goods are getting more and more costly. Now even if you have passed Form Four you can stay at home, failing to get a job. That's our government, oh [groans]. In the past could you fail to get work if you had passed Form Four? Now Form Four is like Grade One. These things of the present are very bad. The present is full of grief.

Like her cousin Baka Ngoni, Baka Jesi was part of the exodus by many of Lupondo's granddaughters from Bango Chiefdom. By contrast to her cousin Baka Ngoni, however, Baka Jesi was one of the few granddaughters who for long kept one foot in the town and the other in the country; and thus she managed to bridge both town and country, while moving between them. In this respect, Baka Jesi, too, like her cousin Baka Ngoni, was something of a pioneer. Having had a household among Shona in the countryside, which allowed her to join her husband in town during the slack agricultural season, she had found a way to maintain herself in town, despite her husband's neglect and desertion. She became very quick, skilful and artistic in knitting sweaters— the one she knitted for my daughter was stunning— and from her handicraft along with some petty trading, she was able to earn enough to pay for the bare necessities for herself and her children and to meet their school fees. But she was now finding it harder to cope with the soaring inflation which had struck so sharply not long after independence. Her experience had made her bitter against the government, which she blamed for increasing poverty. The suffering was all the more unacceptable because she, like many other women in the countryside, had suffered physical abuse and made great sacrifices, looking forward to the promise of Zimbabwe as a country of their own. If more vulnerable than most in her home circle, because she had to provide for herself and her children without support from her husband, she voiced the distress of many people from Bango Chiefdom, both within and outside Lupondo's family, when she said, 'The present is full of grief'.

But what was the *past* like, and how is it to be known, remembered, and perhaps most importantly, brought into powerful communication with the present? And how can that powerful communication be made healing when the present has called so much of the past into question?

The liberation war and its aftermath made these concerns of remembrance and communication vital for Lupondo's granddaughters and their home circle and, of course, not for them alone. In this period, many of the people of Matabeleland found such concerns compelling. There was a widespread experience of senseless loss and anxious bereavement, often due to kin dying in atrocities and without decent burial or wakes. It was well known that there were mass graves into which people had disappeared, leaving no trace for their kin. The need to be cleansed from wartime acts of violence and violation was also widely felt (see Reynolds, 1990, pp. 12–15 on post-war cleansing outside Matabeleland in Musami to the east of Harare).

One response in Matabeleland, both in the towns and in the countryside, was a remarkable increase in the number of mediums known according to their drums as *sangoma* in Sindebele or *changoma* in Kalanga. A great revival took place around these mediums. With it came a fresh surge of attention to their specially costumed embodiment of the dead, their revelatory messages warning people against forgetting the past, their fixing of blame for sorcery and responsibility for neglect of the dead, their herbal prescriptions for cleansing and protection, their dancing and drumming, their blood sacrifices and other ritual acts of therapy.

This is not the place for a full account of what mediums dream, say and do or of what the cult practice is. Very generally, the *sangoma* cult is a cult in which participants seek protection against sorcery and ask for healing through restored communication with the dead. Its revival reveals three important tendencies: first, the growing importance of memorialising war and the violation of the person; second, the expansion across town and country; and third, the emerging interethnic significance of transcultural healing. My aim in the rest of this chapter is to bring to light the links between such tendencies in the *sangoma* revival and change in Lupondo's family—above all in the security circle around his granddaughters permanently resident in the city. It is worth saying also that in speaking of a revival I do not mean to imply that the *sangoma* cult had temporarily disappeared or been in retreat (on its continuing importance and its variable significance in distant parts of east, central and southern Africa, see Janzen, in press). In my usage here, the revival is simply a religious movement greatly invigorated by efforts to revive the past.

Let me first consider the growing importance of the revival for memorialising violence, aggression, and violation of the person. The *sangoma* mediums I saw on my first visit were alien witchdoctors who danced aggressively, brandishing weapons, such as spears and axes, sometimes threatening onlookers. Costumed as warriors, they enacted a counteraggression to attacks by sorcery. Since then, however, and I cannot say when the change took place, it has become common for mediums to wear a mantle of red cloth (in Sindebele, *lembo lebomvu*). The red is for blood, the blood of violence and war, I was told. The significance of this has come in part from a contrast in colours, red and black. The contrast has emblazoned a changing opposition between cults: on the one hand, the *sangoma* cult and, on the other, the regional cult dedicated to God Above, Mwali (on the Mwali cult, see Werbner, 1989, pp. 245–98 and on a comparable opposition elsewhere in Zimbabwe, expressed as between cults of conquerors and autochthons, see Garbett, 1977, pp. 78–80, n.d.; Lan, 1985, pp. 72–111).

Black is the colour of the cloth worn by the possessed, those 'loved by God', in the Mwali cult. The black is said to be for the rain that God lets sow the earth when it is free of pollution, such as comes from the shedding of blood and other violations of the person. The peace and the welfare of the land along with its people have been the overriding concerns of the Mwali cult.

Somewhat opposed concerns and interests have prevailed at times in the *sangoma* cult. The *sangoma* cult has been associated with Ndebele as conquerors. At least one of its mediums, embodying a warrior chief of the past, Mtuwane Dhlo-Dhlo, has spoken on behalf of 'the kingdom of the Ndebele people': he has claimed the authority to call for war or its end (this is my reading of the evidence in Ranger, 1989c). During the revival of the *sangoma* cult and perhaps for a considerable period before that, certain mediums of the *sangoma* cult and their supporters have made attempts to create a merger, or at least a close link between their cult and the Mwali cult. They have gone to great lengths, against resistance from within the Mwali cult, to turn its great pilgrimage centres, containing the shrines of highly prestigious and very widely attended oracles, into places for authoritative communication by *sangoma* mediums also. They have tried to use those sacred central places in ways that memorialise war and the violation of the person.

Among the close kin of Lupondo's granddaughters, the medium most directly involved has been the one embodying an exemplary figure, Hobani. Hobani was an important messenger between the Mwali cult and the Chief Bango of his time. Still remembered as a martyr, having been shot in the back by an American at a Mwali cult shrine during the rebellion of 1896, Hobani exemplified the unarmed, innocent victim of war whose murder left his kin suffering from a vengeful, aggrieved presence as *ngozi*. Towards the end of my recent visit, his kin were planning to make a major sacrifice and consult Hobani through his medium at a cardinal shrine of Mwali; their intent was 'to return him back home', appeasing the *ngozi*.

A similar concern was paramount when Baka Jesi's sister Baka Ngoma became a *sangoma* medium after the liberation war, in 1982. Having been afflicted by throbbing headaches, severe pains across her whole body, and swollen legs so badly enlarged she could hardly move from her house in the city, Baka Ngoma consulted diviners accompanied by her mother Baka Lufu and her brother Lufu. The consultations disclosed, according to Baka Lufu:

> Their forefathers [her children's] were saying that we cast them aside into the open and that we are no longer concerned about them. And Dzilo [her husband's older brother] had spoken saying, 'When I die, you will take out a beast for the child of my younger brother.' Then having become *ngozi* [a vengeful ghost] he was grieving in his heart that his death was not known and recognised. It was a very bad thing, and that is how we came to

do it just as he had spoken. His beast was slaughtered from the pen, and she [Baka Ngoma] was made to suck the blood while it was still fresh. Then it was said, 'Today the *changoma* has come back to your homestead, to the homestead of its father.'

Neglect of the dead and failure to give them due recognition caused Baka Ngoma's affliction, the diviners indicated. In particular, her suffering came because of the wrong done her father's brother Dzilo. It was a wrong that made his ghost a vengeful and aggrieved presence, *ngozi*. The atrocity of his death, unmourned in any wake, haunted his family. In their divinations, they remembered that he had intended to leave one of his cattle for a child of his younger brother, whose widow Baka Lufu he had inherited.

The remembered events concerned 'tears', both literally and figuratively in Kalanga terms. Literally, they were the tears shed by the living when they cried in mourning their loss. Figuratively, the tears were embodied in cattle and everything that came to the living from the dead. By acting upon one aspect of their concern with memory, the figurative embodiment, and putting it right, the intent of family members was to act upon and right the other aspect, the literal expression of loss. In terms of their intent, also, sucking the sacrificial blood fresh from a black beast of Dzilo's, and by his pen, brought the *changoma* back as a spirit within Baka Ngoma and within Dzilo's homestead. In Baka Ngoma's dreams came songs of her own from the dead. It was a communication characterising her as a medium. The refrain of one of these songs, which she later sang in Sindebele and then translated into Kalanga for me, was:

The *sangoma* sleeps in the river, suffering.

This conveyed an image of suffering brought on by abandonment, by people being remote and neglectful when they should be caring, remembering their late forefathers.

Distinct voices of the past, 'the voices of the people of old', spoke through Baka Ngoma as a medium. They were, in turn, those of her paternal grandfather, Lupondo himself, her great grandfather, and her maternal grandfather, but not the voice of Dzilo. It was through the sacrifice that family members worked upon the memory of Dzilo's death and his grieving presence as *ngozi*. They proved that they acknowledged him in death as a kinsman having claims upon them; that they did know and recognise him, despite having been forced to bury him without the respect due him. But the very fact that they could not and would not forget him and his death meant that they could appease but not fully free themselves of his grieving presence.

Second, as the revival expanded, it mobilised people and their resources across town and country. Performances were held wherever mediums and their kin lived or died, now and in the past. A medium, such as Baka Ngoma, whose *changoma* was brought back from the dead in the countryside, 'back to the father's homestead', was expected to make offerings each year at that

*4* Tim's Jewelry Services and Curios, in Bulawayo

home. But she could and did do so also in the city. If originally beer offerings had to be brewed from the family's own grain and in the vicinity of their own homes, in town it came to be acceptable also to offer factory-brewed beer bought from the bars.

In demands on time, money and services, the revival tested brothers and sisters and other close kin. They had to give a powerful and highly valued proof of their responsibility and co-operation across town and country. Often, the kinsmen who enabled women to become mediums were the same brothers who sent their sisters goods from South Africa for sale in the city of Bulawayo and who were regarded as keeping their sisters' needs in mind, while they themselves were based in the countryside. Such a brother was Lufu, who paid for Baka Ngoma's costume and most of her ritual paraphernalia, at the time of her initiation. His donation, like that of other responsible kin, was an endorsement of moral claims across town and country, for it enabled his town-based sister to become a figure having a voice, indeed, several voices, of moral weight and authority in both places.

This view of the medium's importance calls for some qualification. Baka Ngoma told me, that after the *midzimu*, the divinities or shades of the dead, have gone, following a consultation, she never knows what they have said, and she has to hear about that from other people. Like all *sangoma* mediums, she had to speak during drum-induced trance in a representative capacity, and not as herself or in her own right. Another qualification needs to be mentioned, also. At least in Lupondo's family, no two mediums have come from the same group of brothers and sisters, so that in terms of the representation of moral weight and authority, each medium has been representative in and for a distinct part of the family.

Virtually the whole of Lupondo's family in Matabeleland got caught up in the *sangoma* revival, in one way or another. Besides Baka Ngoma, several of Lupondo's granddaughters permanently resident in town and at least one grandson also became mediums. Even family members belonging to churches opposed to mediums found they had to take part. They did so by paying for the costly costumes (Zimbabwe $300, at least, and roughly £100 sterling), by caring for novice mediums during their year-long training and treatment, by attending the mediums' performances, by testifying to the past as it was manifested in present affliction, and by meeting the other obligations of kin to mediums as the embodiment of their grandfathers, great-grandfathers, or even more remote ancestors.

The revival thrived on and, in turn, fostered handicrafts, the production of petty commodities, and petty trade. It was of one piece, in other words, with that informal economic activity upon which so many granddaughters of Lupondo relied to supplement their husbands' earnings as workers. In the circulation across town and country, ritual objects were revalued as 'curios' to be commercially traded for cash; they were then turned into traditional gifts for recovering or repairing the past and thus for healing and protecting the present. Family members bought the mediums' costumes and paraphernalia, the red cloths (Z.$14), axes (Z.$7), staffs (Z.$10.50), ostrich headdresses (Z.$30), skirts (Z.55), leg rattles (Z.$10.50), drums (Z.$10.50), baskets (Z.$3.95), shells (each Z.$0.25 or Z.$0.50), beads, python and other snake bones, herbal roots and clays from the smart display cases of a store in a modern office block on a main street near the city centre of Bulawayo. The store trades under the name of *Tim's Jewelry Services and Curios*. Since 1979 its owner, Timoth Ncube, a businessman and not himself a medium, has travelled widely, collecting virtually all of his 'curios' from remote parts of the country-side for resale in the city. Throughout the growing revival, his trade in 'curios' as ritual costumes and paraphernalia has fluctuated seasonally, his shop assistants told me, according to the flow of people between town and countryside. The demand has been greatest around the holiday seasons, such as at Christmas, when people, coming home to the countryside from the city, 'hear that they have problems', as the shop assistants put it.

Finally, the revival has had considerable interethnic significance. For Lupondo's family, the *sangoma* cult was exotic. It came to them from Ndebele. Although even at the time of my first visit some Kalanga had long before borrowed it, family members turned to it then, in the early 1960s, merely to seek remote and alien witchfinders. At that time, it was not a cult to which anyone in Lupondo's family belonged. Family members first joined, becoming mediums, during the revival. Prior to the revival, and even after it, although less prominently, some of the other women of the family had been possessed by demons, *mazenge*, in their cult of the alien and the wild (see Werbner, 1989, pp. 61–108). In the *mazenge* cult there is also an appropriation of the exotic; the possessed, like the *sangoma* mediums, speak in the language of a neighbouring people, in this case Karanga. But the possessed women perform the ritual of demons at home and only in the homesteads of kin, never in town. And it is possession by women only, not including men as in the *sangoma* cult. During my recent visit, I was told by family members that they still maintain this restriction on home performance and that they had never seen or heard of women being possessed by *mazenge* in town. In the *mazenge* cult Kalanga seek to heal affliction while around women they reconstruct the meaning of domestic life in the countryside. But they do not invoke the dead, seek to communicate with specific ancestors, or reconstruct the past in their presence.

Kalanga could have adapted the demonic cult for healing in town and country. They could have refocused its ritual around their extended concerns, confronting the danger of the alien and the exotic in both places. Instead, they expanded their repertoire of cults. They kept the old one for certain purposes; for others, they borrowed the new one. It is worth saying, although briefly within my present limits, that the borrowing followed a pattern and that the new cult, as it was received, became a systematic variation or transformation of the old.

Family members met their concerns by re-establishing communication with the dead through an exotic cult focused upon aggression and associated with Ndebele and their stereotype of being war-like. As a consequence, family members tied the healing recovery of the past to the reconstruction of their identities in the present. They did so in response to certain recent changes. Among these were their new experiences of living in the midst of ethnic strangers and marrying them, of speaking Sindebele in the city, and even in the countryside, as the region's *lingua franca* and as the main language for many of their children, and of being identified with Ndebele in the quasi-nationalism of the liberation war and its violent aftermath. Yet the healing they received and offered through the cult was even more broadly transcultural. It was drawn from therapeutic practices and prescriptions which had become widespread beyond Ndebele. The cult was open to patients irrespective of their ethnic origins. Among Baka Ngoma's patients in Bulawayo were Kalanga, Ndebele and Shona, and the ease with which she conversed with them in their own language was impressive. In this sense, therefore, participation in the revival, at least by some members of Lupondo's family, can be understood as at once an appropriation of Ndebele identity and a transcendence of it.

Through the revival, voices of the past have been made to speak in the present in order to testify to a truth, deeply felt by many family members, that certain memories have to be kept alive, honoured and never forgotten. Among these are memories of suffering and loss, of lapses from humanity, of the failures of kin, and not merely their triumphs in success or achievement. The tears of the dead must also be the tears of the living.

# Brief Profiles

'Baka' means 'Mother of', and it is the title of a married woman.

WOMEN

BAKA BUDZA, daughter of Lupondo's half brother Kunda and Baka Chedza; mother of six children; born c. 1922 near Marula; reared at Bango Chiefdom; married 1937; divorced 1940; remarried 1944 and divorced 1957; alive and still in the family's neighbourhood, surrounded by numerous members of her own family in 1989.

BAKA BUKA, second wife of Lupondo; born c. 1895 at Bango Chiefdom; died c. 1953; mother of five children. Having been an early girlfriend of Lupondo's, she failed to become his senior wife. In the memory of her son Buka, her suffering was the cause of his grievances against his father Lupondo, and it provided a sentimental source for his rivalry with his half brother Dzilo.

BAKA CHEDZA, wife of Lupondo's half brother Kunda; mother of two married daughters; born c. 1900 near Plumtree; reared at maternal grand-parents at Ndiweni Chiefdom; married 1919 at Taylor's Block; alive in 1989, having gone to the care of her daughter in a distant neighbourhood. Putting her greatest trust in Lupondo's son Dzilo, she testified realistically, in 1960–1, to a series of family quarrels. In 1989, in her old age, she spoke bitterly against the guerrillas for murdering Dzilo; she blamed Mugabe's government for un-leashing the Fifth Brigade and for allowing the extreme rise in the cost of food and clothes.

BAKA CHILALO, widow of Lupondo's full brother Malidzo; mother of two married daughters; born c. 1895 at Mpini Chiefdom near Marula; married at Bango Chiefdom; brought younger sister Baka Tandiwe as co-wife; reared Buka as a herdboy; died in 1960s. Prosperous and influential, she took Buka's side in the rivalry of Lupondo's leading sons, defending Buka in gossip against attacks on his character.

BAKA DZILO, senior wife of Lupondo; mother of eight children; born c. 1890 at Bango Chiefdom near Marula; married c. 1909; died in 1960s. Wealthy, proud of her position and fierce in defence of it, she was a *femme formidable*, much accused of sorcery by her junior co-wife's son Buka.

BAKA LUFU, widow of Lupondo's son Mfila; mother of eight children; born c. 1925 near Marula in Bango Chiefdom; married c. 1942; alive 1989. She spoke with grief and deep questioning about her experiences in the liberation war and its aftermath.

BAKA MILONGA, daughter of Lupondo's son Mfila; mother of one married daughter; born 1946 in Bango Chiefdom; married in Bulawayo early in the 1960s to a Mozambiquean. She was helped by her cousin Baka Ngoni to settle in the city.

BAKA NGOMA, daughter of Lupondo's son Mfila; mother of seven children; born 1949 in Bango Chiefdom; married in Bulawayo to a man from Selukwe. Having become a *sangoma* medium in 1984, she performed in both town and country and had a varied clientele in 1989.

BAKA NGONI, first-born daughter of Lupondo's son Buka; mother of twelve children; born 1945 at Bango Chiefdom; married in 1963 to a Mozambiquean in Bulawayo. A pioneer among the granddaughters who settled permanently in the city, she became centrally active in the forming and sustaining of a security circle.

BAKA SALA, widow of Lupondo's son Buka; mother of four children; born c. 1932 at Bango Chiefdom, Jimmie Farm; reared by mother's brother; married 1953; alive 1989. Her husband's favourite, she became the foil for conflicts with his brothers, and the subject of blame for a change in his character. She achieved the kind of amity with her senior co-wife that enabled her co-wife's children to be reconciled to her, despite Buka's discrimination in her favour.

BAKA TENGA, widow of Lupondo; mother of five children; born c. 1915 at Bango Chiefdom; married c. 1932; rejoined her brother at a distant neighbourhood in early 1940s; alive in 1989. Her husband's favourite, she left their marital hamlet, without breaking up their marriage, accusing her senior co-wife of sorcery at the death of her first born. By 1989 some of her sons had returned to live permanently in the family's neighbourhood. One of her sons, not resident in the chiefdom, was the only member of the family to become a rich entrepreneur, as the owner of stores, a ranch near Bulawayo, and a large herd of cattle. Although his mother's brother had also been one of the richest men in one part of the chiefdom, his own wealth was said to have been derived originally from a large amount of money gained while he was a labour migrant in South Africa.

BAKA YENDA, senior widow of Lupondo's son Buka; mother of four married daughters; born c. 1922 at Bango Chiefdom, Jimmie Farm; reared at Smith Block; married 1942; separated from her husband, two years before his death (ostensibly, to care for her rich brother's substantial homestead); alive in 1989. During the campaign against 'dissidents', her defence of her own and her husband's homestead against the Fifth Brigade became celebrated in stories of her heroism. She and her junior co-wife maintained an appearance of amity, even after the separation from her husband, which was a final expression of her resentment at her husband's discrimination.

## MEN

BUKA, first-born son of Lupondo's second wife; father of nine children; born c. 1909 at Bango Chiefdom; reared by maternal grandfather; married at least four wives (possibly six); divorced two; died 1988. He suffered the indignity of becoming the acting head of the family on the terrible occasion of the murder of his brother and sometime rival Dzilo.

DZILO, senior son of Lupondo's senior wife; father of eleven children; born c. 1912, at Bango Chiefdom; married twice (1936, 1956), succeeded his father as administrative headman. Murdered in 1978 by ZIPRA guerrillas, he became a vengeful and aggrieved presence, *ngozi*, for his bereaved kin.

GWATI, oldest surviving son of Lupondo's second wife; father of seven children; born c. 1914, at Bango Chiefdom in Smith Block; reared by maternal grandfather; married 1945. He was the subject of conflicting appeals by his brothers Buka and Dzilo, some made at divinations; he maintained amity with both the rivals. He insisted he was outraged but not crushed, or resigned to defeat, by the brutal ordeals he was forced to suffer himself, often as a witness, during the liberation war and the campaign against dissidents.

KUMBA, son of Lupondo's second wife; father of six children; born c. 1928 at Bango Chiefdom; married 1945; divorced 1961; died in late 1960s. After his divorce, his children were reared by their mother's brother in another part of the chiefdom, where most of them remained; none returned to the family neighbourhood.

KUNDA, half brother of Lupondo; father of two married daughters; born c. 1896 at Mpini Chiefdom, near Marula; married 1919 at Taylor's Block; died at Bango Chiefdom. Feckless, ineffectual, and often drunk during my first visit, he was virtually a dependent of Lupondo's son Dzilo.

LUPONDO, founding head of his family; father of eighteen children of his own and a number of others with his brother's widows; born c. 1885, Mpini Chiefdom at Marula; married three wives (1909, 1911, 1932) and inherited another three; became an administrative headman; resigned the office to his son Dzilo; died early 1960s. After the liberation war, his granddaughter Baka Ngoma, on becoming a *sangoma* medium, performed as his re-embodiment.

MABUYANI, social biographer of Lupondo's family; father of two children; born 1937, at Boston, Massachusetts, USA; married 1971; carried out fieldwork among Winnebago of Nebraska in 1958 (two months), among Eastern Kalanga in 1960–1 (fifteen months) and 1989 (six weeks), among Western Kalanga in 1964–5 (fifteen months), 1969 (three months), 1974 (one month), 1977 (two months), 1985 (three weeks), and among Tswapong in 1972–3 (fifteen months), 1978; became the Reader in African Anthropology at the University of Manchester in 1990.

MALIDZO, younger full brother of Lupondo; father of eleven children; born c. 1890 at Mpini Chiefdom near Marula; married three wives; died in the late 1930s. The sons of his third wife are now prominent in the family's neighbourhood.

MBULAWA, son of Lupondo's son Tengi; father of two children; born 1958 at Bango Chiefdom; became ZIPRA guerrilla; married, in Bulawayo, a woman from Tjolotjo. After a nervous breakdown in 1988, he was being initiated as a *sangoma* medium in 1989.

MFILA, last-born son of Lupondo's senior wife; father of eight children (one by his levir, Dzilo); born 1914 in Bango Chiefdom at Smith Block near Marula; married 1942; died 1961. Towards the end of his life, he became an ardent member of the Zion Christian Church.

TENGI, son of Lupondo's third wife; father of nine children; born 1940 at Bango Chiefdom; married twice; divorced once. Having been a cook as a labour migrant in Bulawayo, he became a storekeeper and witnessed the Fifth Brigade from the safety of their main base in a nearby chiefdom.

TOBELA, Lupondo's cousin; born c. 1890, at Mpini Chiefdom; married four wives (1918, 1924, 1940, 1947); succeeded his deranged brother as administrative headman; died in 1960s. A maternal kinsman of Chief Jeremiah Ngugama Bango, he was one of the few men of his generation who protested publicly, during a confrontation, against the land use planning under the Land Husbandry Act.

# Sources and Bibliography

MISSION RECORDS

London Missionary Society, Archives

Whiteside, John, Letter from Tjimali near Marulla, 30 December 1912.
Wilkerson, G. J. Letter from Figtree Siding to Secretary L.M.S. 29/1/1911.
Williams, R. C. Superintendent's Report to London Missionary Society 31/–/1909.


OFFICIAL PAPERS

Native Department, Plumtree District, District Archives

Native Commissioner to Provincial Native Commissioner, correspondence: 29 August 1958; 4 April 1961 in Per 5/Chief Banko/61 12 May 1960; 20 May 1960 in 1/2/61; 19 September 1961 in Per 5/Chief Banko/61.
Native Commissioner to Chief Banko 10/3/65 in per/5/Chief Banko/65.
Provincial Native Commissioner to Native Commissioner 17 May 1960.


District Administration, Plumtree District, District Archives

District Administrator to Provincial Administrator in Per 5/Chief Banko: Cable 33/84; 8/6/1984.
District Administrator, Provincial Governor's Draft Speech, Bango Chieftainship, 1986 in Per/3 Bango Chieftainship.
Senior Administrative Officer to Provincial Administrator in Per 5/Chief Banko: 19/8/1981.
Zimbabwe Republic Police Record, Police Voucher 19/3/81 in Per 5/Chief Banko.

Bango Council, National Archives of Zimbabwe, Bulawayo
District Officer, Report 14/4/1979 in SBV 2/1.

Unpublished Report, Native Department, Plumtree District
Hunt, Arthur 1960, The Future of the Cattle Country, Salisbury.

PRIVATE PAPERS

Correspondence in Author's File
Chief Bango, Plumtree to Mrs J. E. Nkomo, London (photocopy).

ARTICLES AND BOOKS

Bhebe, Ngwabi (1988). The Evangelical Lutheran Church in Zimbabwe and
the War of Liberation, 1975–1980. In Carl Hallencreutz and Ambrose Moyo
(Editors), *Church and State in Zimbabwe*. Mambo Press, Gweru.

Chater, Patricia (1985). *Caught in the Cross-Fire*. Zimbabwe Publishing
House, Harare.

Chinodya, Shimmer (1989). *Harvest of Thorns*: Baobab Press, Harare.

Cilliers, J. C. (1985). *Counter-Insurgency in Rhodesia*. Croom Helm, London.

Cliffe, L., Mpofu, J. and Munslow, B. (1980). Nationalist Politics in Zimbabwe: The 1980 Elections and Beyond. *Review of African Political Economy* 18: 44–67.

Clifford, James (1986). On Ethnographic Allegory. In James Clifford and
George Marcus (Editors), *Writing Culture*. University of California Press,
Berkeley.

Deng, Francis (1986). *The Man Called Deng Majok*. Yale University Press,
New Haven and London.

Drinkwater, Michael (1989). Technical Development and Peasant Impoverishment: Land Use Policy in Zimbabwe's Midland Province. *Journal of
Southern African Studies* 15: 287–305.

Eickelman, Dale F. (1985). *Knowledge and Power in Morocco*. Princeton
University Press, Princeton.

Frederikse, Julie (1984). *None But Ourselves*. Penguin Books, New York and
Harmondsworth (paperback).

Gann, L. H. (1965). *A History of Southern Rhodesia*. Chatto and Windus,
London.

Garbett, G. K. (1963). The Land Husbandry Act of Southern Rhodesia. In D.
Biebuyck (Editor), *African Agrarian Systems*. Oxford University Press for
the International African Institute, London.

Garbett, Kingsley (1977). Disparate Regional Cults and a Unitary Field in
Zimbabwe, in R. P. Werbner (Editor), *Regional Cults*. Academic Press,
London.

Hannan, M. (1959). *Standard Shona Dictionary*. Macmillan and Co. Ltd., London.

Herbst, Jeffrey (1990). *State Politics in Zimbabwe*. University of California Press, Berkeley.

Janzen, John (in press). *Ngoma: Cults of Affliction and Ritual Healing in Central and Southern Africa*. University of California Press, Berkeley.

Kriger, Norma (1991). *Peasant Voices*. Cambridge University Press, Cambridge.

Kuper, Hilda (1978). *Sobuza II Ngwenyama and King of Swaziland*. Duckworth, London.

Lan, David (1985). *Guns and Rain*. James Currey, London.

Lawyers Committee for Human Rights (1986). *Zimbabwe: Wages of War*. Lawyers Committe for Human Rights, New York.

Martin, David and Johnson, Phyllis (1981). *The Struggle for Zimbabwe*. Faber and Faber, London.

Mirza, S. and Strobel, M. (1989). *Four Swahili Women*. Indiana University Press, Bloomington.

Mlambo, Eshmael (1972). *Rhodesia, The Struggle for a Birthright*. C. Hurst, London.

Moore-King, Bruce (1989). *White Man, Black War*. Baobab Books, Harare.

Moyo, Sam (1986). The Land Question. In Ibbo Mandaza (Editor), *Zimbabwe, The Politics of Transition 1980–1986*. Codesria Book Series, Dakar.

Munson, Henry Jr (1984). *The House of Si Abd Allah*. Yale University Press, New Haven and London.

Nkomo, Joshua (1984). *Nkomo, The Story of My Life*. Methuen, London.

Radin, Paul (1926). *Crashing Thunder*. D. Appleton and Co., New York.

Ranger, Terence (1970). *The African Voice in Southern Rhodesia, 1898–1930*. Heinemann, London.

Ranger, Terence (1985). *Peasant Consciousness and Guerrilla War in Zimbabwe*. James Currey, London.

Ranger, Terence (1989a). Whose Heritage? The Case of the Matobo National Park. *Journal of Southern African Studies* 15: 217–49.

Ranger, Terence (1989b). Missionaries, Migrants and the Manyika: The Invention of Ethnicity in Zimbabwe. In Leroy Vail (Editor), *The Creation of Tribalism in Southern Africa*. James Currey, London and University of California Press, Berkeley.

Ranger, Terence (1989c). The Politics of Prophecy in Matabeleland. *Paper presented to the Fifth Satterthwaite Seminar*. Colloquium on African Religion and Ritual, Satterthwaite, Cumbria.

Ranger, Terence (forthcoming). *Voices from the Rocks: The Modern History of the Matopos Hills*.

Reynolds, Pamela (1990). After War: Healers and Children's Trauma in Zimbabwe. *Africa* 60: 1–38.

Rosaldo, Renato (1989). *Culture and Truth*. Beacon Press, Boston.

Seidman, G., Martin, D. and Johnson, P. (1982). *Zimbabwe: A New History*. Zimbabwe Publishing House, Harare.

Shostak, Marjorie (1981). *Nisa: The Life and Times of a Kung Woman*. Harvard University Press, Cambridge MA.

Solway, Jacqueline (1990). Affines and Spouses, Friends and Lovers: The Passing of Polygyny in Botswana. *Journal of Anthropological Research*, 46: 41–66.

Werbner, Richard (1964). Atonement Ritual and Guardian Spirit Possession among Kalanga. *Africa* 34: 206–23.

Werbner, Richard (1975). Land, Movement and Status among Kalanga of Botswana. In Meyer Fortes and Sheila Patterson (Editors), *Essays in African Social Anthropology*. Academic Press, London.

Werbner, Richard (1982). Production and Reproduction: The Dynamics of Botswana's North-Eastern Micro-Regions. In R. Hitchcock and M. R. Smith (Editors), *Proceedings of the Symposium on Settlement in Botswana*. Heinemann Educational Books Ltd, Gaborone.

Werbner, Richard (1989). *Ritual Passage, Sacred Journey*. Smithsonian Institution Press, Washington and Manchester University Press, Manchester.

Werbner, Richard (1990). South-central Africa: The Manchester School and After. In R. Fardon (Editor), *Localizing Strategies*. Scottish Academic Press and Smithsonian Institute, Edinburgh and Washington.

# Index